cu/w

POWER IN VERSE
Metaphor and Metonymy
in the
Renaissance Lyric

Those numbers wherewith heaven and earth are mov'd,
Show, weakness speaks in prose, but power in verse.

—Samuel Daniel, "Musophilus"

POWER IN VERSE
Metaphor and Metonymy
in the
Renaissance Lyric

Jane Hedley

The Pennsylvania State University Press
University Park and London

"This Is Just To Say" is reprinted with permission of New Directions Publishing Corporation from William Carlos Williams's *Collected Poems, Volume I: 1909–1939*, edited by A. Walton Litz and Christopher MacGowan. Copyright 1938 by New Directions; and with permission of Carcanet New Press Ltd., Manchester, England.

Lines from "A Prayer for my Daughter" are reprinted with permission of Macmillan Publishing Company from *The Poems of W. B. Yeats: A New Edition*, edited by Richard J. Finneran (Copyright 1924 by Macmillan Publishing Company, renewed 1952 by Bertha Georgie Yeats); and with permission of A. P. Watt Ltd., on behalf of Michael B. Yeats and Macmillan London Ltd.

Lines from "The Love Song of J. Alfred Prufrock" are reprinted from *Collected Poems 1909–1962* by T. S. Eliot, copyright 1936 by Harcourt Brace Jovanovich, Inc.; copyright 1963, 1964, by T. S. Eliot, by permission of the publisher.

Lines from "At Melville's Tomb," from *The Complete Poems and Selected Letters and Prose of Hart Crane*, edited by Brom Weber, are used by permission of Liveright Publishing Corporation. Copyright 1933, 1958, 1966, by Liveright Publishing Corporation.

Library of Congress Cataloging-in-Publication Data

Hedley, Jane.
  Power in verse.

  Bibliography: p.
  Includes index.
  1. English poetry—Early modern, 1500–1700—
History and criticism. 2. Metaphor. 3. English
language—Metonyms. I. Title.
PR535.M37H43 1988   821'.04'0915   87–32745
ISBN 0-271-00623-4

In Memory of

Harold Roy Turner
1906–1986

Margaret Jane Elizabeth Turner
1908–1974

Contents

Preface and Acknowledgments ix

A Note on Texts xi

1 Metaphor and Metonymy: Theoretical Groundwork 1

2 The Lyric in Context: Poesy and the Cult of Elizabeth 15

3 "It may be good": Metonymic Deixis in the Early
   Tudor Lyric 29

4 "Let me imagine, in this worthless verse": Metonymy in
   the Mid-Tudor Auto-Anthologies 59

5 "Your monument shall be my gentle verse":
   Sonneteering and the Metaphoric Way 77

6 "Happy ye leaves": Metaphor, Metonymy, and the
   Phases of English Petrarchism 113

7 "This bed thy center is": The Metonymic Poetry of
   Donne and Jonson 143

Postscript: The Metaphysical Conceit 171

Notes 177

Index 195

Preface and Acknowledgments

I have a double purpose here: to map the history of the English lyric from Wyatt to Donne into consecutive stylistic phases, and to put Roman Jakobson's theory of language to work in a systematic way. Ever since I first encountered his essay on "Two Aspects of Language" ten years ago, the poetry I know best has been helping me to make sense of Jakobson's central notions, while they in turn have clarified the stylistic features of the poetry. I hope I have succeeded, to some degree, in re-creating that two-way process for the readers of this book.

Several people have read the manuscript of this study at different stages of its development and given me helpful suggestions: Joseph Kramer, Barbara Turner, Kim Benston, Carol Bernstein, Robert Burlin, Ulrich Langer, A. C. Hamilton, Margaret Ferguson, Annabel Patterson, Laurence Stapleton, Marjorie Sherwood, Arthur Kinney, and Donald Cheney. Even where I have not followed their advice, it has helped me to clarify my own goals, and this is a better book than it could have been without their help. Sandra Berwind, my dearest friend and best critic, has read every draft and every version with unfailing enthusiasm for what I was trying to do and a gimlet eye for trouble spots and inconsistencies in my argument. She has been so close to this project that I find myself unwilling to indemnify her in the usual way against any liability for its shortcomings, but I will admit to having neglected, once or twice, to act on a suggestion of hers.

Through the process of readying this book for publication, I have been fortunate to have the tactful, alert guidance of Philip Winsor, along with his conscientious editorial staff.

Sabina Sawhney, my editorial assistant, has labored intelligently, and always cheerfully, to verify quotations and rectify inconsistencies in the

Notes. Pennie Mueller has retyped the manuscript more times than she probably cares to remember, with unfailing accuracy and good humor.

I wish to thank the American Association of University Women for a fellowship that enabled me to begin working on this project in 1980–81, and the Trustees of Bryn Mawr College for a junior faculty leave in that same year. Mary Patterson McPherson, president of Bryn Mawr College, has steadily befriended and supported my work.

From the beginning of this project, I had Margaret Temeles to turn to for sympathetic encouragement and practical advice. Without her there are many times when I would, like Diana's unfortunate nymph, have "sat down to rest in middest of the race," and never got up again. I would like also to thank Stephen Salkever for helping me to stay convinced, every day of our life together, that it is a great privilege to be making our living teaching and learning.

My father died just a few months too soon to share my pride and relief at finishing this book, but he always knew that I would. My mother, whom I lost even longer ago, would have mightily enjoyed coming to terms with its argument for herself and going over my prose with a fine-tooth comb. I wish to dedicate the book to both of them, in memory of their having "begot me, bred me, loved me."

A Note on Texts

The spelling and punctuation of all Renaissance texts that are quoted in this study have been modernized, with the exception of Spenser's poetry, which thereby retains the antique flavor Spenser built into it for his own contemporaries. (I will discuss this aspect of Spenser's poetics in chapter 5.) The decision to modernize cannot be taken lightly: there are philosophical considerations to be weighed, as well as practical difficulties. A modernized rendering that claims to stop short of translation and keep the original wording intact must cope somehow with puns, obsolete words that have no modern spelling, and words whose meaning has shifted. In poetry, where words have their acoustic and semantic potentialities more fully enlisted than in prose, these are especially tricky problems, and so is punctuation, because of the special contribution it makes in poems to phrasing and rhythm. Lately also it has begun to be argued—most notably in my own area by Anne Ferry and Thomas Greene—not just that modernization is hard to bring off, but that it is in principle a bad thing to do. It behooves us, these scholars suggest, to keep alert to the distance that divides us from the literary works we seek to interpret and from their cultural context: modernization promotes misunderstanding of how hard it is to recover the past.

My own working assumption is the reverse of this, really: it is that English literature of the sixteenth and early seventeenth century is not less but more accessible to us emotionally, socially, and stylistically than it seems at first to be, and that the strangeness of its authors' habits of spelling and punctuation (they spelled and punctuated both differently *and* less consistently than we do) is estranging only in a superficial way, which may nevertheless discourage us from seeking to know this poetry really well. John Williams, in whose anthology, *English Renaissance Poetry*, I first encountered several of the poems I will work with here, suggests in his preface that "the old, irregular spelling and punctuation give a spurious archaism to poems that were modern in their time, and that are best read today as if they were poems rather than literary specimens." This seems all the truer as we reflect on what is involved and what it is like to read a verbal text "as if it were a poem"—how actively a poem requires to be read, not only in the sense of decoding but also in the sense of performance. Uniform modernization is perhaps the only way to enlist for the reading of Gascoigne's or Ralegh's or even Sidney's poems the same active, confident engagement we have with Shakespeare's poetry—*for all its strangeness*, which we do not thereby fail to notice—whereas we have mostly come to know Shakespeare in texts that have persuaded us, from childhood, of his invincible modernity.

Where I could, I have taken advantage of recent, modernized editions, as follows: for Shakespeare's *Sonnets*, Stephen Booth's edition (New Haven: Yale, 1977); for Sidney's *Defense of Poesy*, Jan Van Dorsten's edition (*A Defence of Poetry*, Oxford University, 1966); Joost Daalder's edition of Wyatt's *Collected Poems* Oxford, 1975); Theodore Redpath's second, revised edition of Donne's *Songs and Sonets* (New York: St. Martin's, 1983); and for Ben Jonson, George Parfitt's Yale University press edition of 1975. Where there was no modernized text available, I have worked from an old-spelling edition and made the necessary adjustments myself. Old-spelling editions differ among themselves, of course—not only as to the caliber of the scholarly work that has gone into them but also in terms of adjustments that stop short of modernization but do enhance readability. In his conservative Clarendon edition of Sidney's poetry, William Ringler has made a number of orthographic adjustments (*u* to *v* and so on) and has modernized the punctuation; this makes for a much more readable text than, for example, Agnes Latham's *Ralegh* (Houghton Mifflin, 1929, repr. Harvard University, 1951, 1985), which adheres more closely to the text of Ralegh's poems as Latham found them in sixteenth-century manuscripts and published anthologies.

For my own purposes, which so often involve comparison of single poems by different poets, it has seemed best to give all quoted texts a comparably modern rendition. Thus, for example, I have modernized Surrey's poems in taking them from F. M. Padelford's edition (University of Washington, revised 1928), to bring them into line with Daalder's Wyatt. Surrey's poems are stiffer-jointed than Wyatt's, and to see why, it is necessary to get beyond the superficial quaintness and stiltedness projected by old spellings and conventions of punctuation, to the more crucial stiltedness of Surrey's syntax. I am indebted to John Williams's anthology for assistance in arriving at modernized versions of some of Surrey's, Gascoigne's and Googe's poems, although I have not always reproduced Williams's version exactly.

Apart from Spenser, the only poet I have taken to be something of a special case is Shakespeare, in the *Sonnets*. I am convinced by Stephen Booth's argument that punctuation of these poems should allow as much as possible for the energy and the ambiguity of their language, and so I defer to his compromise with the Quarto punctuation, which often looks or "sounds" a bit strange as compared with the more thoroughly modernized versions of other editors.

I am also indebted to Robert Durling's wonderfully precise translation of Petrarch's *Lyric Poems* into modern English (Harvard, 1976; Copyright 1976 by Robert M. Durling), which has enabled me to use Wyatt's and Surrey's Petrarchan imitations as a point of departure for my discussion of the phases of English Petrarchism in chapter 6.

1 Metaphor and Metonymy: Theoretical Groundwork

English lyric poetry from Wyatt to Donne falls into three consecutive stylistic phases. *Tottel's Miscellany* presided over the first, making the lyrics of Wyatt and Surrey available for imitation by lesser mid-century poets like Googe, Turberville, and Gascoigne. *The Shepheardes Calender* and Sidney's *Defense of Poesy* ushered in the second, the Elizabethan or "Golden" phase of the 1580s and 1590s. Then, with the turn of the century, John Donne's poetry set a new fashion, the so-called "Metaphysical" mode; meanwhile, Ben Jonson, of the same generation as Donne, reacted in different terms against the stylistic orientation of the Elizabethan poets. Lyric poetry was a courtly prerogative throughout this whole period,[1] and each of these phases is the product of a different moment in the history of the English aristocracy. Wyatt and Surrey were attached to the court of King Henry VIII; Gascoigne, Googe, and Turberville were country gentry whose poetry helped to advertise their aristocratic breeding. In the Elizabethan phase, poetry became an important part of England's national identity and of the ideological apparatus that helped to establish a strong central government. Even the lyric, the least pretentious and least public of literary kinds, became involved in the Elizabethan ideological program. Donne and Jonson began to write their lyrics as the fragile coherence of the Elizabethan regime was beginning to break down, and during the reign of Elizabeth's successor, James I. They are anti-Elizabethan, both in style and stance.

The differences between these three phases are obvious, but they have never been mapped out in a systematic way. C. S. Lewis's classic account of "Drab," "Golden," and "Metaphysical" poetry has scarcely been improved upon, even though Lewis's ideological bias has been challenged and his critical vocabulary is out of date.[2] Partly, the problem has been that "Drab" and "Golden" poetry are different in all kinds of ways whose interrelatedness is not easy to demonstrate. The same is true of the lyrics of Jonson and Donne, who belong to the same stylistic phase. We have not had a linguistic or a literary theory that would enable us to conceive of all these differences, within and between generations, as interrelated features of the same stylistic profile.

I propose to generate stylistic profiles for these three successive phases of English lyric poetry from the semiotic theory of Roman Jakobson. According to Jakobson, all verbal and indeed all symbolic behavior is derived from two interactive processes: selection and substitution; combination and contexture. These processes find their most condensed expression, he explains, as metaphor and metonymy, respectively. The bias of a single piece of writing, of a single writer's oeuvre, or of a literary movement such as Romanticism or Realism, can always be specified in terms of the relative primacy of one or the other process. A metaphoric or metonymic bias will be expressed as stance or outlook, and as style or figurative strategy, both at once. Stylistic innovation occurs whenever a writer or a group of writers privileges the process that had been underplayed or deemphasized by already prevailing canons of representation.

Jakobson based his model of linguistic behavior on Saussurean linguistics and the semiotic theory of C. S. Peirce, in conjunction with clinical research into language acquisition and language loss. He laid it out and briefly illustrated its possible applications in "Two Aspects of Language and Two Types of Aphasic Disturbances," in a monograph that was published by Mouton in 1956.[3] This was a fundamental contribution to semiotic studies, which has by now made an impact in many different areas, including anthropology, film studies, and psychoanalysis.[4] In literary studies, the metaphor-metonymy opposition has gradually become a commonplace of practical criticism.[5] So far, however, the only attempt to use it as the basis for mapping out consecutive phases in the history of literary style is David Lodge's study of modern prose fiction, *The Modes of Modern Writing* (1977).

I have found Lodge's book very helpful, but working with the lyric has brought me to a different understanding from Lodge of some of Jakobson's theoretical principles. I have also found it necessary to push beyond Lodge's notion of what constitutes an adequate history of collective shifts from one of these two poles to the other. I will propose that early Tudor poetry is metonymic, that the collective orientation of Spenser and Sidney and their Elizabethan contemporaries is metaphoric, and that Donne's and Jonson's lyrics bring metonymy once again to the fore. But whereas Donne's and Jonson's relation to precursor poets can be explained in terms of reactive oscillation from one pole to the other, the earlier shift requires a different kind of explanation altogether.

In the next few pages I will set out what are, for my purposes, the bare essentials of Jakobson's theory. These include his definition of "the poetic function of language," from a paper that is even better known than the "aphasia" paper to literary critics in America: "Linguistics and Poetics," originally delivered as the closing address to an interdisciplinary conference on Style at the University of Indiana, whose proceedings were published in 1960.[6] Then I will briefly demonstrate how the theory can be used to map the differences between metaphoric and metonymic writing. Finally, I will address its limitations as an instrument of literary history: these must be squarely faced, if they are to be successfully overcome.

Verbal behavior is governed by two interactive functions: selection and combination. In composing verbal messages, we *select* units from the code and *combine* them into larger wholes: distinctive features into phonemes, phonemes into words, words into sentences, sentences into discourses and conversations. To understand a verbal message of someone else's, we refer each of its constituents simultaneously to the code from which it has been selected and to the context in which it has actually figured. The relation that comes into play as we refer to the code is similarity/difference; the relation that holds contexts together is contiguity.[7] Where oral communication is concerned, what we mean by "context" is the situation in which the message is spoken and heard. If I say, "Have a look at this table, would you—I think there's still something the matter with it," you will understand me to mean one thing by "table" if you are a carpenter and we are standing in my dining room, and something else if you are a statistician helping me to publish a piece of social science research. Meanwhile we share a linguistic code in which "table" has a certain set of possible meanings, one of which the context activates. Where published written discourse is concerned, there is no immediate situation to refer to: the context available to the reader is the rest of the discourse in which the linguistic unit has figured.

The basis of this way of explaining how language works is Saussure's *Cours de linguistique générale*, but it was Jakobson who demonstrated the explanatory power of the Saussurean model of language. He used it to explain some notorious special cases of signification within the domain of ordinary language—shifters and proper names[8]—and also to initiate the systematic study of extraordinary verbal behavior: the speech of aphasic patients, whose linguistic competence has been impaired by brain damage; and verbal art, where the linguistic medium calls attention to itself as a distinctive configuration of signs.

Aphasia blocks one of the two basic functions, entirely or partly, and thereby exposes the domain of the other. In "Two Aspects of Language" Jakobson cites, for example, the behavior of an aphasic patient whose selection function, her capacity to perform linguistic operations based on similarity, had been impaired. "When asked to list a few names of animals, [she] disposed them in the same order in which she had seen them in the zoo; similarly, despite instructions to arrange certain objects according to color, size, and shape, she classified them on the basis of their spatial contiguity as home things, office materials, etc." (p. 249). This patient had lost the ability to relate words to other words in terms of their encoded meanings. She no longer knew what words meant out of context.

Jakobson explains that even a person whose speech is unimpaired will tend to favor one or the other function: either selection or combination. When asked to free-associate with some ordinary noun (Jakobson's example is "hut"), some respondents tend to produce a synonym or antonym or metaphoric substitution ("A hut is a poor little house"); and some refer instead to the contexts in which the word most commonly occurs (thereby producing responses like "burnt out," or "thatch," or "poverty"). In ordinary practical communication, where there is necessarily full cooperation between the two functions, we are not free to express a pronounced bias in favor of one or the other. But in verbal art a writer has greater freedom to control the development of a discourse and to choose its stance.

A piece of writing will be either "metonymic" or "metaphoric," depending on whether the writer has privileged the contiguity or the similarity relation:

> The development of a discourse may take place along two different semantic lines: one topic may lead to another either through their similarity or through their contiguity. The metaphoric way would be the most appropriate term for the first and the metonymic way for the second, since they find their most condensed expression in metaphor and metonymy respectively. (p. 254)

This correlation of metaphor and metonymy with the complementary axes of the Saussurean model of language is Jakobson's most important contribution to literary stylistics. Handbook definitions of metaphor and metonymy are usually taxonomic rather than functional. They enable us to recognize the figure where it occurs, but not to account for its intelligibility or generalize about what it can be used to do. In the case of metonymy, we are told that the name of an attribute or adjunct of a thing is being used to designate the thing itself: "sail" designates "ship," "the crown" refers to "the kingship." Taking Jakobson's approach, we can explain that metonymy enlists the contiguity-relation to situate the explicitly designated object in a larger context or field of objects. The mariner calls out "a sail! a sail!" and if he is at sea rather than in a warehouse, he is understood to have sighted a ship. The sail leads to the ship along the path of contiguity: this is what Jakobson means by defining metonymy as the condensation of a discursive procedure. He would call a piece of writing "metonymic" even if it seems not to require the reader to go beyond the given details—even if the ship is specified along with the sail—provided that it moves from topic to topic on the strength of the contiguity-relation.

Jakobson's object in broadening the traditional scope of the term "metonymy" in this way is to make a theoretical point: namely, that metonymy is the figure which will tend to predominate in a discourse that privileges the contiguity-relation. Nineteenth-century realism is a "metonymic" mode of writing, in this sense, and Jakobson points out that in *War and Peace*, for example, Tolstoy uses metonymy for shorthand references to minor characters after the scene in which each is first described in detail: "hair on the upper lip," "bare shoulders" (p. 255).

Metaphor effects a discursive condensation in terms of the axis of selection/substitution: one word refers simultaneously to two topics and asserts their likeness to one another. The metaphor does not take their similarity for granted but asserts it, often in the face of a difference so great as to make that assertion surprising or bizarre. There has been some disagreement among rhetoricians as to whether simile, whose terms are explicitly compared using "like" or "as," is a special case of metaphor, or metaphor of simile. Taking Jakobson's approach, simile and metaphor fall into place as more and less condensed versions of "the metaphoric way." The most condensed is the most exclusively or purely metaphoric, because it dispenses entirely with the syntagma, whereas similes syntagmatize the assertion of similarity, bringing the axis of combination into play.[9]

Metaphor and metonymy are antithetical figures, in the sense that each runs interference with the function on whose operation the other depends for its intelligibility. Metonymy uses x to say xY on the strength of the contiguity of x and Y, be it spatial or temporal, either in some specific presupposed situation or else in our habitual experience of the world. Metaphor proposes that X be taken for Y, whereas in language and experience they usually belong to different spheres of activity or being. If, then, a metaphor occurs in a discourse whose procedure is according to the axis of combination, it will rupture the fabric of contiguities that discourse is weaving, by importing an element from out of context. Realist writing is not devoid of metaphor, as David Lodge has pointed out,[10] but the realist writer will keep that kind of disruption to a minimum by taking his or her metaphoric vehicles, as well as their tenors, from the descriptive context.

By the same token, the more thoroughly "metaphoric" a piece of fiction is, the less stability the fictional world will be apt to have in terms of ordinary chronology and scenic locale. Whereas metonymic writing is "set toward the context," and metonymic fictions often claim to be true history, metaphoric fictions are "self-focused" by repetitions and recurring motifs, or by paradigmatic relationships between their events, places, and characters. The more obvious these patterns are, as Lodge points out, the less incentive there is to take the fiction for an excerpted piece of actual history, and the more it will seem to constitute a "total metaphor" for the human condition.[11] Metonymic writing only purports to depict some part of the lives of some particular group of people more or less arbitrarily chosen, and will usually allow the reader to glimpse a more extensive range of happenings and of social relations that it has not, but presumably might have, included. A metaphoric work will present us with a social microcosm, or it may depict a society that is set over against the world of the reader as being very different from it. Pastoral is a metaphoric mode, in this sense.

Relative to prose, poetry favors "the metaphoric way," because what Jakobson calls the "poetic function" of language[12] disarms the contiguity-relation in favor of the principle of similarity/dissimilarity. Poetry uses the soundshape of language, the signifying substance itself, to superimpose on the syntagma patterns whose fundamental principle is equivalence. Meter, which measures out the signifier in isochronic units, is the most important of these patterns: each line of iambic pentameter consists of ten syllables, five equally stressed alternating with five equally unstressed, and the poetic structure—be it blank verse, be it a sonnet—is constituted by the repetition of that unit, regardless of the length and the structure of the syntagma in which it is lodged. Rhyme is another pattern of equivalence that overrides the syntagma, fostering semantic interplay between syntactically unrelated words that sound alike. By virtue of these patterns, which are gratuitous from the standpoint of practical communication, the message's "set toward the context" is weakened. Its syntax is not able to limit each word to one meaning only: additional meanings may be triggered by the metric structure or the rhyme scheme, or simply by the way in which these patterns synchronize the discourse.[13] Beyond the referential function the message ostensibly has for its speaker and addressee, it hangs together for the reader of the poem as a distinctive configuration of signs.

This is what Jakobson means by the "poetic function" of language, whereby "the principle of equivalence is projected from the axis of selection into the axis of combination," and the message becomes "self-focused." The easiest way for a poet to collaborate with the poetic function of language, especially in highly patterned forms like the sonnet, sestina, or villanelle, is not to tell a story or develop a complicated piece of argumentation but to elaborate a thematic kernel through a series of interlinked variations. The similarity-relation, and hence "the metaphoric way," becomes the line of least resistance for the development of the poem's subject, whatever it be.

The argument of this sonnet of Shakespeare's takes the metaphoric way. Its occasion is the speaker's doubt as to the adequacy of a metaphoric equation, which his love for the poem's addressee had moved him to make but now moves him beyond:

> Shall I compare thee to a summer's day?
> Thou art more lovely and more temperate:
> Rough winds do shake the darling buds of May,
> And summer's lease hath all too short a date;
> Sometimes too hot the eye of heaven shines,
> And often is his gold complexion dimmed;
> And every fair from fair sometime declines,
> By chance or nature's changing course untrimmed:
> But thy eternal summer shall not fade,
> Nor lose possession of that fair thou ow'st,
> Nor shall death brag thou wand'rest in his shade,
> When in eternal lines to time thou grow'st.
>   So long as men can breathe or eyes can see,
>   So long lives this, and this gives life to thee.

(Sonnet 18)

This poem's message is highly redundant. After the initial assertion of difference within similarity ("more lovely," "more temperate"), its argument simply rings changes on that assertion in a series of equivalent claims, first about "summer" and then about "thee." These claims accumulate paratactically in one- or two-line units: the argument has been fitted to the form, in the sense that each line is a whole clause. The fit between syntax and sonnet structure gives the rhyme scheme prominence and fosters semantic linkage between the rhyming words, most of which are verbs or predicate-nouns: shines/declines; fade/shade; owest/growest. Like-beginnings and alliteration help still further to reinforce the parallelisms on which the argument depends for its rhetorical power.

Whereas the speaker's assertions about ordinary summer in 11. 3–8 are plausible metonymies, the "eternal summer" he predicates of his addressee is a paradox, a combination that is not intelligible *prima facie*, but only as a function of our being able to manipulate encoded substitution-sets. We must recognize that "eternal" is being substituted for an opposite like "ephemeral," which would have been a perfectly acceptable adjective for "summer." Thus the case for "thy" superiority to a summer's day depends upon a metaphoric violation of combinational/contextual norms. The violation is rendered more acceptable when "thy eternal summer" finally gets located not in the world but in the poem's "eternal lines." The move from paradox to self-reference is earned by the rhyme, the alliteration, the high message-redundancy, the coincidence between syntactic and poetic units—in short, by all the ways in which the poem calls attention to its own "lines." As we read through Shakespeare's sonnets in the 1590 Quarto order, and come upon this one after seventeen which propose that the beloved immortalize himself through procreation, its argument seems to arise from the experience itself of re-sonneting the same injunction seventeen times. The poet has apparently discovered by doing this that a poem's proper business is not to deliver a message in some particular context but to be an autonomous verbal configuration, which lends its message a longer "lease" by lifting it out of context.

Jakobson's "poetic function" is a real improvement over the "aesthetic function" of the Russian Formalists, because it keeps poems and nonpoems in the same domain of verbal behavior and allows for the recognition that some poems are more self-focused than others. The referential and the poetic function, "self-focus" and "set toward the context," are given by his theory as opposite but not mutually exclusive tendencies. The same goes for the antithetical figures, metaphor and metonymy: thus poetry has a metaphoric bias relative to prose, because the poetic function of language collaborates with the metaphoric way of developing a discourse, but not all poems are equally metaphoric. For example, as compared with Shakespeare's sonnet 17, this free-verse poem of William Carlos Williams's is highly metonymic in its orientation:[14]

> This Is Just To Say
>
> I have eaten
> the plums
> that were in
> the icebox
>
> and which
> you were probably
> saving
> for breakfast
>
> Forgive me
> they were delicious
> so sweet
> and so cold

This poem has neither meter nor rhyme scheme. Had it appeared on a kitchen table somewhere, without line divisions, it would simply be a message about some plums, a note left in the kitchen late at night for its author's wife to read the next morning.

In order to make sense of the poem's message, we must infer a highly specific context from its language: a kitchen; a certain time-frame; a conventional husband-wife relation. It stands for a larger situation that must be produced by our reading. Because it is presented to us out of context, we do perceive it as a synchronic configuration: thus it acquires a three-part structure, with a stanza given to statement of fact, a stanza to acknowledgment of the claims of household economics, and a clinching stanza to the sweetness and coldness of the plums themselves, which thereby take priority over the domestic order of regular mealtimes and balanced diet. But in being so like a merely practical message, the poem makes us feel a little silly about doing this sort of reading. After all, this was "just to say" that some plums tasted good. Williams's note thus resists the poetic function of language. He has contrived, we could say, an oxymoronic relation between "self-focus" and "set toward the context."

Whereas a metaphoric bias is consistent with a lot of good work in intricate closed forms like the sonnet, we might expect a poet whose bias is metonymic either to find such forms uncongenial and fail to handle them successfully, or else to use them subversively, in an ironic way. Here is a poem of Michael Drayton's that subverts the sonnet's metaphoric bias and its tendency to be self-focused. It has the form of a Shakespearean sonnet, but the message it carries is strongly "set toward the context," especially in its opening and closing lines.

> Since there's no help, come, let us kiss and part—
> Nay, I have done: you get no more of me;
> And I am glad, yea, glad with all my heart
> That thus so cleanly I myself can free.
> Shake hands forever, cancel all our vows,
> And when we meet at any time again,
> Be it not seen in either of our brows
> That we one jot of former love retain.
> Now at the last gasp of love's latest breath,
> When, his pulse failing, Passion speechless lies,
> When Faith is kneeling by his bed of death,
> And Innocence is closing up his eyes,—
>> Now if thou wouldst, when all have given him over,
>> From death to life thou mightst him yet recover.[15]

To make sense of the "since" clause that opens this poem, we must suppose the speaker to have been involved in a love affair that he is finally now ready to end. What the particular circumstances are that have brought him to this pass, why he is convinced "there's no help," he does not say, but a contemporary reader of the poem would have no more trouble producing a context for his words than Williams's readers have in presupposing a kitchen and a husband-wife relation of a certain kind to contextualize "This Is Just To Say." Insofar as the language of Drayton's poem requires us to do this kind of interpretive work, it overcomes the tendency of the sonnet form to close in upon itself and be a self-sufficient verbal icon. This happens again in the last two lines of the poem, where the *allegoria* of Passion on his deathbed takes an unexpected turn, to disclose that the speaker is not quite convinced there's no help, after all—not really ready, in other words, to bring the relationship to closure. By introducing a feminine rhyme into the couplet, Drayton weakens its closural force and thereby conveys irresolution by way of the sonnet's formal properties.

Whereas Williams made a poem out of a strongly contextualized written message, Drayton has made a poem out of an oral utterance in a face-to-face encounter. His speaker's words are embedded in a larger situation that unfolds in terms of the things he says to his partner from one line to the next. "Nay, I have done" implies that a parting kiss has been exchanged between lines one and two. In line 5 "Shake hands forever" is probably not to be taken literally, but its imperative mood reinforces the illusion of face-to-face leavetaking. In Shakespeare's sonnet 17 the poet-lover uses the form to create a space apart from the vicissitudes of daily intercourse with the beloved where an ideal image of him can be preserved. The central metaphor is a paradox—"eternal summer"—that violates the conditions of ordinary spatiotemporal experience, in order to envision love's emancipation from those conditions—from change, from the natural process of aging. Drayton's lover also resorts to metaphor, in the third quatrain of his sonnet, apparently as an attempt to objectify and distance himself from his not-quite-extinguished passion for the lady. But his little allegorical scene is tightly tied to the immediate present, the "now" of the utterance itself, and is thereby vulnerable to incursion from the immediately contiguous social setting. In the couplet just such an incursion takes place, as the lady is given a role to play in the allegorical scene. Ostensibly the lover has been seduced by her physical contiguity into a redirection of the metaphor, and a subversion of the poetic form he had meant to use to "free himself cleanly" from her. If the whole performance comes across as a calculated piece of seduction on his part, that is because of the ironic relation that obtains between the sonnet form and the verbal encounter it is used to stage: we cannot help noticing how good a fit has been contrived between the structure of the sonnet and the self-reversal it dramatizes.

Once the metaphoric bias of the sonnet had been established in English by Shakespeare, Edmund Spenser, and the early sonnet-work of Sir Philip Sidney, it became possible to resist or subvert that bias, as Drayton has done here, in order to insist on the lover's responsiveness to the pressure of his immediate circumstances and to demonstrate his resourcefulness as a suitor. Chronologically this subversive moment overlaps with the moment it presupposes, in which the iconic, monumentalizing power of the sonnet form was discovered and institutionalized by the Elizabethan poets of the 1580s and 1590s. A fuller account of the history of the English sonnet will be given in chapter 5; here I have just been using sonnets to show what kind of account can be given of a poem on the strength of the claim that it is metaphoric and self-focused, or metonymic and set toward the context.

By now, some of my readers have probably begun to object that sixteenth-century writers were well trained, and highly self-conscious, in terms of categories I am prepared to ignore in favor of a linguistic model I have no historical warrant for using to explain their poetic practice. Jakobson's complementary axes do indeed produce a different alignment of stylistic features from the traditional schemes/tropes dichotomy. According to that classification, as it was usually given in Renaissance handbooks, schemes consist of syntax-and-sound manipulation; tropes alter the meanings of words. Thus, for example, any kind of repetition, including meter, is a "scheme"; on the other hand, metonymy is a "trope," along with metaphor, because it uses the word for the cause to signify the effect, the word for the container to signify the contents, and so on.

Of course we cannot afford to be ignorant of the role these poets' rhetorical training played in their own writing. But let us not exaggerate its importance. There is no reason to suppose that their training *explicated* their practice for them, except in relatively superficial ways. "A pretty epanorthosis, and withall a paranomasia," chortles the editor of *The Shepheardes Calender* in his gloss to one of the eclogues, but his appreciation does not take him beyond a taxonomic labeling of these figures. Linguistic competence is unconsciously held: grammar only helps us describe our native language after we have learned to use it, and we learn to write good prose from reading and writing, not from grammar lessons. The same is true of what we might analogously call "poetic competence": it is acquired by "imitation and exercise," as Sidney points out in his *Defense of Poesy*. Language is a system of interdependent variables, such that some of the things a writer deliberately intends constrain him to do other things he will not have intended, in the same sense, at all. This study will be valuable precisely to the extent that Jakobson's model can generate a new account of such interdependencies, making relationships visible that are obscured by traditional habits of classification.[16]

The trouble with Jakobson's model, as a basis for literary stylistics, is that it fosters an approach to literary history that is ahistorical. It produces synchronic hypostases which can then be played off against each other as if literature were a closed system with its own internal rhythm of oscillation. In 1933 Jakobson defended the Russian Formalist school against the Soviet Marxist allegation that it had "[failed] to grasp the relationship of art to real life," and insisted that "none of us has ever proclaimed the self-sufficiency of art."[17] The Russian Formalists did indeed assume that language and verbal art are historically conditioned social practices: this emerges from the writings of Ejxenbaum and Tynjanov as well as Jakobson himself. But in the "aphasia" essay, which is from a later, more scientific phase of his career, he depicts language as a brain function rather than a social practice, and he neglects to situate his examples of metonymic and metaphoric bias in historical terms. He does therefore seem to be proclaiming the self-sufficiency, if not of art, then at least of the history of art:

> The primacy of the metaphoric process in the literary schools of romanticism and symbolism has been repeatedly acknowledged, but it is still insufficiently realized that it is the predominance of metonymy which underlies and actually pre-determines the so-called "realistic" trend, which belongs to an intermediary stage between the decline of romanticism and the rise of symbolism and is opposed to both. . . . The same oscillation occurs in sign systems other than language. A salient example from the history of painting is the manifestly metonymical orientation of cubism, where the object is transformed into a set of synecdoches; the surrealist painters responded with a patently metaphorical attitude.
>
> ("Two Aspects of Language," pp. 255–56)

What we seem to have here is an autonomous rhythm of oscillation from metaphor to metonymy and back again.

When David Lodge, whose native tradition is Anglo-American formalism, set out to map the modes of modern writing in terms of Jakobson's model, he treated the diachronic or "historical" dimension of his typology in just this way. Reflecting on his own undertaking in a later essay, Lodge reasoned as follows:

> If we combine Jakobson's typology of discourse with the Russian Formalist theory of literary dynamics as a process driven by the automatization and defamiliarization of perception, a new style being developed because the old style has exhausted its expressive possibilities, then we have an explanation of why there seems to be a cyclical rhythm to literary history; why innovation is so often a return to the last fashion but one in some respects; why,

within the modern period, phases of metaphoric experiment seem to alternate with phases of metonymic realism. If Jakobson is right, there is nowhere for writing to go except between these two poles.[18]

Lodge does here suppose literary history to be an autonomous domain, and proposes to define novelty or change as a dynamic internal to that domain.

To be sure, the bias of predecessor artists has sometimes been the most important motive for novel fashions of representation, but there are almost always other kinds of contributory pressures, and their importance relative to each other cannot be taken for granted; it is a matter of historical contingency. Often changes in literary fashion betoken ideological shifts whose causes are extraliterary. Sometimes they reflect changes in the value accorded to different kinds of writing, relative to each other and to other political and social practices. As soon as we try to map successive phases in the literature of some particular national group at some particular time in its history, relations between the literature and the circumstances of its production begin to claim our attention as having helped to determine its stylistic orientation from one phase to the next. Circumstances of production are especially likely to be important where a collective change in orientation is not accompanied by manifestos or self-conscious theorizing, so that it seems to have occurred without any explicit collective intention to write differently, or look at the world differently, or define what counts as appropriate subject matter differently from before.

In England in the sixteenth century, the shift from Elizabethan metaphoric writing to the metonymic writing of Donne and Jonson is expressed as reaction and innovation within the institution of English "poesy." The earlier shift, which can be dated for convenience in 1579, when *The Shepheardes Calender* was published, reflects a change in the status of poetry as a social practice. Both shifts were ideologically motivated, so that our frame of reference for both must be the political life of Elizabethan and post-Elizabethan England. In chapter 2 I will begin to sketch that larger frame of reference, to explain poesy's emergence as a national institution during the reign of Elizabeth.

2 Historical Context: Poesy and the Cult of Elizabeth

During the sixteenth century a massive economic, political, and social reorganization occurred in England, whose outcome was the "nationalization" of politics. "The person of the monarch," explains the political historian Wallace MacCaffrey, "became the focus of a single national political world with centripetal force powerful enough to draw into its orbit all rivalries, personal, local, or dynastic."[1] The monarch's status as head of both church and state served to strengthen England's identity as a nation, vis-à-vis the rest of Europe. The emergence of a capitalist economy in the context of a stable, centralized political regime brought her into the international arena, where she competed with France and Spain to develop foreign markets and open up new territories for commercial empire-building. National self-consciousness reached its apogee during the 1580s, with the defeat of the Spanish Armada, when it seemed that England had finally achieved internal stability and world-historical importance.

As a reflex of the emergence of English nationhood, "poesy" emerged as a national institution, and came to be seen as having its own vernacular history and an intrinsic hierarchy of genres. Along with this status came a change in the relation that was understood to obtain between a poem and the political and social context in which it was produced. The change in poetry's institutional status was the catalyst of a shift from metonymic, context-implicated writing to metaphoric, self-focused writing that took place from one generation of Tudor poets to the next. Wyatt and Surrey, and their mid-century imitators and readers, conceived of poetry's relation to political and social life as one of metonymic participation; the Elizabethan poets reconceived it as one of metaphoric representation.

Poetry began to be regarded as a national institution as early as 1557, when Tottel published the poetry of Wyatt and Surrey "to the honor of the

English tongue, and for profit of the studious of English eloquence,"[2] to demonstrate that English was as good a language for poetry as Latin or Italian. But before 1580, as Eleanor Rosenberg explains in her study of Elizabethan literary patronage, most vernacular publication had "a recognizable utility." Until the latter part of Elizabeth's reign "poetry remained an avocation of gentlemen. . . . When lyrics, prose and verse romances, and dramatic writing did begin to appear in quantity, these compositions usually offered moral—and therefore utilitarian—justification."[3]

Typical of that kind of justification are the letters to "Reverend Divines" and to "the youth of England" which George Gascoigne published with the second edition of his poems in 1575.[4] He assures the Right Reverend that he receives no money for publishing the *Posies*, and that he did not do it "out of a vainglorious desire to be thought a pleasant poet." He offers them as a demonstration that it is possible to write "both compendiously and perfectly in our English tongue," and to advertise his own qualities of mind, in the hope of obtaining serious employment. He assures his readers that moral profit may be obtained from the collection as a whole, despite the inclusion of some chaff with the grain, "some verses more sauced with wantonness than with wisdom." His rationalization for including this material is that the example of his youthful follies may teach young men what to avoid. Many of the poems in the volume have elaborate headnotes or narrative settings: it seems they are being offered to the reader as exemplary social performances, lessons as to how a young gentleman should (or should not) behave in polite society.

With the next generation of Elizabethan writers poetry was still a gentlemanly pastime, but it was also more than that, and began to have a different kind of legitimacy. Sidney and Spenser cast themselves quite self-consciously as the creators of "English poesy," both in the sense of presenting themselves as England's Petrarch, England's Vergil, and also in the sense of making a native tradition of poetry visible to their contemporaries. Wyatt and Surrey had used Petrarchan models, but Sidney plays his love poetry off against Petrarch's, disparaging the conventions of Petrarchist poetry in order to claim a more sincere originality for his own. In the *Defense of Poesy*, which began to circulate in manuscript about 1580, he includes a survey of English poesy from More and Wyatt up to the present, and urges his contemporaries to improve the quality of their nation's literature in every genre. *The Shepheardes Calender* was published in 1579 with an elaborate editorial apparatus, to celebrate Spenser's debut as an English poet.[5] E.K.'s introduction includes a learned discussion of the pastoral mode, so that readers will have a context in which to admire the literary performances as such. In the arrangement of the eclogues, native verse forms like the fourteener and the roundelay are played off against foreign imports, the sestina and the classical ode: the other shepherds admire Colin Clout's ability to handle these more pretentious and difficult forms. Their admiration calls attention to Spenser's having put the lyric on an equal footing with that of other great nations, past and present. A few years later he published the first three books of an English epic that was to do for his country what Vergil's *Aeneid* had done for Rome: celebrate its founding, disclose its destiny, immortalize its national heroes.

We find Gascoigne upbraiding the prospective audience of his *Posies* for assuming that a poem's occasion will always have been a real event in the poet's life. Some have thought, he scornfully observes, that the Lord Vaux wrote "I loathe that I did love" on his deathbed; "the pleasant ditty of the noble Earl of Surrey (beginning thus: 'In winter's just return') was also construed to be made indeed by a Shepherd."[6] Gascoigne's own writing was especially vulnerable to this kind of misunderstanding. *The Adventures of Master F.J.*, whose ostensible purpose is to re-create the social context in which F.J.'s poems were originally written and circulated, reads like a realistic novel of manners in a contemporary setting. For the second edition, Gascoigne added an edifying moral and pretended to have translated an Italian novella, so that he could not be accused of publishing local gossip.

Elizabethan fictions are more obviously fictive than *Master F.J.*, and their fictive status is often enhanced with framing devices which set the fictional world apart from the world of their readers: prologues and epilogues, or an editorial apparatus that places the work generically and calls attention to its literary antecedents, as E.K. does in *The Shepheardes Calender*. Often the frame will instruct the reader to regard the fiction itself as a "total metaphor" for the human condition. A classic example of this is the proem to the second book of *The Faerie Queene*, where the poet explains how to get to Faeryland:

> Right well I wote most mighty Soveraine,
>   That all this famous antique history,
>   Of some th'aboundance of an idle braine
>   Will iudged be, and painted forgery,
>   Rather then matter of iust memory,
>   Sith none, that breatheth living aire, does know,
>   Where is that happy land of Faery,
>   Which I so much do vaunt, yet no where show,
> But vouch antiquities, which no body can know.
>
> But let that man with better sence advize,
>   That of the world least part to us is red:
>   And dayly how through hardy enterprize,

Many great Regions are discovered,
　　Which to late age were never mentioned.
　　Who ever heard of th'Indian *Peru*?
　　Or who in venturous vessell measured
　　The *Amazons* huge river now found trew?
Or fruitfullest *Virginia* who did ever vew?

Yet all these were, when no man did them know;
　　Yet have from wisest ages hidden beene:
　　And later times things more unknowne shall show.
　　Why then should witlesse man so much misweene
　　That nothing is, but that which he hath seene?
　　What if within the Moones faire shining spheare?
　　What if in every other starre unseene
　　Of other worldes he happily should heare?
He wonder would much more: yet such to some appeare.

Of Faerie lond yet if he more inquire,
　　By certaine signes here set in sundry place
　　He may it find; ne let him then admire,
　　But yield his sence to be too blunt and bace,
　　That no'te without an hound fine footing trace.
　　And thou, O fairest Princesse under sky,
　　In this faire mirrhour maist behold thy face,
　　And thine owne realmes in lond of Faery,
And in this antique Image thy great auncestry.[7]

We travel to Faeryland by accepting a metaphoric substitution. It is at once an "antique image" and a "new world." The poet is claiming that it is no less really there than the lands that had recently been discovered by European explorers; but whereas those lands are unforeseen extensions of the already-known world, this land is the already-known world newly envisioned.

In his *Defense of Poesy*, Sidney explains that poesy is a better teacher than history could possibly be. Had Nature ever produced "so right a prince as Xenophon's Cyrus," the historian, with his "bare was," would be citing him as a particular individual who once ruled especially well. The poet uses him paradigmatically, "[bestowing] a Cyrus upon the world to make many Cyruses."[8] In the same way, Faeryland confronts the historian's chronological sequence of wars and rulers with a synchronizing paradigm of good and bad rulership. King Arthur's reign and Queen Elizabeth's are contemporaneous in Faeryland. Elizabeth may find herself mirrored in Gloriana, and also, though the poem never tells her this explicitly, in Lucifera, Gloriana's counterimage in the first book. Poesy's relation to actual human experience thus becomes an ahistorical relation of metaphoric correspondence. This is Sidney's assumption whether he is generalizing about the entire body of writing classifiable as poesy, or whether he is explaining the value of some particular work, like the *Cyropedia*, for readers of all times and places.

He makes this assumption also in his treatment of literary genre. George Puttenham, author of *The Art of English Poesy*, who was Gascoigne's contemporary,[9] regarded literary kinds almost as modes of social behavior. "What is most remarkable about Puttenham's discussion of poetic kinds," observes Louis Montrose admiringly, "is his conception of poetry as a body of changing cultural practices dialectically related to the fundamental processes of social life."[10] Puttenham begins his discussion of decorum by defining it as "the good grace of everything in its kind," but this turns out not to be a principle of conformity to the prescribed conventions of literary kinds. Instead, as Daniel Javitch has pointed out, Puttenham's examples assimilate literary decorum to models of propriety and impropriety in the conduct of social life.[11] Sidney's way of dealing with genre is to posit a synchronic hierarchy of poetic kinds that corresponds to the hierarchy of species intrinsic to the divinely created natural order. Here again, poesy's relation to history or to ongoing social life is taken to be one of metaphoric correspondence rather than metonymic participation.

As far as lyric poetry is concerned, the change from writing that is metonymic, implicated in history and social life, to writing that is metaphoric and self-focused was assisted by printing, which altered the status of the lyric between Wyatt's generation and Sidney's. *Tottel's Miscellany* was the first printed collection of lyric poetry in English. The poets themselves had not had this sort of dissemination in view: they wrote their poems for oral performance or for private circulation in manuscript. For their original audience, these poems were stylized social gestures. For mid-century readers that is still what they ostensibly were, but at such a distance as they were from their original context, and in view of Tottel's having seen fit to publish them, their status was slightly altered. Tottel's headnotes attribute these stylized gestures to "the lover," a generalized anonymous figure who stands for the entire class to which he belongs. The mid-century "auto-anthologists"[12] tried to give this anonymous lover some individuality and a bit of a social context: they framed their poetry with elaborate headnotes and sometimes explanations of how particular poems came to be written. Meanwhile, however, it was becoming customary to encounter the lyric at a distance from its originating occasion. In the poetry of the 1580s and 1590s, instead of headnotes to overcome that distance, we find it thematized by the poems themselves, with the claim to be conferring immortality on the love they celebrate or the beloved they praise. Wyatt and Surrey and their mid-century imitators never make this claim; the Elizabethan poets are continually doing so. Lyric poetry remained for them a social pastime, but it had also come to be seen as a publishable art form, an enduring literary "monument."

As this happened, the potentialities of fixed forms like the sonnet and the sestina, in which a high degree of internal organization begets a highly self-focused message, came to be better understood and better exploited. The assumption ceased to be made that a poem's message should be couched in the same sort of language and empowered by the same rhetorical strategies as we use to do our business outside of poetry. Gascoigne cautions the would-be poet to "beware of rhyme without reason," and not to use an unnatural word order in deference to the meter. He has no notion of allowing poetic structures themselves to play a part in shaping the argument and releasing the semantic potentials of a poem's language. The Elizabethan poets' attitude toward the medium itself is manifestly different. Spenser used an archaizing diction to put his poems at a distance from ordinary speech situations. He and Daniel and Shakespeare used poetic forms like the sonnet and the Spenserian stanza in such a way that the poetic form becomes the controlling armature of the discourse. What we encounter among these poets is a collective willingness to exploit the poetic function of language to the fullest.[13]

Their collective attitude toward poetic structures and poetic language was indirectly fostered, as we have seen, by the emergence of English poesy as a national institution; and the reverse is also true. Self-focused, metaphoric writing readily became the vehicle of a nationalist ideology, a cult of the monarch which was also a cult of the state. Most of the poetry of the 1580s and 1590s is love poetry, and the erotic paradigm it puts forth is one that sublimates desire, suspends the laws of ordinary experience, and lifts the object of desire into a special aesthetic realm, where it becomes the cynosure of the lover's inner eye. This paradigm could be used interchangeably for private courtship and for the depiction of the Elizabethan courtier's public, political posture. The erotic ideology of the lyric forms part of a larger ideological configuration, to which other kinds of writing contributed also—especially pastoral and chivalric romance.[14]

Elizabeth's regime was economically and politically fragile: Wallace Mac-Caffrey explains (p. 97) that in the absence of a paid bureaucracy or a professional army, its stability depended on "arduous and constant wooing of the body politic." The pulpit and the printing press, controlled as they both were by a centralized system of political patronage, figured importantly in this ideological program, and so did the entertainments staged for Elizabeth's summer "progresses" through the countryside. Much of the poetry of the 1580s and 1590s was part of a collective effort to envision the queen as the divinely appointed center of a unified kingdom. Apotheosis of the monarch masked the fragility of the newly emergent nation, positing for it a divinely given invulnerability to challenge, both from without and from within.

At the same time that worship of the Virgin Mary was being suppressed in the interest of an English national religion, the queen allowed herself to become the focus of a many-faceted secular cult, which was all the more effective for being eclectic. Secular rituals were invented to celebrate her Accession Day, and she lent herself enthusiastically to these rituals, as if she realized that they fostered social cohesiveness in the same way as the discredited festivals of the Catholic church had done. She acquired a galaxy of symbolic names, each of which could express a different version of the national interest.[15] As Judith or Deborah, she stood for the Protestant cause against the European Catholic menace; as Diana, she had refused to compromise England's autonomy through marriage to a foreign prince; as Astraea, she presided over the administration of justice throughout the realm, and as Cynthia, over English naval power. In this way the cult of the monarch helped to articulate and consolidate an English national identity. Roy Strong argues that it was crucial to the success of Elizabethan statecraft, because it helped to contain the momentum of religious iconoclasm in the wake of the Protestant Reformation.[16] The short-term result of the Reformation had been to enhance the status of the monarchy, but its long-term tendency was to undermine the king's authority and challenge the privilege of the aristocracy. The cult of Elizabeth helped to keep that tendency in check, for the forty-year duration of her reign.

Of all the symbolic names she acquired, Laura seems perhaps least able to serve as a rallying point for English nationalism. But Laura had already been made capable of fusing an imperial with a personal theme in Petrarch's *Trionfi*, which was just as well known in England as the *Canzoniere* from the time of Henry VIII. As Frances Yates explains in *The Imperial Theme in the Sixteenth Century*,[17] the imperial panoply of the Roman triumph is conjoined in this work with a Christian allegorical conception of spiritual warfare: Laura appears as the central figure in the Triumph of Chastity. In this context, Laura became a public figure: her chastity took on religious and political overtones. The way in which the cult of Elizabeth appropriated Laura's symbolic value for its own purposes is clearly illustrated by this sonnet of Ralegh's, which was published with *The Faerie Queene:*

> Methought I saw the grave, where Laura lay,
> Within that temple, where the vestal flame
> Was wont to burn, and passing by that way
> To see that buried dust of living fame,
> Whose tomb fair love, and fairer virtue kept,
> All suddenly I saw the Faery Queen:

At whose approach the soul of Petrarch wept,
And from thenceforth those graces were not seen.
For they this Queen attended, in whose stead
Oblivion laid him down on Laura's hearse;
Hereat the hardest stones were seen to bleed,
And groans of buried ghosts the heavens did pierce,
   Where Homer's spright did tremble all for grief,
   And cursed th'access of that celestial thief.[18]

Ralegh's allegory capitalizes on the pun that enables Laura's name to cite Petrarch's fame—his "laurels"—as a poet of the Italian vernacular, at the same time that it refers to the lady herself. Ralegh is celebrating Spenser's leading role in the creation of an English vernacular poesy—hence the reference to "Homer's spright" as well as to the ghost of Petrarch. The personal, erotic tenor of Petrarch's relation to Laura has not disappeared in this sonnet but is assimilated to a public, political tenor, as Gloriana's poet, England's poet, inherits the fame of illustrious predecessors.

The cult of Elizabeth encompassed versions of English national history, both religious and secular, which represented her regime as the culmination of a providential design to bring peace, justice, and true religion back to the earth.[19] In the religious version, promulgated to justify the Anglican reform, Elizabeth was hailed as the modern counterpart of the Roman emperor Constantine, who put an end to the persecution of the early church at the beginning of the Christian era. In secular terms also, her regime was celebrated as a return or rebirth of empire: the Tudors claimed to be descended from King Arthur, and ultimately from the Trojan hero Brute. Polydore Vergil had tried to discredit these claims in the history he wrote for Henry VII, but they persisted because they helped confirm the Tudor prerogative to rule a united Britain and gave the nation a sense of continuity in the wake of the baronial wars.

The cult of Elizabeth used structures which were static, synchronistic, and centripetal to depict the course of English history, the nature of political power, and the dynamics of political action. The nation became a nest of concentric circles with a fixed center. Political power was depicted as an emanation or effluence from that center, occupied by the queen on behalf of God himself. Political action was envisaged not in terms of progress or change but as a circular process whereby power is disseminated from the center and then gathered back into the center as tribute or homage. The popularity of both pastoral and chivalric romance during the last quarter of Elizabeth's reign is owing to their aptitude for representing the political order and for making sense of history in precisely these ways. Along with the

Petrarchan love sonnet, these two literary kinds were especially privileged by the emerging institution of English poesy during the 1580s and 1590s, because they lent themselves, as "metaphoric" fictions, to the Elizabethan ideological program.

Beginning in the 1570s, pastoral entertainments were regularly incorporated into Elizabeth's yearly summer progresses into the countryside: one of Gascoigne's very last writings and one of Sidney's very first were scripts for events of this kind.[20] Louis Montrose explains that these entertainments had an ideological function similar to that of the Accession Day celebrations that Roy Strong discusses in The Cult of Elizabeth. They projected a vision of rural life that masked the social upheavals produced by the shift that England was undergoing from a feudal agrarian economy to a centralized market economy. The pastoral vision sublimated the material conditions of peasant life and "mystified" the conflicts of interest that actually obtained between the peasants and the landowning aristocracy.[21] Entertainments like the one that was held at Sudeley in 1591, which Montrose describes in some detail, affirmed "a benign relationship of mutual interest between the Queen and the lowly, between the Queen and the great, and among them all" (p. 179).

The pastoral mode could be used for social criticism and political satire: as Puttenham explained in The Art of English Poesy (p. 38), it enabled the poet "under the veil of homely persons, and in rude speeches, to insinuate and glance at greater matters." But even as an instrument of political commentary or criticism, the pastoral metaphor had an apolitical bias, because it lifted contemporary events and persons out of context and assimilated them to essentializing, transhistorical paradigms. The Shepheardes Calender is a very topical work, as E.K. is continually reminding us with his efforts to identify the shepherds as contemporary public figures or friends of the poet: and yet it is "a calender for every year."[22] As such, it naturalizes Tudor despotism[23] and moots the question of social or political change. When it is used for social criticism, the pastoral metaphor implies that the exploitation of one social class by another is as inevitable and natural as wolves and foxes, or winter and rough weather.

Where it is used to honor the queen, as it is for example in the April eclogue of The Shepheardes Calender, pastoral represents Tudor despotism as not just a benign but a natural state of affairs. As Eliza Queen of Shepherds, Queen Elizabeth has no political business to do. Colin Clout's vision cites her essential virtues as a ruler and places her at the center of an ideally harmonious community. He gives her a mythical genealogy: "She is Syrinx daughter without spotte, / Which Pan the shepheardes God of her begot." E.K. explains that it would not be fitting for a shepherd to seem to know of "a Queen's royalty." But as a poet, Colin is able to envision it; Eliza carries the genealogy of Elizabeth I of England in her face:

> Tell me, have ye seene her angelick face,
>   Like *Phoebe* fayre?
> Her heavenly haveour, her princely grace
>   can you well compare?
> The Redde rose medled with the White yfere,
> In either cheeke depeincten lively chere.
>   Her modest eye,
>   Her Maiestie,
> Where have you seene the like, but there?

> (11.64–72)

E.K.'s gloss for this stanza consists of a brief narrative:

> By the mingling of the Red rose and the White, is meant the
> uniting of the two principal houses of Lancaster and of York: by
> whose long discord and deadly debate, this realm many years was
> sore travailed, and almost clean decayed. Till the famous Henry
> the seventh, of the line of Lancaster, taking to wife the most
> virtuous Princess Elizabeth, daughter to the fourth Edward of
> the house of York, begat the most royal Henry the eighth . . . , in
> whom was the first union of the White rose and the Red.

> (p. 434)

This is a perfect example of the way in which the pastoral metaphor effects
translation from diachronic into synchronic terms and gives a political fact
the status of a fact of nature. As a political paradigm, the vision of Eliza is
static, hierarchic, and centripetal. It represents the queen not as a political
actor but as the center or source of the nation's prosperity, harmony, and
stability.

Ostensibly, pastoral and epic are antithetical genres or modes: epic is a
narrative mode that treats of war and the founding of nations—the legacy of
Cain; pastoral is a lyric mode characterized by nostalgia for "a world of
unalienated labor synchronized with the orderly cycles of nature"
(Montrose).[24] The heroes of epic are ambitious for personal and national
glory; the ethos of pastoral is an ethos of lowly contentment. When Spenser
wrote an epic that incorporates pastoral digressions and Sidney brought his
two noble princes among the shepherds of "Arcadia," they were both producing a generic paradox that throws the antithesis between the two genres
into high relief. But the merger was facilitated by the kind of epic both of
them were writing—chivalric romance. In this kind of epic, whose ideological
project is to justify despotism, heroic action is sublimated as courtship or

courtiership and the narrative line, with its burden of heroic exploit, is a
circle that returns to its point of origin.

In *The Faerie Queene*, Gloriana and Elizabeth herself and all the other
figures who stand for aspects of her greatness are imaged as centers of radi-
ance or wells of inspiration, both for the active heroism of the questing
knights and for the contemplative eulogy of the poet himself. According to
Spenser's original conception, each of the quests was to have been initiated
at the court of Gloriana, during her annual feast, and each of the knights
would finally return there to dedicate his victory to the queen. Each of the
quests would thus have extended the purview of Gloriana's glory by articulating a part of its hypothetical domain. This original conception was never
realized, but in the "Cantos of Mutabilitie" Spenser brought his unfinished
poem to closure in such a way as to disclose the ideological implications of its
narrative structure and give the Elizabethan political order a higher sanction. The rebellious titaness Mutabilitie insists that she should be acknowledged ruler of the cosmos instead of Jove, because change is the primary fact
of nature; but Nature herself is appealed to, and she confirms Jove "in his
imperiall see" by explaining that change is a universal principle but not the
ultimate ground of being:

> I well consider all that ye have sayd,
>   And find that all things stedfastnes doe hate
>   And changed be: yet being rightly wayd
>   They are not changed from their first estate;
>   But by their change their being doe dilate:
>   And turning to themselves at length againe,
>   Doe worke their owne perfection so by fate:
>   Then over them Change doth not rule and raigne;
> But they raigne over change, and doe their states maintaine.[25]

Nature's judgment provides a metaphysical rationale for the structure of the
entire poem, with its accumulating series of parallel quests. Each of the
quests is the "dilation" of a particular virtue; each of the knights is working
out his own perfection in terms of the virtue whose patron he is, whose
"pattern" he becomes. Twelve books would have completed the paradigm of
"twelve private moral virtues," and fully dilated the pattern of "a gentleman
or noble person."[26]

As Sidney went about to transform his pastoral romance into an epic, he
too gave heroic exploit a metaphoric or paradigmatic status, in keeping with
his account of how the epic poet bestows a Cyrus upon the world to make
many Cyruses. The two young princes, Pyrocles and Musidorus, are forced
to use heroic narrative as a strategy for courting the princesses, Philoclea and

Pamela: they have to assume disguises to gain entry into the pastoral enclave, and the story each of them tells of his pre-Arcadian career becomes a way to let his beloved know who he really is. Disguised as the shepherd Dorus, Musidorus tells Pamela the true history of the noble prince Musidorus; and then to confirm that he is himself that noble prince, he rigs up an opportunity to perform for her on horseback. Pamela, describing this performance to her sister, marvels at how Musidorus began and concluded every demonstration of horsemanship "with his face to me-wards, as if thence came not only the beginning but ending of his motions."[27] It is the same with his narrative, which thereby delivers up heroic prowess as erotic homage.

During the 1580s and 1590s, a great deal of erotic homage was addressed directly to the queen herself. Among her closest courtiers, the rhetoric of erotic sublimation and idealization was routinely used to depict the ruler-to-subject relation. As Leonard Tennenhouse points out in connection with what he calls the Elizabethan "literature of clientage," the language of amorous eulogy and love-complaint became the language of court politics not only because it could express the "irrational logic" of the patronage system but also because it masked the economic needs which made that system an effective instrument of government.[28] Elizabeth insisted on her royal prerogative to dispense political patronage arbitrarily, on the strength of her own assessment of the candidate's worthiness. She must be appealed to as a goddess, with absolute power to redress her suitor's predicament but no obligation to do so.

And thus the queen became for her poets, in the 1580s and 1590s, the transcendent focus of political and personal aspiration. Their poems depict her as "Eliza, Queen of Shepherds": as Gloriana, sending out her knights one after the other to achieve their self-perfection by extending her empire; and as Cynthia, whose magnetic force controls the troubled, obsessive life-rhythms of the Ocean.[29]

The centripetal force of the Elizabethan ideological program, its effectiveness in sublimating political conflict within the aristocracy and containing the momentum of religious iconoclasm, did not survive the queen herself. King James and his court did not have native English roots, and he did not continue the Elizabethan tradition of broadly based public festivity and ceremonial.[30] Stuart Britain was more cosmopolitan, but less cohesive internally, than Elizabethan England had been. Spain was no longer a threat, and so the national interest was no longer such an effective deterrent as it had been in the 1590s to factionalism within the aristocracy. James allowed the patronage system to deteriorate by awarding honors and offices lavishly but indiscriminately; and he allowed the rituals to lapse which had helped to sublimate personal ambitions and political rivalry at court. "Of court, it

seems, men courtesy do call," and courtesy presupposes a rigorous obser-
vance of hierarchy: "to bear oneself aright / To all of each degree as doth
behove," as Spenser puts it in the sixth book of *The Faerie Queene* (FQ VI, ii,
1). As hierarchy collapses, lateral antagonisms have freer play:

> Prince, father, subject, son, are things forgot,
> For every man alone thinks he hath got
> To be a Phoenix, and that there can be
> None of that kind, of which he is, but he.

"This is the world's condition now," according to Donne's *First Anniversary*,
published in 1611. The reason he gives is that

> She that should all parts to reunion bow,
> She that had all magnetic force alone,
> To draw, and fasten sundered parts in one;
> She whom wise Nature had invented then
> When she observed that every sort of men
> Did in their voyage in this world's sea stray,
> And needed a new compass for their way;
> She that was best, and first original
> Of all fair copies; and the general
> Steward to Fate; she whose rich eyes, and breast,
> Gilt the West Indies, and perfumed the East;
> Whose having breathed in this world, did bestow
> Spice on those isles, and bade them still smell so,
> And that rich Indie which doth gold inter,
> Is but as single money, coined from her;
> She to whom this world must itself refer,
> As suburbs, or the microcosm of her,
> She, she is dead; she's dead: when thou know'st this,
> Thou knowest how lame a cripple this world is.[31]

Interestingly enough, this passage does *not* refer to the death of Queen
Elizabeth in 1603. Marjorie Nicolson tried to argue that it really must be
about the queen, after all,[32] and it is easy to see why: this is the very language
of the cult of Elizabeth. But the "she" whose death this poem ostensibly
celebrates is a public nonentity, a little girl named Elizabeth Drury who died
at age fifteen. Ben Jonson is said by Drummond to have "told Mr. Donne, if
it had been written of the Virgin Mary, it had been something." The rejoin-
der attributed to Donne, "that he described the Idea of a Woman, and not as
she was," misses the real force of Jonson's objection.[33] The symbolic status of

the Virgin Mary was collectively, institutionally authorized, and the same is true of Queen Elizabeth, as we have seen. The problem is not that Elizabeth Drury could not possibly have been as virtuous as Donne makes her out to be: it is that the symbolic importance he ascribes to her has no collective, institutional sanction. The eulogist's claim on her behalf is a demonstration of his own thesis that the world is undergoing a crisis of authority in relation to all the frameworks that have traditionally afforded paradigms for collective orientation: political, religious, scientific-cosmological.

As a particular private person drawn from Donne's immediate neighborhood, Elizabeth Drury resists translation to the synchronic plane of religious and mythic archetypes that is invoked by his claims about her. Her status in relation to the rest of the world is merely metonymic, and so to designate her as its center of coherence is to turn the Elizabethan world picture into an anamorphic projection. Synchrony is forced back under the aegis of diachrony; metaphor, of metonymy. The poet asserts his prerogative to give traditional values a purely personal sanction, and thereby gives the metaphoric ideology of the Elizabethan moment a kind of ghostly afterlife.[34]

Donne's poetry is thoroughly metonymic in its orientation: he reacted against the Elizabethan poets' collective endorsement of the poetic function of language and reasserted the importance of the message-to-context relation. But this is not simply a reversion to the stance of Wyatt or Gascoigne. The change in the status of poetry in general and of the lyric in particular that had been promoted by the Elizabethan political program and fostered by the printed book was irreversible: the lyric would remain an autonomous verbal icon. Donne did not alter its status by privileging the message-to-context relation; what he did was foreground or thematize that relation, as a way to subvert the idealistic, synchronistic perspective of Elizabethan metaphoric writing.

3 "It may be good": Metonymic Deixis in the Early Tudor Lyric

'They told me you had been to her,
   And mentioned me to him:
She gave me a good character,
   But said I could not swim.

He sent them word I had not gone
   (We know it to be true):
If she should push the matter on,
   What would become of you?

I gave her one, they gave him two,
   You gave us three or more:
They all returned from him to you,
   Though they were mine before.

If I or she should chance to be
   Involved in this affair,
He trusts to you to set them free,
   Exactly as we were.

My notion was that you had been
   (Before she had this fit)
An obstacle that came between
   Him, and ourselves, and it.

Don't let him know she liked them best,
   For this must ever be
A secret kept from all the rest,
   Between yourself and me.'

'That's the most important piece of evidence we've heard yet,' said the King, rubbing his hands; 'so now let the jury——' 'If any one of them can explain it,' said Alice (she had grown so large in the last few minutes that she wasn't a bit afraid of interrupting him), 'I'll give him sixpence. *I* don't believe there's an atom of meaning in it.' The jury all wrote down on their slates, '*She* doesn't believe there's an atom of meaning in it,' but none of them attempted to explain the paper.

'If there's no meaning in it,' said the King, 'that saves a world of trouble, you know, as we needn't try to find any. And yet I don't know,' he went on, spreading out the verses on his knee, and looking at them with one eye; 'I seem to see some meaning in them, after all. "*said I could not swim—*" you can't swim, can you?' he added, turning to the Knave. The Knave shook his head sadly. 'Do I look like it?' he said. (Which he certainly did *not*, being made entirely of cardboard.) 'All right, so far,' said the King; and he went on muttering over the verses to himself: ' "*We know it to be true*"—that's the jury, of course—"*If she should push the matter on*"—that must be the Queen—"*What would become of you?*"—What indeed!—"*I gave her one, they gave him two*"—why, that must be what he did with the tarts, you know——'

'But it goes on "*they all returned from him to you*",' said Alice. 'Why, there they are!' said the King triumphantly, pointing to the tarts on the table. 'Nothing can be clearer than *that*.'

Into the climactic scene of *Alice in Wonderland,* where the Knave of Hearts is on trial for stealing some tarts, Lewis Carroll interjects a poem that is unintelligible, because it will not permit successful recuperation of its deictics or "shifters." Alice sees immediately that its message is indecipherable—"*She* doesn't believe there's an atom of meaning in it." The King of Hearts, on the other hand, needs a piece of evidence that the knave stole the tarts. This, he finds, will do very nicely, if he assumes that "I" refers to the knave, that he is himself the "you" being addressed, that "they" in the third stanza refers to the tarts on the table in front of him, and so on. The king fails to acknowledge that what he is reading is a poem, but the challenge to which he responds with naive literal-mindedness is one that most poems confront their readers with, and his misreading highlights the kind of interpretive work that almost all poems give their readers to do. We render a poem's message intelligible by producing a hypothetical context for its "I" and "you," its present and present-perfect tenses, its time and place adverbials, its demonstrative pronouns. A poem uses deictics to carry a context around with it, in the same way that "forty sails" carry around with them the fleet of ships to which they metonymically refer.

The semiotician C. S. Peirce classified deictics—along with, for instance, road signs—as "indexical symbols," because, like the act of pointing, they are in existential relation with the objects they designate. They are also known as "shifters," because although they have constant general meanings, their meanings are in another sense variable.[1] "I" always means "the one who is saying 'I'," and so the particular person it designates will shift back and forth in a conversation with each change of speaker. Similarly "here" designates wherever the speaker happens to be, and she takes "here" with her wherever she goes. Deictics are all of those words that give a verbal message its orientation, temporal, spatial, and interpersonal, from the addresser's or speaker's vantage point.[2]

In an oral exchange, the parties to the communication are there to be pointed at by their own "I's" and "you's"; in a lyric poem, of course, they are not. Jonathan Culler explains in *Structuralist Poetics*[3] that for the lyric one of the fundamental conventions of reading is the interpretive move whereby the reader produces the situation that is indicated by all of the poem's deictics: "One morning the poet was in bed with his mistress and, when awakened by the sun which told him that it was time to be up and about his affairs, he said, 'busie old foole, unruly Sunne . . .'" To illustrate this interpretive move, Culler has chosen a well-known poem of John Donne's, "The Sun Rising":

> Busy old fool, unruly Sun,
> 　　Why dost thou thus,
> Through windows, and through curtains, call on us?
> Must to thy motions lovers' seasons run?
> 　　Saucy pedantic wretch, go chide
> 　　Late schoolboys, and sour prentices,
> 　　Go tell court-huntsmen that the King will ride,
> 　　Call country ants to harvest offices;
> Love, all alike, no season knows, nor clime,
> Nor hours, days, months, which are the rags of time.
>
> 　　Thy beams, so reverend and strong
> 　　Why shouldst thou think?
> I could eclipse and cloud them with a wink,
> But that I would not lose her sight so long:
> 　　If her eyes have not blinded thine,
> 　　Look, and tomorrow late, tell me

> Whether both Indias, of spice, and mine,
>   Be where thou leftst them, or lie here with me.
> Ask for those Kings whom thou saw'st yesterday,
> And thou shalt hear: 'All here in one bed lay.'
>
>   She is all States, and all Princes I,
>   Nothing else is:
> Princes do but play us; compar'd to this,
> All honor's mimic, all wealth alchemy.
>   Thou, sun, art half as happy as we,
>   In that the world's contracted thus;
>   Thine age asks ease, and since thy duties be
>   To warm the world, that's done in warming us.
> Shine here to us, and thou art everywhere;
> This bed thy center is, these walls, thy sphere.[4]

Ostensibly, this poem's speaker is oblivious to our need to know where he is, to know that the woman he loves is there with him, and so forth. We have to figure these things out for ourselves, by construing his deictic references: his "I" and "thou" and "us" and "thus" and "here." From our point of view, his utterance is a metonymy: it is part of a larger situation that must be produced by our reading of the poem.

The appropriateness of the term "metonymy" for this relationship between the speaker's utterance and the context it presupposes will perhaps be more obvious if we specify the relationship more precisely, as metonymy of effect for cause. We must infer from the speaker's words the situation that has prompted or caused them—the poem's occasion, as it is often called. In this poem deictic references are strategically supplemented by appositive phrases, so that the speaker can give us crucial information without seeming to be aware of our need for it. The sun is not merely addressed ("thou"), but apostrophized ("unruly Sun"). "Thus" and "here" are explained ("through windows"; "through curtains"), although the word "bedroom" never appears. The poem's occasion is too complex and specific to have been conveyed by deictic references alone, but they are the crucial agents of its metonymic strategy. They are what has enabled Donne to give a convincing representation of spontaneous oral delivery.

Spatial, temporal, and social deixis will all work together to anchor a lyric poem to the here and now of the one who says "I": "now" is to some degree implied by "here," and vice versa. But each of these dimensions may also be elaborated independently and out of proportion to the others. A spatial dimension is projected by means of place adverbials and demonstratives: "here," "there," "this place." A temporal matrix is brought into play through verb tense and time adverbials. A social context is presupposed with personal pronouns, especially "I" and "you."

Deictic orientation is so important for the lyric that standard definitions usually make its proper business out to be the depiction of somebody speaking. Barbara Herrnstein Smith has suggested that we think of the lyric as "the imitation or representation of an utterance."[5] Meyer Abrams, in his *Glossary of Literary Terms*, says a lyric is "any fairly short, non-narrative poem presenting a single speaker who expresses a state of mind or a process of thought and feeling."[6] There are poems, however, for which a definition like Abrams's is not very appropriate, and might even be misleading.

On the Life of Man

What is our life? a play of passion,
Our mirth the music of division;
Our mothers' wombs the 'tiring houses be,
Where we are dressed for this short comedy;
Heaven the judicious sharp spectator is,
That sits and marks still who doth act amiss;
Our graves that hide us from the searching Sun,
Are like drawn curtains when the play is done;
Thus march we playing to our latest rest,
Only we die in earnest, that's no jest.[7]

This poem's interest is enhanced for many readers if they suppose it to have been written to express Sir Walter Ralegh's state of mind while he awaited execution for treason; but no such situation is implicit in the poem's language. Whereas "The Sun Rising" is full of deictic references to a particular context of utterance, Ralegh's poem eschews such reference entirely: there is not even an "I" to hold responsible for the question and its answer. The pronoun "we" is a shifter, but Ralegh's "we" has nowhere to shift: it is coextensive with "man." In Donne's poem the present tense is contextualized by time adverbials, imperatives, verbs in past and future tenses that gesture backwards and forwards from a particular vantage point. Ralegh's unvarying present tense is uncontextualized, and thus atemporal. His copular verbs are like equal signs in an equation.

Ralegh's poem is the sort of message that linguists often illustrate with the sentence, "A bachelor is an unmarried man." Such statements are metalinguistic: their function is to inform us about the conventions of the code we are using. "A bachelor is an unmarried man" tells us that "unmarried man" is what "bachelor" normally signifies. Metalinguistic statements are context-independent; and so is this poem. It correlates a broad, basic definition of "life"—the interval between birth and death; the activities which fill that interval—with an equally broad and basic definition of "play"—stage presentation; musical performance; jest. The Donne poem, by contrast, is strongly "set toward the context":[8] it differs from the Ralegh poem in the same way that the sentence "I have been here since yesterday" differs from "A bachelor is an unmarried man."

The degree to which a poem is set toward the context by deictic references can vary between the extremes that I have used Donne's and Ralegh's poems to exemplify. In Ralegh's poem, virtually nothing has been done to give the utterance a specific occasion or vantage point. Donne's poem is intricately situated in terms of all three dimensions: temporal, spatial, and social or interpersonal.

My discussion of the lyrics of Wyatt and Surrey will focus on their metonymic use of deixis. For these two members of the Tudor aristocracy, writing as they did for oral performance or for immediate circulation in manuscript, lyric poetry was an intrinsic part of social life. Their poems are highly context-oriented and context-implicated: they have specific occasions. If we are nevertheless able to read them at a distance from, and even in ignorance of, those occasions, that is because they have used deixis to project a larger context for the social gestures their speakers make. Deixis is Wyatt's most important figurative device, and it is responsible for the characteristic terseness and sometimes obscurity of his poems. Time is the most important and most skillfully articulated dimension of the context a poem of his will use deictic references to presuppose. Surrey was less skillful than Wyatt in terms of that dimension. His use of deixis is on the whole simpler, and for Surrey spatial orientation was the most important means of giving a poem a particular occasion.

"It is not until we reach Donne and Shakespeare and the sixteenth century draws to its close," remarks Raymond Southall, "that we experience anything comparable to the sharp and refreshing sense of personal contact which is occasioned by such poems as 'They fle from me,' 'Eche man me telleth' and 'It may be good.' "[9] What creates that sharp sense of personal contact is Wyatt's metonymic use of deixis. Typically, a poem of his will be strongly set toward a context that is presupposed by the poem's language without being fully explicated. His poems seem to depict a man thinking aloud to himself, or addressing someone else out of a shared past that has put them on intimate terms. In order to make sense of what the speaker is saying, the reader must hypothetically produce the situation that lies behind his words. Often a lyric of Wyatt's situates itself at a turning point: the speaker's words presuppose an interpersonal rupture or propose a break with the past. The manipulation of verb tense, time adverbials, and pronouns is these poems' most important figurative strategy.[10]

Of the three poems Southall mentions, the most emphatically and ellipti-
cally metonymic is "It may be good," which seemed to Southall to epitomize
the courtier's predicament at the court of Henry VIII. The poem's subject or
theme is the state of mind that is summarized in its refrain: "For dread to fall
I stand not fast." This state of uneasiness is represented as being habitual for
the speaker, but it has an immediate cause or trigger also: the event, propo-
sition, or whatever is presupposed by the poem's very first word.

> It may be good, like it who list,
> But I do doubt: who can me blame?
> For oft assured yet have I missed,
> And now again I fear the same:
> The windy words, the eyes' quaint game,
> Of sudden change maketh me aghast:
> For dread to fall I stand not fast.
>
> Alas, I tread an endless maze
> That seeketh to accord two contraries
> And hope still, and nothing hase,
> Imprisoned in liberties,
> As one unheard and still that cries,
> Always thirsty, and yet nothing I taste:
> For dread to fall I stand not fast.
>
> Assured I doubt I be not sure;
> And should I trust to such surety
> That oft hath put the proof in ure
> And never hath found it trusty?
> Nay, sir, in faith it were great folly.
> And yet my life thus do I waste:
> For dread to fall I stand not fast.[11]

The poem's first two lines also presuppose an audience that knows enough
about "it" and about past disappointments of the speaker's to have its own
opinion as to whether he should go after "it" or not. By itself the phrase "like
it who list" might pass for a reference to mankind in general, the verbal
equivalent of a shrug of the shoulders; but in combination with "who can
me blame," it acquires the force of a reference to the speaker's immediate
social milieu. Donne probably would have provided more specific clues as to
what it was that triggered the speaker's outburst, and Tottel seems to have
been trying to do just that when he published the poem in his *Miscellany*: he
changed line 5 to read "The words that from your mouth last came."[12] But

Tottel's change is not an improvement; we really do not need to know more. The idiom of amorous courtship—the commonplace oxymorons, the word "game"—leaves us in no doubt as to the *kind* of thing "it" is. At the same time, the utterance seems to dramatize its speaker's taciturnity. It consists of very short sentences, most of whose verbs are specific about his desires and feelings but are not given direct objects or adverbial complements to specify just *what* he was assured of, hopes for, has often missed. The references that he does make to these things are all metonymies—"the windy words, the eyes' quaint game"—or else metaphors whose tenors must be guessed at, although this is not hard to do: thirst, imprisonment, "an endless maze." In combination, all these ways of not quite giving us the particulars seem to dramatize the theme of the poem: the speaker's unwillingness to "hase" (i.e., "hazard") anything.

The manipulation of verbal and adverbial deixis is especially interesting in this poem. Each stanza begins and ends in the present tense, and that present tense is assisted by "now again," "still," and "thus" to convey not only "this is how it always is for me" but "on this particular occasion I again experience a familiar feeling." Meanwhile in subordinate clauses, what has often happened in the past is adduced as having brought about the speaker's state of uncertainty: "And should I trust . . . That oft have put the proof in ure / And never have found it trusty." In these lines the perfect tense is made capable by the adverbs "oft" and "never" of a deep perspective into past time, but keeps its purchase on the present vantage point of the one who says "I," who now experiences the cumulative force of past experience. In the first and third stanzas Wyatt uses the perfect participle "assured" to give "I" simultaneous predicates in different tenses and thereby to put assurance and uncertainty in an oxymoronic relation: "Assured I doubt I be not sure." The possibility of a different stance is broached ("And should I trust . . . ?") but then immediately mooted, by another sentence that gives "I" contradictory predicates. The structure of these sentences seems to show us how past experience keeps the one who says "I" from adopting a more trusting or hopeful posture.

Many of Wyatt's poems not only tell us about the feelings of a frustrated lover but seem actually to dramatize his state of mind. This is owing to his dexterity in the deictic manipulation of verb tense. He will situate his speaker firmly in the immediate present, with the help of time adverbials, present-perfect verb forms, and past-present antitheses. Past events will be presupposed in embedded phrases and clauses, so that the utterance is consistently focused by its main clauses on a present attitude or dilemma or project:

> Since that so oft ye have made me to wake
> In plaint and tears and in right piteous case,

Displease you not if force do now me make
To break your sleep, crying "Alas! alas!"

(Egerton, 73, 11.9–12)

Alas, madame! for stealing of a kiss,
Have I so much your mind then offended?

(Egerton, 44, 11.1–2)

The past always figures in his poems not as narrated history but in terms of
its bearing on the present, or of the aspect it wears with hindsight:

I am mistaken wonderly,
For I thought nought but faithfulness,
Yet I remain all comfortless.

(Egerton, 62, 11.12–14)

It was no dream: I lay broad waking.
But all is turned thorough my gentleness
Into a strange fashion of forsaking,

(Egerton, 37, 11.15–17)

Who list to live in quietness
By me let him beware,
For I by high disdain
Am made without redress,
And unkindness alas hath slain
My poor true heart all comfortless.

(Egerton, 89, 11.8–13)

Ye know my heart, my lady dear,
That since the time I was your thrall
I have been yours both whole and clear,
Though my reward hath been but small:
So am I yet, and more than all.

(Egerton, 41, 11.1–5)

The answer that ye made to me, my dear,
When I did sue for my poor heart's redress,
Hath so appalled my countenance and my cheer
That in this case I am all comfortless,

(Egerton, 90, 11.1–4)

In the first two of these passages, the speaker is struck by a paradoxical discontinuity between past and present, and this is conveyed by the juxta-position of present and preterit verbs. In the second he uses a passive con-struction ("is turned") to record the change from one state of affairs to another and thereby avoids a dynamic mediation, such as the perfect tense would accomplish, between what used to be and what is now. In the last three passages, this kind of mediation does occur. The last one makes it especially easy to see how the perfect tense will represent the relation between past events and present feelings as a psychological dynamic: "Did so appall . . ." would have been grammatically and metrically acceptable, but the perfect tense implies that the "appalling" has been a gradual process, culminating in the speaker's present condition.

In Wyatt's poetry psychological states and interpersonal relationships are almost always given a finite time-frame. Here, for example, is a translation of his that departs in small but significant ways from its original:

> Such vain thought as wonted to mislead me,
> In desert hope, by well assured moan,
> Maketh me from company to live alone
> In following her whom reason bid me flee.
> She fleeth as fast by gentle cruelty,
> And after her my heart would fain be gone,
> But armed sighs my way do stop anon,
> 'Twixt hope and dread locking my liberty.
> Yet as I guess under disdainful brow
> One beam of pity is in her cloudy look
> Which comforteth the mind that erst for fear shook,
> And therewithal bolded I seek the way how
> To utter the smart that I suffer within:
> But such it is, I not* how to begin.
> *ne wot - don't know

(Egerton, 56)

Robert Durling's more exact prose translation shows that Petrarch's poem adheres to a frequentative present tense, the tense of "what happens to me from time to time."

> Full of a yearning thought that makes me stray
> away from all others and go alone in the world,
> from time to time I steal myself away from myself, still
> seeking only her whom I should flee;

and I see her pass so sweet and cruel that my soul
trembles to rise in flight, such a crowd of armed
sighs she leads, this lovely enemy of Love and me.

If I do not err, I do perceive a gleam of pity on
her cloudy proud brow, which partly clears my
sorrowing heart:

then I collect my soul, and, when I have decided to
discover my ills to her, I have so much to say to
her that I dare not begin.[13]

(*Rime*, 169)

Petrarch is talking about an enduring state of yearning that is intensified by
a recurrent wish-yet-inability to speak of his suffering to the one who is
responsible for it. The frequentative present tense lifts his dilemma out of
time, thereby helping to give it a wholly subjective status. Wyatt's changes of
tense work toward grounding the inability to speak in a particular encounter
with the lady. The speaker's dilemma becomes an interpersonal episode at a
particular point in time. Wyatt has split the frequentative present tense of
Petrarch's first quatrain into a frequentative past ("wonted to mislead") and a
present that then, increasingly, seems to refer to the present moment of the
utterance itself. In the sestet, Petrarch's "cor doglioso" ("sorrowing heart")
becomes "the mind that *erst* for fear shook" but is *now* comforted by a "beam
of pity" from the lady. The changes do not quite work, but their tendency is
toward the kind of predicament Wyatt handled more successfully in "It may
be good."

The same tendency is discernible in a sonnet of Petrarch's that both Wyatt
and Surrey translated, "Amor che nel penser mio viva e regna" (*Rime*, 140).
Petrarch's Amor, Surrey's "Love that liveth and reigneth in my thought,"
becomes in Wyatt's translation "The long love that in my thought doth
harbor." Surrey's is the more faithful translation; Wyatt has shifted the mode
of representation of psychological experience from achronic allegory toward
temporal metonymy. Petrarch's speaker is in love; Wyatt's has been in love for
a long time.

Wyatt's lyrics are often laconically brief and suggestive, without being
fragmentary or incomplete, by virtue of depicting an utterance that metonymically cites a larger context. A good example of this is a translation of a poem
of Serafino whose wording is very close to the original:

What needeth these threatening words and wasted wind?
All this cannot make me restore my prey.
To rob your good* iwis** is not my mind,

> Nor causeless your fair hand I did display.
> Let love be judge or else whom next we meet
> That may both hear what you and I can say.
> She took from me an heart, and I a glove from her:
> Let us see now, if the one be worth the other.
> *property **certainly

(Egerton, 48)

The achievement of this poem is to make the utterance it imitates believably presuppose a situation whose most important datum is a nonverbal act. The speaker does not tell his addressee things she already knows: "I have stolen your glove and you are angry." But the poem conveys these things to the reader, partly through deictic references that force us to presuppose an interpersonal crisis ("*these* threatening words"), and partly by means of the speaker's hypothetical appeal for arbitration to someone who, like the reader, was not there to see him steal her glove. The same pretext serves for disclosure of something we could not have literally seen even if we had been there: the lady's theft of his heart. Thus the poem functions as a metonymy for a whole little two-character scene, and beyond that for an interpersonal "histoire" that gets projected backward and forward from within the poem itself.

That Wyatt could reproduce the metonymic strategy of the Serafino poem on his own is demonstrated by another little poem of his which has the same length and metric structure:

> Lux, my fair falcon, and your fellows all,
> How well pleasant it were your liberty!
> Ye not forsake me that fair might ye befall,
> But they that sometime liked my company,
> Like lice away from dead bodies they crawl:
> Lo, what a proof in light adversity!
> But ye, my birds, I swear by all your bells,
> Ye be my friends, and so be but few else.

(Hill MS., 168)

In the same way as the Serafino translation, this poem conveys much more than its speaker actually says, and there is an ironic relation between the small part of his world that is highlighted or "foregrounded" and all the rest that is implicit or "backgrounded." His falcons are right there in the room with him; he is looking at them as he speaks. He prefers their company to that of the fair-weather friends who have abandoned him, and whom he relegates with the deictic vagueness of his allusion—"they that sometime liked my company"—to the outermost periphery of his consciousness. But it is really they who have placed themselves there, whereas his birds are not able to forsake him: the bells he refers to in the next-to-last line are attached, as we must suppose, to the harness that keeps them from flying away. "I swear by all your bells" conveys that he knows this perfectly well and suspects that there is no one, including his best friends in the animal kingdom, who would not choose to desert a man when his luck runs out. As in the Serafino translation, the next-to-last line is pivotal. It makes just that reference to the context that is necessary to disclose the speaker's situation fully to us.

Wyatt's poems are not always perfectly successful at situating a speaker out of his own mouth at a particular juncture in his ongoing social life. Where this has not been successfully managed, the poem seems to call for more background information.

> Sometime I fled the fire that me brent
> By sea, by land, by water and by wind;
> And now I follow the coals that be quent
> From Dover to Calais against my mind.
> Lo, how desire is both sprung and spent!
> And he may see that whilom was so blind,
> And all his labor now he laugh to scorn,
> Meshed in the briers that erst was all to-torn.
>
> (Egerton, 59)

Clearly this poem turns on a contrast between how the poet-lover used to feel and how he feels now: the fire that once burned him is quenched, the desire he once felt is spent; his eyes are opened; he can laugh now at what used to give him pain. The opposition between flying and following in the first four lines is in an ironic relation to all of the others; and whereas it is easy enough to understand that the lover fled when his desire was at full strength, it is not obvious why he should now be following, against his will, "the coals that be quent." For this to come clear, we would need more information about the journey.

Raymond Southall assimilates this poem to the Anne Boleyn affair, and suggests that its occasion was a trip King Henry had arranged to make to Boulogne, to meet with the King of France, in 1532. Anne went with him; they were married later that same year. Wyatt accompanied the royal party; he had been Marshal of Calais since 1528. This information seems to be just what is needed to account for the flying-following paradox of the first four lines. But Southall's reading of the rest of the poem is less convincing: he takes Wyatt to be "[expressing] trepidation . . . at the thought that the king, ill enough done by already, may discover how very badly he is being used."[14] Southall's reading is based on the assumption that "he" in line 5 and thereafter refers to Henry: "he may see that whilom was so blind." More likely, "he" is the "I" of the first four lines, who now that his desire is spent can assume a posture of scornful detachment in relation to his former blindness. Many of Wyatt's poems use a particular personal experience to rediscover the validity of a proverbial commonplace. The shift from first to third person here is surely an instance of this kind of generalizing move, with the fifth line—"Lo how desire is both sprung and spent!"—acting as a bridge between narration and reflection.

In this poem the speaker's utterance has not served as an adequate metonymy for his situation. Clearly, however, biographical information is not an infallible remedy for the sort of difficulty this makes for the reader. Southall's discovery of King Henry behind this poem's "he" is a little like the King of Hearts' seeming to have discovered a valuable piece of evidence in the case of the missing tarts.

As John Stevens has pointed out in his study of *Music and Poetry in the Early Tudor Court*, lyrics like Wyatt's were above all social gestures, "gambits in a game of love."[15] A contemporary audience would presumably have been able to guess at what "it" referred to in "It may be good," or who "they" were "that sometime liked my company" in "Lux, my fair falcon." Their guesses would have been a way of playing the game along with the disaffected lover. It may have been unwise to be any more explicit concerning these poems' occasions, especially in the ones that allude to Wyatt's involvement with Anne Boleyn. Had he been writing for a different kind of publication, he might have written poems whose metonymic strategy is not so challenging and sometimes problematic.

But one of his own poems tells us that even his original audience complained of his obscurity. The poem's way of responding to this complaint shows that Wyatt had taken the measure of his own strategy and was disappointed to find that his contemporaries could not or would not do the kind of interpretive work that it challenges.

> Me list no more to sing
> Of love nor of such thing
> How sore that it me wring,
> For what I sung or spake,
> Men did my songs mistake.
>
> My songs were too diffuse,
> They made folk to muse.
> Therefore, me to excuse,
> They shall be sung more plain,
> Neither of joy nor pain.

From this point on, for six stanzas, the poem just goes on *ad nauseam* piling up proverbial commonplaces: untasted fruit will rot; treasure that is locked away is worthless; *carpe diem*. In the midst of this the poet pauses like an officious preacher or schoolmaster to call his readers to attention:

> Therefore fear not to essay
> To gather, ye that may,
> The flower that this day
> Is fresher than the next:
> Mark well, I say, this text.

His songs used to have occasions in his emotional life: that kind of poem "made folk to muse." This kind of poem does not invite them to go beyond its explicit statements, which have the same out-of-context self-sufficiency as Ralegh's "On the Life of Man." Would folk rather have this kind of aphoristic preachment than the kind of poem that is "diffuse" in the sense of allowing its language to have a larger field of reference? Would they rather have poems from which the one who says "I" completely disappears except as a monitory finger that directs their attention to impersonal commonplaces?

> If this be under mist
> And not well plainly wist,
> Understand me who list:
> For I reck not a bean,
> I wot what I do mean.
>
> (Devonshire, 130)

Ironically, such commonplaces turn out to have their own kind of inscrutability here, precisely because they are not in any way contextualized or motivated. Usually in Wyatt's lyrics commonplaces are brought in to serve as an interpretive gloss for particular experiences:

> It was not long ere I by proof had found
> That feeble building is on feeble ground
>
> (Egerton, 71, 11.17–18)

> . . . I leave off therefore,
> Sithens in a net I seek to hold the wind.
>
> (Egerton, 7)

> The bell tower showed me such a sight
> That in my head sticks day and night:

> There did I learn out of a grate,
> For all favor, glory or might,
> That yet *circa Regna tonat.*
>
> (Blage MS., 143, 11.16–20)

The particular experience gives the commonplace fresh currency, and the commonplace gives the particular experience exemplary force. "Me list no more to sing" is perplexing not because its speaker's situation is inadequately presupposed but because its "text" has no context at all.

When Richard Tottel published Wyatt's lyrics after his death, he tried to help his readers produce the contexts they presuppose by giving many of them headnotes like "The lover complaineth that his love doth not pity him," or "To his love whom he had kissed against her will." Ironically, these headnotes must have been partly responsible for the failure of Wyatt's mid-century imitators to reproduce his metonymic strategy. The translation from Serafino that I have already cited as one of Wyatt's most perfectly metonymic poems appeared in *Tottel's Miscellany* with the heading, "To his love from whom he had her gloves."[16] The heading spoils the fun of the poem for the reader, which is like the fun of anticipating the answer to a riddle. George Turberville used this poem as a model for one of his, but obviously did not learn anything from its strategy of deictic presupposal:

To a Gentlewoman from whom he took a Ring

> What needs this frowning face?
>   what means your look so coy?
> Is all this for a ring,
>   a trifle and a toy?
> What though I reft your ring,
>   I took it not to keep;
> Therefore you need the less
>   in such despite to weep:
> For Cupid shall be judge
>   and umpire in this case,
> Or who by hap shall next
>   approach into this place.
> You took from me my heart,
>   I caught from you a ring;
> Whose is the greatest loss?
>   Where ought the grief to spring?
> Keep you as well my heart,
>   as I will keep your ring,

And you shall judge at last
   that you have lost nothing.
For if a friendly heart,
   so stuffed with staid love,
In value do not pass
   the ring, you may reprove
The reaving of the same:
   and I of force must say
That I deserved the blame
   who took your ring away.
But what if you do wreak
   your malice on my heart?
Then give me leave to think
   you guilty for your part;
And when so e'er I yield
   to you your ring again,
Restore me up my heart
   that now you put to pain.
For so we both be pleased
   to say we may be bold
That neither to the loss
   of us hath bought or sold.[17]

In the Serafino/Wyatt original, the lover's appeal to Cupid "or else whom next we meet" is a pretext for referring to the lady's grievance against him and a means of grounding his utterance as of a particular point in time: he has just stolen her glove, and she has been scolding him, and a passerby might happen along at any moment. In Turberville's poem, the appeal to Cupid becomes a bit of rhetorical persiflage, because it is not needed for reader orientation: other arrangements have already been made for referring to what the speaker did to anger the gentlewoman. Whereas Wyatt's poems are sometimes imperfectly metonymic through not saying enough, Turberville fails of metonymy here by saying too much: his poem's most obvious defect is that it is too prolix. In the Serafino/Wyatt poem just enough, and just the right things, are said to bring the whole situation into focus by means of a part that seems in proportion small.

Modern readers of Wyatt are better able than Tottel's original readers to work with the kind of poem that metonymically presupposes its own occasion, because we have had Donne's more vivid and obvious metonymies to teach us how.[18] Both Donne and Wyatt imitate utterances that are highly context-oriented and context-implicated, but Donne made more extensive use of spatial and interpersonal deixis than Wyatt. Wyatt's poems tend to be metonymic not of a scene but of a relationship or a psychological process. The Serafino translation is more Donne-like than most of Wyatt's lyrics, in its presupposal of a physical as well as a temporal context for the utterance.[19] Wyatt's poems usually presuppose an active listener but do not fully dramatize an interpersonal encounter. Often, as in "It may be good" and "Each man me telleth," the speaker does not explicitly address an interlocutor until near the end of the poem. Often deictic formulas like "whoso list" will gesture toward a larger social world that remains, for the reader, just out of range or out of focus. Typically the center of the poem's field of force is the "I" who speaks and the temporal juncture from which he speaks. Hence the impression of neurotic egotism, alienation, even paranoia that one gets from reading too many of Wyatt's lyrics at a sitting.

Another hallmark of Wyatt's dexterity as a metonymic poet is the way in which he handles the refrain-poem: a refrain of Wyatt's will change its meaning as the same words get recontextualized from stanza to stanza. Sometimes the shift is the instrument of a new insight or a change in the speaker's attitude. In "My lute, awake," for example, the meaning of the repeated phrase "I have done," as in "My lute be still, for I have done," completely changes in the poem's penultimate stanza. In every other stanza this refrain uses the present-perfect tense to refer to the immediate present of the song's delivery, helping thus to create the impression that the singer is still actively trying to "have done" with his fruitless effort to pierce the heart of the impervious lady:

> As to be heard where ear is none,
> As lead to grave in marble stone,
> My song may pierce her heart as soon.
> Should we then sigh or sing or moan?
> No, no, my lute, for I have done.
>
> (Egerton, 66, stanza 2)

In the next-to-last stanza, the refrain does not mean "I have finished," but instead becomes part of a prediction that the lady will come eventually, when she is "withered and old," to experience the same frustrated longing that he has gone through for her sake: "Then shalt thou know beauty but lent, / And wish and want as I have done." The shift in meaning reflects a shift on the singer's part from the short to the long view of his disappointment. By achieving that longer view, he becomes able to have done, in the original sense of the phrase, and thereby bring his song to a satisfying closure in the very next stanza:

Now cease, my lute: this is the last
Labor that thou and I shall waste,
And ended is that we begun.
Now is this song both sung and past:
My lute, be still, for I have done.

In another of Wyatt's most impressive refrain-poems, the speaker is explicitly concerned with a problematic code-to-context relation:

In eternum I was once determed
For to have loved, and my mind affirmed
That with my heart it should be confirmed
        In eternum.

Forthwith I found the thing that I might like,
And sought with love to warm her heart alike,
For as me thought I should not see the like
        In eternum.

To trace this dance I put myself in press;
Vain hope did lead, and bade I should not cease
To serve, to suffer, and still to hold my peace
        In eternum.

With this first rule I furthered me apace,
That as me thought my truth had taken place
With full assurance to stand in her grace
        In eternum.

It was not long ere I by proof had found
That feeble building is on feeble ground,
For in her heart this word did never sound—
        In eternum.

In eternum then from my heart I kest
That I had first determed for the best:
Now in the place another thought doth rest
        In eternum.

                                            (Egerton, 71)

Each of the first four stanzas uses the repeated phrase "in eternum" in a
sentence where it means "forevermore," but its connotations are subtly different from one setting to the next. In the second stanza, it helps to express

the lover's conviction that the woman he chose to love was peerless; in the third, it lends a certain grimness to his fidelity; in the fourth, it gives his pledge, and the "assurance" he thought it had reciprocally elicited, the status of a binding contract. In the penultimate stanza, instead of changing its meaning, the phrase is momentarily emptied of meaning: he does not use it in a sentence but cites it as a mere "word." What he discovered, finally, was that his own mind was the only context in which the notion of a permanent commitment "had taken place." In the last stanza he does not tell us what "other thought" has replaced it, perhaps because there is no word for that thought, or perhaps to convey, as in "Me list no more to sing," that he no longer cares whether he is understood or not.

Surrey's poems are not as strongly set toward a presupposed context of utterance as Wyatt's are. His speakers strike conventional poses: they complain of grief, they swear to be true, they rail upon Cupid, with bold, simple rhetorical gestures. Whereas Wyatt's "I" is usually speaking from a critical juncture in an interpersonal "histoire," Surrey's will expatiate from a particular state of mind without acknowledging its implication in a dynamic train of events. If a poem of his discloses how the lover came to be in love or in pain, it almost never uses embedded clauses and shifters to put what has happened in relation to what is being urged or felt in the present. Surrey resorts to simpler expedients: the paratactic "and then" of narrative, "and eke" of catalogue. In several of his poems verb tense is clumsily handled precisely where Wyatt showed himself adept: where it is a question of articulating the bearing of past experience on the present, or of negotiating between what has been wont to happen and what is in the offing here and now.

In this translation, for example, Surrey needed but did not introduce a perfect tense to help him render the involuted hypotaxis of Petrarch's ballata:

> I never saw you, madam, lay apart
> Your cornet black, in cold nor yet in heat,
> Sith first ye knew of my desire so great,
> Which other fancies chased clean from my heart.
> While to myself I did the thought reserve
> That so un'ware did wound my woeful breast,
> Pity I saw within your heart did rest;
> But since ye knew I did you love and serve,
> Your golden tress was clad alway in black,
> Your smiling looks were hid thus evermore,
> All that withdrawn that I did crave so sore.
> So doth this cornet govern me, alack!

> In summer, sun; in winter, breath of frost;
> Of your fair eyes whereby the light is lost.[20]

The poem turns upon the difference between how the lady used to behave
before she knew of her lover's desire, and how she has behaved ever since, up
to the present moment of his complaint. The poem should take its departure
from the speaker's vantage point in the present: "Lady, I have never seen you
put aside your veil" is how Robert Durling begins his prose version of the
original.[21] The long "since" clause in the sestet should also be thrown into
the present-perfect tense. In Surrey's version the before-since antithesis is
blurred by his persistence in the preterit, and then the last three lines lurch
into the present, where the speaker should have positioned himself to begin
with.

In another poem of Surrey's, "When youth had led me half the race," it is
perhaps even clearer that something is wrong with the tense structure.[22] The
lover explains in the first two stanzas that at a certain point he paused to
reflect upon how he had spent his youth:

> When youth had led me half the race
> That Cupid's scourge did make me run,
> I looked back to meet the place
> From whence my weary course begun.
>
> And then I saw how my desire
> By ill guiding had let* my way;
> Whose eyes, too greedy of their hire,
> Had lost me many a noble pray.
> *hindered

There follows for several stanzas a past-tense narrative account of how he saw
himself as having behaved, up to that point: he had, as we say, worn his
heart on his sleeve.

> For when in sighs I spent the day,
> And could not cloak my grief by game,
> Their boiling smoke did still bewray
> The fervent rage of hidden flame.

In the last two stanzas of this poem, the lover explains that now he behaves
very differently: "all too late," he knows how to dissemble and keep his
feelings a secret. Oddly enough, however, he never reverts to the vantage
point he had established for reflection in the poem's opening stanzas:
instead, he moves into a frequentative present tense, using a pivotal "but" to

create a simple binary opposition between "how I used to behave" and "how I behave now":

> But all too late Love learneth me
> To paint all kind of colors new,
> To blind their eyes that else should see
> My sparkled cheeks with Cupid's hue.
>
> And now the covert breast I claim
> That worships Cupid secretly,
> And nourisheth his sacred flame
> From whence no blazing sparks do fly.

(Poem 15)

Here, for comparison, is a sonnet of Surrey's that does successfully articulate the same relationship between the lover's present condition and a moment of reflective self-evaluation in the recent past:

> The fancy which that I have served long,
> That hath alway been enemy to mine ease,
> Seemed of late to rue upon my wrong
> And bade me fly the cause of my misease.
>   And I forthwith did press out of the throng,
> That thought by flight my painful heart to please
> Some other way, till I saw faith more strong.
> And to myself I said, "Alas! those days
>   In vain were spent, to run the race so long."
> And with that thought I met my guide, that plain
> Out of the way wherein I wandered wrong
> Brought me amidst the hills in base Bullayn;
>   Where I am now, as restless to remain,
>   Against my will, full pleased with my pain.

(Poem 9)

This poem's discourse is a little clumsy, so that the last six lines are hard to make sense of; but there is no loophole in its tense structure. The first main clause is in the past tense, but includes a subordinate clause in the present-perfect tense which is assisted by the adverbs "long" and "alway" to encompass the recent occasion with which the main clause is concerned. Within the account of what the speaker did on that occasion, we are told of a moment in which he said to himself that he had been wasting his time up to that point. Here that moment is successfully embedded in a narrative that carries him back again into the present: line 10 is the link that was missing in the other poem between the two retrospective vantage points. Perhaps the

reason why Surrey was successful here with a very complicated tense structure is that his speaker's vantage point in the immediate present, from which
the poem begins and to which it returns in the last three lines, is geograph-
ically reinforced: "Brought me *amidst the hills in base Bullayn* / Where I am
now . . ." Surrey seems to have least difficulty keeping his purchase on a here
and now from which to "express a state of mind or a process of thought and
feeling" in poems where the "here" is concretely specified.

Surrey's single best poem, "So cruel prison," takes its departure from a
vantage point in the present whose physical location is not just a setting for
reflection but the stimulus that has triggered it:

> So cruel prison, how could betide, alas,
> As proud Windsor, where I, in lust and joy,
> With a king's son my childish years did pass . . .

In this poem, the kind of paratactic listing to which he often resorts to give
his poems a middle is powerfully motivated by the setting itself, in several
different ways at once. The speaker is physically imprisoned at Windsor
Castle; he is nostalgically inclined to let each of its features trigger a different
memory; and together these memories constitute an idyllic conspectus of his
boyhood:

> The large green courts, where we were wont to hove,
> With eyes cast up unto the maidens' tower,
> And easy sighs, such as men draw in love.
>
> The stately sales,* the Ladies bright of hue,
> The dances short, long tales of great delight,
> With words and looks that tigers could but rue,
> Where each of us did plead the other's right.
> *rooms
>
> The palm-play, where, despoiled for the game,
> With dazèd eyes oft we by gleams of love
> Have missed the ball, and got sight of our dame,
> To bait her eyes which kept the leads above.
>
> The gravelled ground, ...
> . . . .
> The secret groves, ...
> . . . .
> The wild forest, ...
> . . . .

> The void walls eke, that harbored us each night;
> Wherewith, alas, revive within my breast
> The sweet accord, such sleeps as yet delight,
> The pleasant dreams, the quiet bed of rest.

Surrey's account of his "childish years" has no internal diachronic structure: what he recalls is the daily round of activities, organized according to the physical layout of the castle and its environs. Between the complaint and its spatial context, three kinds of contiguity-relation obtain. The second, nostalgia, puts the first, imprisonment, and the third, boyhood happiness, in an ironic relation to each other:

> "O place of bliss! renewer of my woes!
> Give me accompt where is my noble fere,
> Whom in thy walls thou diddest each night enclose,
> To other lief,* but unto me most dear."
> *beloved

> Echo, alas, that doth my sorrow rue,
> Returns thereto a hollow sound of plaint.
> Thus I, alone, where all my freedom grew,
> In prison pine with bondage and restraint:

> And with remembrance of the greater grief,
> To banish the less, I find my chief relief.

> (Poem 31)

In this way Surrey solved a problem that more often defeated him, especially in lyrics that approach this one in length: the problem of how to situate a speaker metonymically out of his own mouth while he expresses an attitude from within that situation. In another Windsor poem, in order to give his speaker a view of the surrounding countryside from a particular vantage point, he used a description in the past tense to pose himself against the walls of Windsor Castle:

> When Windsor walls sustained my wearied arm,
> My hand my chin, to ease my restless head,
> Each pleasant plot revested green with warm,
> The blossomed boughs, with lusty vere* yspread,
> The flowered meads, the wedded birds so late,
> Mine eyes discovered . . .
> *green

By the end of the poem, the verb tenses are gravitating toward a vantage point in the immediate present:

> . . . Then did to mind resort
> The jolly woes, the hateless short debate,
> The rakehell life that 'longs to love's disport.
> Wherewith, alas! mine heavy charge of care,
> Heaped in my breast, brake forth against my will;
> And smoky sighs, that overcast the air;
> My vapored eyes such dreary tears distill,
> The tender spring to quicken where they fall;
> And I have bent to throw me down withall.
>
> (Poem 30)

Tottel tried to remedy the tense-discrepancy between the beginning and the end of the poem by throwing more of its verbs into the present tense.[23] Apparently, however, neither Tottel nor Surrey thought the present tense appropriate for the detailed self-situating image with which it commences. Obviously Surrey wanted to cite a particular occasion of reverie but could not decide between past-tense narration and present-tense dramatization. "So cruel prison" avoids the problem by keeping to a frequentative present tense, the tense of "how it is with me here these days."

So do Surrey's two most often anthologized sonnets: "Alas, so all things now do hold their peace" and "The soote season, that bud and bloom forth brings."[24] Both poems presuppose a vantage point out of doors from which the speaker looks around him. But in neither poem is he standing anywhere in particular, and in neither poem is he doing any retrospection. All that is needed for deixis, therefore, are definite articles and verbs in the present tense, to deliver a metonymic catalogue of what he sees around him.

> The soote* season, that bud and bloom forth brings,
> With green hath clad the hill and eke the vale;
> The nightingale with feathers new she sings;
> The turtle to her make* hath told her tale.
> Summer is come, for every spray now springs;
> The hart hath hung his old head on the pale;
> *sweet, soft
> *mate

> Alas, so all things now do hold their peace,
> Heaven and earth disturbed in nothing;
> The beasts, the air, the birds their song do cease;

The nightes chare* the stars about doth bring.

*chariot

Obviously Surrey was inclined toward the kind of metonymic writing that Wordsworth is famous for: place-inspired reverie. But he never successfully got beyond paratactic structures of narration and exposition to the hypotactic, context-sensitive formulations Wyatt used for metonymic presupposal.

The lyrics of Wyatt and Surrey are set toward situations in the external world: the coming of spring, a journey to Calais or Boulogne, a lady's intractability or infidelity. The poem-to-context relation is metonymic: the speaker's utterance participates in a larger situation, which is presupposed by his deictic references. The Elizabethan lyric is apt instead to outpicture an inner world, or to create a special, self-focused world of its own. In this often anthologized blazon from Spenser's *Amoretti*, for example, poetic conceits transplant the beautiful feminine body from the real world to a special aesthetic realm:

> Ye tradefull Merchants, that with weary toyle,
>   do seeke most pretious things to make your gain;
>   and both the Indias of their treasures spoile,
>   what needeth you to seeke so farre in vaine?
> For loe my love doth in her selfe containe
>   all this world's riches that may farre be found:
>   if Saphyres, loe her eies be Saphyres plaine,
>   if Rubies, loe hir lips be Rubies sound:
> If Pearles, hir teeth be pearles both pure and round;
>   if Yvorie, her forhead yvory weene;
>   if Gold, her locks are finest gold on ground;
>   if silver, her faire hands are silver sheene.
> But that which fairest is, but few behold,
>   her mind adornd with vertues manifold.[25]

(*Amoretti*, 15)

We do not suppose there are merchants within earshot of this speaker, any more than we suppose the lady's body to be made of ivory. All the deictic gestures he makes are patently nonliteral: they do not attach the utterance to an external situation, but enable it to render an imaginative projection. Merchants are addressed for the sake of the poem's central conceit: so that they can be associated with a centrifugal, far-ranging commercial endeavor. The poem plays off against that endeavor the centripetal, imaginative act of the lover: "For loe my love doth in her selfe containe / All this world's riches." The poetical deictic "lo" points to a mental projection, a figment of the lover's imagination.

The middle of the poem correlates a paradigm of conventionally precious substances with the standard list of features in which feminine beauty is supposed to inhere. Each equation proposes an ontological paradox: in this way lady and treasure are transformed into mental objects. But then the couplet proposes transcendence of this kind of equation, based on the visualizable properties of mental objects: "that which fairest is, but few behold." As her physical properties were played off against merchant's treasure, so her body's treasure is said to be surpassed by her mind's.

This poem is metaphoric by virtue of its projective deictics, its metaphoric equation-making, and the way its argument is structured. It transacts a movement that has nothing to do with contiguities in space and time, and everything to do with selection and substitution, likeness and unlikeness: from far to near, from centrifugal to centripetal seeking; from nature's riches to love's and mind's riches.

Wyatt apparently never composed a blazon, and this is the closest Surrey ever comes to one:

> From Tuscan came my lady's worthy race,
> Fair Florence was sometime her ancient seat;
> The western isle whose pleasant shore doth face
> Wild Chambare's cliffs did give her lively heat.
> Fostered she was with milk of Irish breast;
> Her Sire an earl, her dame of prince's blood;
> From tender years in Britain she doth rest,
> With a king's child, where she tastes ghostly food.
> Hunsdon did first present her to mine eyen,
> Bright is her hue, and Geraldine she hight*;
> Hampton me taught to wish her first for mine,
> And Windsor, alas! doth chase me from her sight.
> Beauty of kind*, her virtues from above,
> Happy is he that may obtain her love.
> *is called
> *by nature

(Poem 29)

As early as the Renaissance, this poem gave rise to a biographical tradition whereby, as Hyder Rollins explains in his introduction to *Tottel's Miscellany*, Surrey and Geraldine "became the English equivalent of Dante and Beatrice or Petrarch and Laura.[26] But this speaker's priorities are conspicuously different from Dante's or Petrarch's: his admiration yields not an apotheosis of his lady's beauty but an account of her lineage. J. W. Lever infers a "distrust of Petrarchan idealizations," and remarks that "it required some boldness" to admit to such different priorities in a sonnet.[27] It has subsequently been argued that this is not a lover's blazon at all, because Elizabeth Fitzgerald was only nine years old when Surrey wrote it; his motive must really have been to pay her family a compliment.[28]

Such a poem is bound to prompt biographical story-telling, because it gives the biographer a lot of proper names to work with. But whatever Surrey's actual feelings may have been for Elizabeth Fitzgerald, the nature of his speaker's interest in Geraldine is perfectly clear, and Tottel's headnote is in keeping with it: "Description and Praise of his Love Geraldine." When we put Surrey's poem alongside Spenser's, it is obvious they are comparable. Both celebrate a lady in whom physical beauty and spiritual beauty are perfectly combined; for both, beauty is the symptom of aristocracy, a noble property more than an instrument of Eros. Both poems are idealistic. The difference is that Surrey's idealism is invested in history: Geraldine's beauty and virtue matter to her admirer as the gifts of providence working through one of England's noblest families. Spenser translates the lady from historical space-time to a wholly visionary locus that displaces the external world. His poem calls attention to the fiction-making power as such. Surrey's uses that power to shape his historical material so that it will seem to tell its own story.

All Surrey's statements refer to the external world, and the poem is firmly anchored to that world by deixis and proper names. In fact their manipulation is the secret of Surrey's art in organizing the poem's material: Geraldine is "my lady" from the outset, so that the narrative account of her upbringing is contained and motivated by her impact on the speaker; but her name is withheld until it can be flourished to celebrate her maturity, the speaker's first meeting with her, and his admiration in the present, all together.

The structure of the poem's discourse is as conspicuously reliant upon spatiotemporal contiguities as Spenser's is upon relations of similarity and difference. As Geraldine grows up, she also moves closer and closer to the speaker's vantage point. The tenth line is the climax of this chronological and geographical progress, Geraldine's "coming out" as an English beauty, from whom Windsor separates the speaker just at the moment for which it seemed her destiny and his had prepared them both. The aphoristic couplet is motivated by the speaker's predicament: from Windsor, all he can do is generalize wistfully about what a prize she will be for someone differently situated than he.

This poem's metaphors are rhetorical conveniences, mostly: place names are personified so that they push the young lady toward her meeting with the speaker and then "chase me from her sight," but such expressions are too few and too weakly metaphorical to constitute an extended conceit. The structural figure that holds the poem together is metonymy: Geraldine is the scion of a noble family, who keeps the family line she carries sound and strong insofar as she is given the right nourishment, bodily and spiritual.

The difference in stance and figurative strategy between Surrey's and Spenser's poems is a classic case of the difference between the metonymic writing of the Tudor "courtly makers" and the metaphoric poetry of the Elizabethans—Sidney, Spenser, Shakespeare, and the sonneteers and pastoralists of the 1590s.

4 "Let me imagine, in this worthless verse": Metonymy in the Mid-Tudor Auto-Anthologies

Between Wyatt's generation and Sidney's falls a group of writers who read and imitated Wyatt's and Surrey's poetry: country gentry who had studied at the universities and the Inns of Court. These are the first English poets to have their own poetry published in printed anthologies. *Tottel's Miscellany*, which had given them models for imitation, had also given them the idea that there was a potential readership for lyric poems beyond the small circle of the writer's personal friends. Publication helped them to advertise their aristocratic breeding and education, with an eye to attracting favorable notice from higher-placed, wealthier members of the aristocracy who might have employment to offer, or influence at court.

The *Eglogs, Epytaphes, and Sonnettes* of Barnabe Googe were published in 1563, at the instigation of his friend George Blundeston. Googe, in a prefatory letter, explains that Blundeston had given them to a printer while he was out of the country, and he had reluctantly allowed them to be published to save the printer from losing his investment. Two or three years later, George Turberville had his collected poems published: the date cannot be precisely established, because no copy of the earliest edition has survived. Both Googe's and Turberville's anthologies are heterogeneous collections of occasional poetry. Interspersed with courting poems and love complaints there are poems addressed to friends which debate whether friendship is more precious than wealth, argue that the country is to be preferred to the court, and so on. Googe's anthology includes several poems in which he and a friend exchange generalizations about a common topic like love or ingratitude. Turberville prints short "sonets" of Googe's, to which he replies.

The most elaborate and interesting of these anthologies appeared in 1573: *A Hundreth sundrie Flowres bounde up in one small Poesie. Gathered partely (by translation*) *in the fyne outlandish Gardins of Euripides, Ovid, Petrarke, Ariosto, and others: and partly by invention, out of our owne fruitefull Orchardes in Englande: Yelding sundrie sweete savours of Tragical, Comical, and Morall Discourses, both pleasaunt and profitable to the well smellyng noses of learned Readers.* This purports to be an anthology of the work of several young gentlemen, of whom "Master Gascoigne" was the only one who had not insisted on concealing his authorship behind a nom de plume or a Latin motto. In a prefatory letter, "G.T." explains to his friend "H.W." that he obtained all the poems directly from their authors, along with explanations of how they came to be written in the first place. "I found none of them so barren," he writes to H.W., "but that (in my judgment) had in it *Aliquid Salis*, and especially being considered by the very proper occasion whereupon it was written."[1] H.W., in turn, explains in a letter to the reader that he thought the poems worthy of sharing with a wider audience, and so has asked "A.B.," a publisher friend of his, to have them printed. There is also a prefatory letter from A.B., who suggests to the reader that G.T.'s professed reluctance to betray his young friends into print is a ruse whereby he and H.W. can both avoid taking full responsibility for the decision to publish. The impression created by this three-tiered editorial framework is that a literary hoax of some kind is afoot, and sure enough: in 1575, in a second edition entitled simply *The Posies of George Gascoigne Esquire*, Gascoigne admits to having written or translated all of the poems. G.T. may possibly have been George Turberville, who was a friend of his, but it is more likely to have been Gascoigne himself, in view of *The Adventures of Master F.J.*, which had originally passed for G.T.'s reconstruction of a love affair that occasioned a series of poems. In the *Posies* Gascoigne turned the *Adventures* into a fable, and claimed that it had been "translated out of the Italian riding tales of Bartello."

George Whetstone's *Rocke of Regard*, which was published in 1576, is obviously modeled on *The Posies*. The editorial format is similar, and so is the range of different kinds of poetry. Corresponding to "The History of Dan Bartholmewe of Bathe," in Gascoigne's anthology, is "The Inventions of P. Plasmos": both consist of a series of poems framed by a Reporter's account of how they came to be written. In Whetstone's anthology there is also a melodramatic romance in prose in which the hero, like Gascoigne's F.J., uses poems to respond to the "chances and changes" of courtship.

The collective bias of these four poets is metonymic, but deixis is not an important figurative strategy in their poems. The poem of Turberville's that was discussed in chapter 3 is typical of their work, in being both longer than the poem it is modeled on and more like a discursive argument in prose. We are left in no doubt as to its occasion, but the poem does not strategically presuppose that occasion in the way that Wyatt's poem does. To structure their poems the mid-Tudor poets tended to fall back on narration, or else on the expository structures their training in rhetoric had taught them to use. The result is versified narrative or versified argument: couplets or quatrains or poulter's measure become the metric vehicle for a discourse whose shape is just that of the argument or the story it delivers.

At its best, this approach produced Googe's epitaph for Nicholas Grimald:

> Behold this fleeting world, how all things fade,
> How everything doth pass and wear away,
> Each state of life, by common course and trade,
> Abides no time, but hath a passing day.
>
> For look as life, that pleasant Dame, hath brought
> The pleasant years, and days of lustiness,
> So Death our foe consumeth all to nought,
> Envying these, with dart doth us oppress,
>
> And that which is the greatest grief of all,
> The greedy Gripe* doth no estate respect,
> But where he comes, he makes them down to fall,
> Ne stays he at the high sharp-witted sect.
> *vulture; slang for money lender
>
> For if that wit, or worthy eloquence,
> Or learning deep, could move him to forbear,
> O Grimald then thou hadst not yet gone hence
> But here hadst seen full many an aged year.
>
> Ne had the Muses lost so fine a flower,
> Nor had Minerva wept to leave thee so,
> If wisdom might have fled the fatal hour
> Thou hadst not yet been suffered for to go.
>
> A thousand doltish geese we might have spared,
> A thousand witless heads, death might have found
> And taken them, for whom no man had cared,
> And laid them low, in deep oblivious ground.
>
> But Fortune favors fools, as old men say,
> And lets them live, and takes the wise away.[2]

This is what C. S. Lewis called "good Drab," and Douglas Peterson, who has done more than any other scholar to define the strengths of Drab poetry, singles it out as one of Googe's best.[3] Googe's skill has been deployed along the axis of combination: his sentences are firmly structured and well paced, and the iambic pentameter line lends a solemn cadence without distorting the syntax. The poem's strength is that of a good piece of rhetoric: from proverbial generalizations at the outset, the argument comes down to the particular case and then broadens out again, this time into a more energetic denunciation of the way that things proverbially are, as if by naming the particular man who epitomized "the high, sharp-witted sect" the speaker had quickened his own world-weariness into anger.

This metonymic strategy of naming a particular person to represent an entire species or "sect" is one of the hallmarks of mid-Tudor poetry. It can do either of two things: give a private individual public importance, or invigorate well-worn generalizations by fastening them to a particular time and place. Googe's epitaph for Nicholas Grimald does the former. Gascoigne does the latter in his "Arraignment of a Lover," by introducing his own first name into a conventional "court of love" situation:

> At Beauty's bar as I did stand,
> When False Suspect accused me,
> George (quod the Judge) hold up thy hand,
> Thou art arraigned of Flattery:
> Tell therefore how thou wilt be tried.
> Whose judgment here wilt thou abide?[4]

The upshot of this trial is that George the lover is condemned to be hanged at Tyburn, "all but the head." He appeals for pardon to Beauty herself, on the grounds that "if I have been untrue, / It was in too much praising you." Beauty at last reprieves him, on the condition that he be henceforth at her beck and call. Apparently some of Gascoigne's original readers responded to his metonymic strategy with naively literal-minded speculation about his personal life, as if some particular love affair lay behind the poem. In his preface to *The Posies* he cites this poem as one of those that "(being written in jest) have been mistaken in sad earnest." A better reading would be one that acknowledged the generalizing force of allegorical abstractions like Beauty, and took the "Arraignment" for a tongue-in-cheek confession that whenever poor George meets a beautiful woman, hyperbolical admiration is bound to result.

This poem of Googe's makes a particular application of an extended similitude, to much the same effect:

> The little fish that in the stream doth fleet
> With broad forth-stretched fins for his disport,

When as he spies the fish's bait so sweet,
In haste he hies, fearing to come too short;

But all too soon, alas, his greedy mind
By rash attempt doth bring him to his bane,
For where he thought a great relief to find,
By hidden hook the simple fool is ta'en.

So fareth man, that wanders here and there,
Thinking no hurt to happen him thereby;
He runs amain to gaze on Beauty's cheer,
Takes all for gold that glisters in the eye,

And never leaves to feed by looking long
On Beauty's bait, where bondage lies enwrapt,
Bondage that makes him sing another song,
And makes him curse the bait that him entrapped.

Neville, to thee, that lovest their wanton looks,
Feed on the bait, but yet beware the hooks.[5]

The poem has the same rhetorical virtues as the epitaph for Nicholas Grimald. The structure of its argument is simple, obvious, and firmly controlled.
The analogy between lovers and fishes is symmetrically balanced, with two
quatrains given to elaboration of the little fish's predicament, and two to the
folly of its human counterpart. In the couplet, Googe deflates his own
magisterial solemnity by compressing the analogy toward metaphor proper at
the same time as he gives it a particular application. The piece of advice he
had been building up to, as it turns out, is "Neville, you poor fish, be
careful."

As Wyatt and Surrey practiced the "occasional" lyric, the poem itself is a
part that signifies a larger whole. Wyatt, as we have seen, was more successful
at producing this kind of poem than Surrey, because of his greater skill in the
manipulation of deictic presupposal. A poem of Wyatt's will depict the
utterance of feelings and wishes at some particular juncture in the speaker's
interpersonal life. At the same time, it will give the reader access to the
situation that motivates the utterance, without explicit narration or exposition. Mid-Tudor poems do not work this way: either they begin with first-
person narration, and then use a version of "Oh then (quoth I)" to introduce
the lyric utterance itself, or they have more or less elaborate headnotes and
framing narratives to explain their occasions. These devices, along with their
propensity for proper-naming the poem's speaker or its addressee, have the
effect of turning the generic figure of "the Lover," from Tottel's headnotes,

into a particular individual whose social performance the reader is being invited to witness and respond to as such.

In Turberville's *Epitaphes, Epigrams, Songs and Sonets* published in 1567, a prefatory "Argument" in verse explains that most of them were generated by the ups and downs of "Tymetes' " lengthy courtship of "Pyndara," who seemed for a while to return his love but finally married someone else.

> Thus ever as Tymetes had the cause
> Of joy or smart, of comfort or refuse,
> He glad or griefful wox, and ever draws
> His present state with pen, as here ensues.[6]

Along with Tymetes' poems to Pyndara, Turberville includes a few of hers to him. Many of the poems are also fitted out with contextualizing headnotes. Some of these resemble Tottel's:

> The lover to his careful bed declaring his restless state

> Of certain flowers, sent him by his love upon suspicion of change

but many of them are lengthier and more detailed:

> To his lady, that by hap when he kissed her and made her lip bleed, controlled him and took disdain

> To his friend T. having been long studied and well experienced, and now at length loving a gentlewoman that forced him not at all

G. K. Hunter has suggested that the purpose of this kind of editorial apparatus was "to create, in some sense, a cultured social world which the reader [could] join for the price of the book."[7] Whether or not this was its purpose, its effect is to give the poem-to-context relation a different kind of importance than it has in Wyatt's poetry. Instead of the context being implicated in the poem, the poem is assimilated to the motivating anecdote or explanation that has been proffered to contextualize it.

Of all the mid-century anthologies, the one that most highly elaborates and complicates the poem-to-context relation is *A Hundreth sundrie Flowres.* Having promised to furnish an account of the "very proper occasion" of each of his young friends' poems, G.T. launches right into the adventures of Master F.J., which are presented to the reader like a connected series of unusually well-developed headnotes. For the *Posies* Gascoigne recast G.T.'s narrative as an exemplary fable, but the original version ends abruptly with the last of F.J.'s poems to Mistress Elinor, after which G.T. apologizes for his long-windedness and promises to introduce the poems of other young gentlemen more briefly, "adding nothing of mine own, but only a title to every poem, whereby the cause of the writing of the same may the more evidently appear." Many of the ensuing "titles" are quite extensive and vivid in their depiction of how this or that poem came to be written. The overall impression is of a lively interest taken, on the reader's behalf, in the social uses to which poems can be put and the social interests they promote. Even the translation of a penitential psalm is motivated by a personal anecdote: Gascoigne was riding from Chelmsford to London and dwelling in his mind on how he had misspent his youth, when he was caught unprepared by a shower of rain, "in a jerkin without a cloak," and decided that this was a message from the Almighty to which he had better respond with a gesture of repentance.

In the letters he prefaced to the *Posies*, Gascoigne acknowledges that some of the *Hundreth sundrie Flowres* had been found by "Reverend Divines" to be offensively "wanton" and "lascivious"; and he assures these critics that in this new edition his poems have been "gelded from all filthy phrases" and "beautified with addition of many moral examples." He nevertheless reprints poems whose headnotes call attention to the immorality of their author's purposes, in order to enlist our admiration for his shrewdness as a social gamesman. Here, for example, is a riddle whose headnote tells us it was used at a dinner party to flirt with a married woman:

> I cast mine eye and saw ten eyes at once,
> All seemly set upon one lovely face:
> Two gaz'd, two glanc'd, two watched for the nonce,
> Two winked wiles, two frowned with froward grace.
> Thus every eye was pitched in his place.
> And every eye which wrought each other's woe,
> Said to itself, alas why looked I so?
> And every eye for jealous love did pine,
> And sigh'd and said, I would that eye were mine.
>
> (*Posies*, pp. 47–48)

Throughout the meal, the young man who tells this riddle has been passionately gazing at his mistress while she returned him occasional glances, a former lover of hers eyed them both suspiciously, her brother tried to catch her eye with warning winks, and her husband looked on at all this complicated eye-play with a frown. Given the situation that is epitomized by the ten-eyed monster in the riddle, none of the owners of the other four pairs of eyes can afford to expound its meaning, and none of the dinner guests offers to do so. "At last the Dame herself answered on this wise: 'Sir,' quod she, 'because your dark speech is much too curious for this simple company, I will be so bold as to quit one question with another.' " She then puts together a monster of her own, out of the conventional paradoxes of a lover's predicament. Ostensibly, her reason for congratulating the young man is that he has told the assembled company a riddle no one could solve. What he has actually done, as she knows perfectly well, is force them all to pretend not to be able to solve the riddle, to avoid naming the game that has been going forward right under her husband's nose. The poem-to-context relation is all-important here, not only for solving the riddle but also to give it the status of a complicated social gambit.

In the *Rocke of Regard*, Whetstone apologizes in much the same terms as Gascoigne for having included "some verses that savor more of wantonness than wisdom."[8] The range of different kinds of occasions his poems presuppose is similar to Gascoigne's, and his contextualizing strategies are similar, but the poem-to-context relation tends not to be so interesting in Whetstone's anthology. In connection with "The Inventions of P. Plasmos," for example, the "Reporter" tells less of a story than the Reporter of Gascoigne's "History of Dan Bartholmewe of Bathe": Whetstone's Reporter continually abbreviates his explanations of how Plasmos's poems came to be written, in favor of didactic generalization about the youthful follies they illustrate. In Whetstone's tale of Rinaldo and Giletta, Rinaldo uses poems in the same way that F.J. does, to express his feelings and to impress the lady and her friends with how skilled he is in "the exercises of a perfect courtier." But there is no danger of mistaking Whetstone's melodramatic tale for a piece of local gossip, as *The Adventures of Master F.J.* had been mistaken by many of its original readers, what with Rinaldo trying to drown himself in the river Po and then withdrawing to the forest to live on nuts and berries until the opportunity presents itself to thwart his rival's marriage plans and slay him in a duel.

F.J.'s performance as a love poet is more realistically circumstanced, and the poem-to-context relation is also more complex, because G.T. suggests to us that the young man's attitudes and motives were actually quite different from what the poetry makes them out to be. At one point, for example, he pauses to try to explain why F.J. preferred the married, promiscuous Elinor over her virtuous, unmarried sister-in-law: "we see by common experience," he observes, "that the highest flying falcon doth more commonly prey upon the corn fed crow and the simple shiftless dove, than on the mounting kite: and why? because the one is overcome with less difficulty than that other" (*Posies*, p. 404). Meanwhile F.J. had been courting Elinor with conventional poetic conceits:

What wonder seemeth then, when stars stand thick in skies,
If such a blazing star have power to dim my dazzled eyes?

(Posies, p. 385)

Whereas F.J. professes here to be an abject admirer of the lady's heavenly perfection, G.T. attributes to him the posture of a bird of prey who has singled out the easiest mark he could find. There is an ironic disparity between the poems and the contextualizing narrative, which not only draws our attention to the role F.J. uses poems to play but also creates the possibility of seeing that role as a way to dissemble hidden motives.

The way that these four poets use narratives and explanatory headnotes and proper names to attach their poems to extrinsic settings is an expression of their collective metonymic bias. Another expression of that bias is their way of handling metaphor. In their poetry metaphor is a discursive strategy that enlists the axis of combination to keep both terms explicit and to keep them distinct. Their poems are full of extended similitudes and of what George Puttenham called "mixed allegory"[9]—continued metaphor that uses copular equations or genitive and appositive constructions to keep both of its terms continuously explicit, so that the vehicle does not displace the tenor or pull it out of context. Googe's poem about the lover and the little fish is typical of the way these poets use metaphor discursively, to furnish the scaffolding for a poem's argument.

A related habit of theirs is to have the poem's speaker derive the vehicle for a similitude or a continued metaphor from his immediate, external environment, so that the metaphor is doubly motivated by the context of his message. In one of Googe's poems, the little fly that was buzzing around his candle as he sat musing in lovelorn solitude becomes the pretext of a complaint in which he plays off his own unhappiness against the carelessness that belongs to a lower level of the scale of being. The device is motivated by his situation, as he sets it up; he is all alone, the house around him is hushed, he is predisposed to notice something that he would not under other circumstances have bothered to notice or to think about:

> Once musing as I sat,
>   and candle burning by,
> When all were hushed I might discern
>   a simple silly fly
>
> That flew before mine eyes,
>   with free rejoicing heart,
> And here and there with wings did play
>   as void of pain and smart.

> Sometime by me she sat,
>   when she had played her fill,
> And ever when she rested had
>   about she flittered still.
>
> When I perceived her well,
>   rejoicing in her place,
> O happy fly quoth I, and eke,
>   O worm in happy case.
>
> Which of us two is best?
>   I that have reason? no:
> But thou that reason art without
>   and therewith void of woe.
>
> I love and so dost thou,
>   but I live all in pain,
> And subject am to her alas,
>   that makes my grief her gain.[10]

The comparison that structures this speaker's argument seems to have been generated by the very predicament he uses it to "muse" about. The same could be said about the prison metaphor in a poem of Turberville's that situates the lover where he will happen to notice a prison that stands near his lady's lodging just as he is casting around for a way to express his frustration at being rejected by her. But a poem that exemplifies this strategy better than either of these is "Gascoigne's Good Night," where an extended similitude is recommended as a format for bedtime prayer. Instead of giving in thoughtlessly to exhaustion, it is suggested that we use the ordinary givens of bedtime to remind ourselves that sleep is a sort of rehearsal for death, from which the body will arise no more but the soul will awake into eternity. The prayer that we would produce in this way would go as follows:

> I see that sleep is lent me here, to ease my weary bones,
> As death at last shall eke appear, to ease my grievous groans.
> My daily sports, my paunch full fed, have caused my drowsy eye,
> As careless life in quiet led, might cause my soul to die:
> The stretching arms, the yawning breath, which I to bedward use,
> Are patterns of the pangs of death, when life will me refuse:
> And of my bed each sundry part in shadows doth resemble
> The sundry shapes of death, whose dart shall make my flesh to tremble.
> My bed itself is like the grave, my sheets the winding sheet,
> My clothes the mould which I must have, to cover me most meet:

The hungry fleas which frisk so fresh, to worms I can compare,
Which greedily shall gnaw my flesh, and leave the bones full bare:
The waking cock that early crows to wear the night away,
Puts in my mind the trump that blows before the latter day.

(Posies, pp. 58–59)

The prayer makes an exhaustive inventory of the "bedward" situation, rein-
terpreting each of its details in the light of the sleep-death analogy. Metonymy furnishes the vehicles for metaphor, so that the prayer is firmly
anchored in an already-given context, and asserts its hope of salvation
against the recalcitrance of the already given.

Whereas the Elizabethan poets would use metaphor to displace the external world with a self-focused poetic realm, Gascoigne and his contemporaries
used it metonymically, to deal with an extrinsic, already-given situation in
terms of its own already-given constituents. That situation might be as
general as "the human condition": another of Gascoigne's poems, entitled
"Gascoigne's Good Morrow," takes for its metaphoric vehicles birdsong, the
coming of day, the rainbow after a storm, and so on, to demonstrate that any
"earthly sight" whatsoever is a "token" of our spiritual destiny. Or, it might
be as local and specific as a hunting party on the estate of the Lord Grey
de Wilton.

As the discursive scaffolding of a poem's argument, mixed allegory is even
easier to use than similitude, because both terms of the metaphor can be
carried along together by an allegorical narrative. It is also a more elastic
frame, because it can be indefinitely extended along the narrative line, pull-
ing in new settings or additional characters to suit the convenience of the
poem's argument as it develops. Here is a characteristic sample of this kind of
allegorical writing, from one of Googe's eclogues:

> Then doth the brainless fool
> Cast bridle off, and out he runs,
>   neglecting Virtue's school;
> Then doth the Devil give him line,
>   and let him run at large,
> And Pleasure makes his mariner,
>   to row in Vice's barge,
> Then up the sails of wilfulness
>   he hoyses* high in haste
> And fond affection blows him forth,
>   a wind that Pluto placed;
> Then cuts he swift the seas of sin,
>   and through the channel deep,

> With joyful mind, he fleets apace,
>   whom Pleasure brings asleep.
> *hoists

In *Elizabethan and Metaphysical Imagery*, Rosemond Tuve cites this very passage to show how allegory should *not* be handled.[11] She explains that in effective allegorical writing, like Spenser's, the metaphoric image-complex gives a richer articulation to its tenor than discursive statement possibly could. In an allegorical image like that of the monster Error or the giant Orgoglio in the first book of *The Faerie Queene*, there has been "a circuitous routing of ideas through the slow channels of expanded sensuous imagery": the nature of Pride or Error is implicit in every detail of a visually elaborate image. Here, instead, we are given both tenors and vehicles in a sort of parallel catalogue. Each tenor is explicitly correlated with its vehicle by means of a genitive or appositive construction. It looks as if Googe could have told us just as much about sin without a ship allegory.

But when a poem's speaker takes his allegorical vehicle from the situation in which he finds himself and then uses it to turn that situation to his advantage, this way of using continued metaphor can be very effective indeed. Allegory becomes a social gambit or an instrument of moral suasion, as it is enlisted to bring about a shift of the perspective in terms of which a particular situation is viewed. Gascoigne used allegory as well as similitude in this way: continued metaphor was not for him the instrument of a "visionary geography" but a rhetorical strategy and a social tactic.

This is also the way that his contemporary, George Puttenham, seems to have thought of allegory. "The use of this figure is so large," he says in the *Art of English Poesy*, "and its virtue of so great efficacy as it is supposed no man can pleasantly utter and persuade without it, but in effect is sure never or very seldom to thrive and prosper in the world, that cannot skilfully put [it] in ure" (p. 186). In his earlier definition of metaphor (pp. 178–79), Puttenham lists "necessity" first among its motivating "causes," and necessity is the motive Tuve highlights, pointing out that metaphors were commended by classical and Renaissance rhetoricians "as a means of getting around the inadequacies of language economically, of making a reader think connections which language does not actually say."[12] But when he comes to discuss "continued metaphor," Puttenham stresses its rhetorical and social efficacy. To exemplify *allegoria* and its subspecies, one of which is *ironia*, he draws at least as often upon social anecdotes as upon poems.[13]

Considered "properly and in its principal virtue," says Puttenham, allegoria is "when we do speak in sense translative and wrested from the own signification, nevertheless applied to another not altogether contrary, but having much conveniency with it . . . as for example if we should call the commonwealth a ship, the prince a pilot, the counsellors mariners, the storms wars, the calm and [haven] peace, this is spoken all in allegory" (p. 187). What Puttenham means by conveniency, presumably, is that the allegory's tenor and vehicle share some leading characteristics, so that our use of the one to put the other in perspective is comprehensible to others and does not violate decorum. Ironia, as a special case of allegoria, would occur when to designate some A as B is conspicuously inappropriate or "inconvenient," in this sense. Allegory proper would shade into or involve irony if a shift of perspective occurred such that conveniency must be apprehended as inconveniency, or a different basis for conveniency began to be cited.

This is what happens in "Gascoigne's Woodmanship," which is arguably the best single poem that was produced by any of these mid-Tudor poets. An elaborate headnote was published with it, which explains that it was originally conceived as a face-saving strategy. The Lord Grey de Wilton had included Gascoigne in a hunting party on his estate, but he proved ridiculously inept—missed his aim, failed to shoot when he had a good opportunity, killed a pregnant doe by mistake. "Your woodman" explains that this, metaphorically speaking, is the story of his life.

> My worthy Lord, I pray you wonder not,
> To see your woodman shoot so oft awry,
> Nor that he stands amazed like a sot,
> And lets the harmless deer, unhurt, go by.
> Or if he strike a doe which is but carren,
> Laugh not good Lord, but favor such a fault,
> Take will in worth, he would fain hit the barren,
> But though his heart be good, his hap is naught.
> And therefore now I crave your Lordship's leave,
> To tell you plain what is the cause of this:
> First if it please your honor to perceive
> What makes your woodman shoot so oft amiss,
> Believe me Lord, the case is nothing strange,
> He shoots awry almost at every mark,
> His eyes have been so used for to range,
> That now God knows they be both dim and dark.
>
> (*Posies*, p. 348)

He proceeds to tell his autobiographical story under the aegis of the metaphor he has picked up from the situation that occasioned the poem: at every stage of his career to date, he has failed to "hit the mark."

Gradually, however, the value his failure carries is altered. Increasingly, what he would have had to do to be successful must strike his audience as morally repugnant. As a student, he failed because he did not work hard enough to master difficult material. At court he failed through being gullible: "He thought the flattering face which fleereth still, / Had been full fraught with all fidelity." As a soldier, he failed because he would not rob his men of their pay or treat them as cannon fodder: "And nowadays, the man that shoots not so, / May shoot amiss, even as your woodman doth." Because the controlling metaphor stays the same, the shift in perspective is gradual. The speaker's confessions of inadequacy become more and more ironic; as the context changes, the reader finds his or her assessment of Gascoigne's Woodmanship increasingly at odds with the world's.

In the meantime, the poem itself is an impressive piece of woodmanship. The strategy of picking up an allegorical vehicle that lies to hand and recontextualizing it so as to change its meaning little by little is one that shows respect for the recalcitrance of the poem's original givens, as well as for the intelligence of the audience the allegorist hopes to persuade to a different view. His concluding gambit is to set up a hypothetical instance of woodmanship and expound it for himself. He rejects, this time, the most obvious reading, and chooses instead to turn the killing of a "carrion" doe into a divinely inspired mistake whereby persistence in folly begets wisdom:

> Let me imagine in this worthless verse,
> If right before me, at my standing's foot
> There stood a Doe, and I should strike her dead,
> And then she prove a carrion carcase too,
> What figure might I find within my head,
> To 'scuse the rage which ruled me so to do?
> Some might interpret by plain paraphrase,
> That lack of skill or fortune led the chance,
> But I must otherwise expound the case;
> I say Jehovah did this doe advance,
> And made her bold to stand before me so,
> Till I had thrust mine arrow to her heart,
> That by the sudden of her overthrow,
> I might endeavor to amend my part,
> And turn mine eyes that they no more behold
> Such guileful marks as seem more than they be:
> And though they glister outwardly like gold,
> Are inwardly but brass, as men may see:
> And when I see the milk hang in her teat,
> Methinks it saith, Old babe now learn to suck,
> Who in thy youth couldst never learn the feat
> To hit the whites which live with all good luck.

Thus have I told my Lord, God grant in season,
A tedious tale in rhyme, but little reason.

(Posies, pp. 351–52)

In this context, the designation of his own verse as "worthless" is a far from simple gesture, because the poem itself has all along been challenging its audience to recognize a discrepancy between what is truly worthy and what the world rewards. The assertion of his prerogative to "imagine" an event that defies "plain paraphrase" looks almost like the discovery of a poet's prerogative to invent "things better than nature bringeth forth . . . not enclosed within the narrow warrant of her gifts, but freely ranging only within the zodiac of his own wit." But Gascoigne did not share the aesthetic idealism Sidney professes in his *Defense of Poesy*. The strength and the limitation of his poetry is that it is "interested," and hence closely tied to actual situations in the world. The poem's closing lines acknowledge that, free as he may be in his own poem to control what happens and what it signifies, from a practical standpoint he remains at the mercy of his most important auditor: only the Lord Grey can make the poem worth something to him in practical terms, if he decides to offer him employment.

Gascoigne's writing is most interesting when it is most "interested": when he is experimenting with the practical application of an allegory or a similitude to a "real-life" situation. In chapter 5, I will argue that his strongly metonymic bias kept him, along with his contemporaries, from discovering how to exploit the poetic function of language, whose tendency is to lift a verbal message out of context and render it self-focused. Here I want to make the related point that when you conceive of metaphor as a strategy for putting a poem's occasion in perspective, what follows from this view is the realization that live conversation is a more flexible and socially sensitive medium for this way of using metaphor than a poem can be. We can infer that Gascoigne had this kind of appreciation of the implications of his own leading motive for metaphor from *The Adventures of Master F.J.*, where he plays off against F.J.'s poetry the social performance of a woman who writes no poems but is a more ambitious and sophisticated allegorist than F.J. himself.

G.T.'s contextualizing narrative highlights, from time to time, the clumsiness from a practical point of view of using poems to seduce a woman. During the beginning stage of the courtship, for instance, F.J. runs into Elinor by accident before he has had a chance to produce a legible copy of the poem he had composed to make his next move with her. The conventional role he uses poems to play turns out to be pretentious and rather wooden under the circumstances: when he writes a poem to Elinor that hyperbolically praises her as his "Helen," she is annoyed instead of flattered because she mistakes his metaphor for a proper name and figures he must have written the poem for some other woman. Meanwhile, however, all the characters are continually using allegorical devices in a very sophisticated and graceful way, in the conversations they improvise from day to day: devices which help them to communicate without ever having to come flat out and say what they want from each other and what they know about one another's desires and purposes.

The character who enjoys this the most and does it the most skilfully is Elinor's sister-in-law, Frances, who wants F.J. for herself. When she discovers that he is in love with her brother's wife, she offers to be his confidante and go-between in a conversation that generates, spontaneously as it seems, an allegorical game between them:

> "for by this Sun," quoth he, "I will not deceive such trust as you shall lay upon me, and furthermore, so far forth as I may, I will be yours in any respect: wherefore I beseech you accept me for your faithful friend, and so shall you surely find me." "Not so," quoth she, "but you shall be my *Trust*, if you vouchsafe the name, and I will be to you as you shall please to term me." "My *Hope*," quoth he, "if you be so pleased." And thus agreed, they two walked apart from the other Gentlewomen, and fell into sad talk, wherein Mistress Frances did . . . both instruct and advise him [how] to proceed in his enterprise.
>
> (*Posies*, pp. 402–3)

The Hope-Trust allegory seems to arise unpremeditated between F.J. and Frances, as a way to establish conventions for friendship. By taking on these allegorical names, both of them claim acquaintance with the tradition of adulterous courtship: Frances offers to be F.J.'s ally against Elinor's "Daunger," and the allegory enables her to make the offer without impropriety.

What Frances is really hoping, though, is that in the long run, when her sister-in-law tires of F.J. as she always does of her lovers, he will be converted by their friendship to the better course of loving someone he has learned he can trust. What Frances hopes for, and what F.J. thinks it means to call her his Hope, are ironically at odds, and Frances is willing to keep F.J.'s interpretation in play for the time being, so that his own experience can gradually bring about recontextualization of the metaphor and change what it means to him. "Experiment" is the word she herself uses for this undertaking, and it is a more flexible strategy than F.J.'s poems, because of being more closely in touch with the chances and changes of the affair as it develops.

The outcome of her experiment is not, however, what Frances had *hoped* for: when Elinor throws him over, F.J. decides never to *trust* a woman again. In the second version of the *Adventures* we are told that he spent the rest of his days "in a dissolute kind of life," while the woman who had offered to be his Hope "did shortly bring herself into a miserable consumption: whereof (after three years languishing) she died."

In *Master F.J.*, just as in "Gascoigne's Woodmanship," the attempt to use a continued metaphor to convert someone else to a different way of looking at an already-given situation is finally deprecated as being unrealistic. "Let me imagine, in this worthless verse," says the Lord Grey's woodman. John Donne, who made the poem-to-context relation critical once again after an intervening phase of self-focused, metaphoric writing, would assert the poet's prerogative to "imagine" much more daringly than Gascoigne was willing to do. The woodman in Gascoigne's poem knows that the figure he has "found within [his] head" may very well not have changed anyone's mind, although he wishes that it may have done so.

5 "Your monument shall be my gentle verse": Sonneteering and the Metaphoric Way

The sonnet is a highly self-focused message. Because it is complete in fourteen lines, and because of its high degree of internal organization, the tendency of the form is to close in upon itself and constitute its own little word-world. The rhyme scheme, and the line units it delimits, converts the diachronic line of the unfolding argument into a synchronic array of phrases and clauses; the fixed length is short enough that it will all hang together in the mind as a simultaneous unity. The meter and rhyme scheme, patterns which are gratuitous from the standpoint of ordinary message delivery, weaken its referential orientation—what Jakobson would call its "set toward the context." A certain opacity of the signifier is produced by the sound patterns which bind its words together.

The easiest way to collaborate with the formal properties of the sonnet is to keep your argument simple, redundant, and metaphoric. Especially in the English or "Shakespearean" sonnet, which is composed of three quatrains and a couplet, the line of least resistance to the form is the kind of argument that progresses by reiterative reformulation of one idea. Here, for example, is one of Shakespeare's most often anthologized sonnets:

> That time of year thou mayst in me behold,
> When yellow leaves, or none, or few, do hang
> Upon those boughs which shake against the cold,
> Bare ruined choirs, where late the sweet birds sang.
> In me thou seest the twilight of such day
> As after sunset fadeth in the west,
> Which by and by black night doth take away,
> Death's second self, that seals up all in rest.
> In me thou seest the glowing of such fire,

> That on the ashes of his youth doth lie,
> As the death-bed whereon it must expire,
> Consumed with that which it was nourished by.
> This thou perceiv'st, which makes thy love more strong,
> To love that well which thou must leave ere long.[1]

The divisions into which the rhyme scheme divides the fourteen lines have been allowed to delineate the units of this poem's argument and to set up a paradigmatic relation between them. The entire argument of the first twelve lines could be boiled down to "As you see, I am growing old." It is reiterated with three different metaphors, all initiated in the same way: ". . . thou mayst in me behold," "In me thou seest . . . ," "In me thou seest . . ." Each is developed in the same way also: the first half of the quatrain compares human middle age with a corresponding stage in an extrahuman natural cycle; the second half compounds the metaphor by giving its nonhuman vehicle human attributes. The differences between the metaphors are mutually reinforcing: the temporal cycle represented by the natural-process metaphor shortens with each quatrain; meanwhile in the compounding metaphor the emphasis on death increases and the life-death opposition is progressively intensified—from nostalgic opposition of winter and summer in the first instance to paradox in the third. In this way the impact of aging becomes more intense with each reformulation. There is a progression from one version of the argument to the next, but it is neither logical nor chronological. Instead, it is constituted by multiple relations of equivalence and contrast.

Architectonically this sonnet of Daniel's is not as complex as Shakespeare's, but it is similarly organized, in parallel quatrains that develop its argument paradigmatically:

> If this be love, to draw a weary breath,
> Paint on floods, till the shore cry to the air:
> With downward looks, still reading on the earth
> The sad memorials of my love's despair;
> If this be love, to war against my soul,
> Lie down to wail, rise up to sigh and grieve me:
> The never-resting stone of care to roll,
> Still to complain my griefs, whilst none relieve me:
> If this be love, to clothe me with dark thoughts,
> Haunting untrodden paths to wail apart;
> My pleasures horror, Music tragic notes,
> Tears in my eyes, and sorrow at my heart:

If this be love, to live a living death;
O then love I, and draw this weary breath.[2]

Shakespeare built his argument climactically, from quatrain to quatrain. Daniel's quatrains are not so coherent and distinct: his poem is a catalogue, with the conditional clause "If this be love" repeated at intervals to keep its project of defining love in focus as the list of typical behaviors lengthens. The poem is all one sentence, which must be apprehended as an expanding synchronous whole until it becomes complete in the fourteenth line. The clause of conclusion, when it finally comes, repeats the wording of the initial clause of condition but substitutes a finite predicate for its infinitive—"O then love I"—and grounds that predicate in the present moment of the utterance itself: "this weary breath." With the a-rhyme returning as the couplet rhyme, the poem's message is strongly self-focused by the contrapuntal relationship between its first and its concluding lines. Thus even as it refers to a particular finite moment, "this weary breath" is subsumed by the poem into the infinite present of "a living death," which epitomizes the lover's paradoxical situation. The catalogue of infinitive phrases, notwithstanding the speaker's claim to have derived it from personal experience, takes on in this sonnet the generalizing force of a definitional paradigm for the predicament of being in love.

Happy ye leaves when as those lilly hands,
    Which hold my life in their dead doing might,
    Shall handle you and hold in loves soft bands,
    Lyke captives trembling at the victors sight.
And happy lines, on which with starry sight
    Those lamping eyes will deigne sometimes to look
    And reade the sorrowes of my dying spright,
    Written with teares in harts close bleeding book.
And happy rymes bath'd in the sacred brooke,
    Of *Helicon* whence she derived is,
    When ye behold that Angels blessed looke,
    My soules long lacked foode, my heavens blis.
Leaves, lines, and rymes, seeke her to please alone,
    Whom if ye please, I care for other none.[3]

This is the first sonnet of Spenser's *Amoretti* sequence. Just as in Shakespeare's and Daniel's sonnets, the argument here is built up in parallel quatrains which reiterate the same idea—that the most important reader of the sequence is the beloved herself, who is also their instigator or Muse. The

Spenserian rhyme scheme hooks the quatrains together like links in a chain—*a b a b, b c b c, c d c d*—and their parallel arguments are also chain-linked. The first quatrain, which addresses the leaves of the ensuing book in anticipation of their being handled by the lady, introduces "sight" into the military metaphor of the third line, and sight then becomes the principal tenor of the second quatrain, where "lines" and "eyes" take over from the first quatrain's leaves and hands. The last line of the second quatrain anticipates the "sacred brooke of Helicon" with its blood and tears that express the lover's suffering. The brook, in the third quatrain, becomes a sacramental antidote for the bleeding of the heart, and the "harts close bleeding book" is transformed into "happy rymes" as the lady's status alters from despotic victor to Muse.

Taken as a whole, the poem's argument is progressive not logically or chronologically, but in the sense that the "victors sight" which strikes fear into her captives has become "that Angels blessed lookè" by the third quatrain: the progression is built metaphorically, out of paradigmatic relations of likeness and difference. In the couplet, the apostrophes that had initiated each of the quatrains are collected into one line, and the poem ends with a new assertion that has been earned by the cumulative force of its variations on a theme.

This way of capitalizing on the sonnet's formal characteristics is typical of Elizabethan sonneteering—especially of Shakespeare, Daniel, and Spenser. These three poets are also the ones who gave the English sonnet sequence its generic project—to immortalize the beloved by going to war with Time. They go to war with Time in their sequences by recuperating diachrony into synchrony, at the level both of the individual sonnet and of the sequence as a whole.

There has been general agreement among historians of the English sonnet that its naturalization to England occurred as two separate initiatives with a thirty-year hiatus in between. Wyatt and Surrey together developed a rhyme scheme which continued to be more popular among English poets than the Petrarchan octave and sestet: three quatrains, each with its own pair of rhyme-words, and a concluding couplet. In "Certain Notes of Instruction for the Making of English Verse," Gascoigne defined the sonnet in terms of this rhyme scheme, and his definition helped to standardize it. But he and his generation did not have good success with the sonnet. Lisle John notes, in a book-length study that was for many years the definitive treatment of English sonneteering, that the history of the sonnet from 1557, when *Tottel's Miscellany* was first published, until 1591, when *Astrophil and Stella* started all of Sidney's contemporaries writing sonnet sequences, is "an unaccountably brief chronicle of scattered and inferior verse."[4] Historians credit Thomas

Watson with introducing the sonnet sequence into England in 1582 with his *Hecatompathia or Passionate Century of Love*. The elaborate editorial apparatus of the *Hecatompathia* flourishes Watson's debts to Italian and French models; and yet, as Hallett Smith remarks, "the annotator of Watson seems wholly unaware of the priority of Wyatt and Surrey in introducing Petrarchan motifs into English."[5] The Elizabethan poets were working from Italian models with the help of the *Pleiade* group in France: C. S. Lewis explains that they "had no need of such scanty help as Wyatt's sonnets could give them," and opines that "the Elizabethan sonnet might not have been very different if Wyatt had never lived."[6]

In 1971 William Harris challenged this account of English Petrarchism as two unrelated phases of translation and imitation thirty years apart. It was his finding that almost three times as many sonnets were published between 1557 and 1582 as Tottel had published from the work of the preceding twenty-five years. Obviously, then, "interest in, and experiments with, the new form continued strong" during this mid-century period.[7] And it is not true, as Harris pointed out, that no one before Watson was putting sonnets together in a sequence. Gascoigne wrote "seven sonnets in sequence" in response to a challenge by his friend Alexander Neville; other poets of his generation also experimented with linked runs of sonnets. But Harris's findings have not and probably will not change the history of English sonneteering. Almost none of this mid-century work ever finds its way into anthologies: it is indeed inferior verse. The reason for this is that Gascoigne and his contemporaries did not understand what the potentialities really were of either the sonnet or the sonnet sequence.

The form of the sonnet developed by Wyatt and Surrey is more hospitable to metonymic writing than the Petrarchan form with its asymmetrical bipartite structure and its unified octave. The English sonnet not only increases from five to seven the number of rhymes allowable within the fourteen lines; it also subdivides the form differently. As J. W. Lever has demonstrated by close comparison of Wyatt's and Surrey's sonnets with their Italian originals, narration and propositionizing became easier to do in three quatrains and a couplet than they had been in the Petrarchan octave-sestet. The Petrarchan octave turns in upon itself: "the second sub-stanza of four lines is carried back to the first by the integral rhyme scheme [*a b b a a b b a*]; the progressive logic of syntax is overborne by the . . . rhyme; and a stasis results."[8] The sestet, where syntax and rhyme can reinforce each other in correlated three-line units, is apt to be used to work out the implications of the experience projected in the octave. If you introduce a couplet rhyme into the sestet, as Wyatt began to do, you throw its structure out of balance "by suggesting logical deduction instead of rational correlation." When you replace the octave by a series of quatrains, each with its own set of rhyme words, you forego the integrative unity of the octave and the asymmetrical complementarity of octave and sestet. The form that results is not as inherently self-focused as the Petrarchan sonnet: it will lend itself to a message that is linear and discursive, the kind of argument that consists, as Lever puts it, of "a chain of observations logically linked."[9] This is the kind of argument that Surrey used the sonnet to carry. His Petrarchan translations undo the self-focused, synchronic coherence of their originals, turning Petrarch's metaphors into similes or analogies, taming his paradoxes with "but" and "whereas," reformulating synchronic simultaneity as diachronic sequence. Gascoigne carried this tendency still further, to the point where the sonnet broke down into a series of stanzas.

Take, for example, the "sonnet sequence" he composed for Neville. The "theme" he was given, as he explains in a headnote, was the adage, *Sat cito, si sat bene*—"no haste but good," equivalent to the more familiar proverb "haste makes waste." Gascoigne undertook to "prove" the adage, which he does by recounting his own career at court. To make the seven sonnets into a "sequence," he repeats the last line of each sonnet as the first line of the next.

In haste post haste, when first my wandering mind
Beheld the glistering Court with gazing eye,
Such deep delights I seemed therein to find,
As might beguile a graver guest than I.
The stately pomp of princes and their peers,
Did seem to swim in floods of beaten gold,
The wanton world of young delightful years
Was not unlike a heaven for to behold.
Wherein did swarm (for every saint) a dame,
So fair of hue, so fresh of their attire,
As might excel dame Cynthia for fame,
Or conquer Cupid with his own desire.
　　These and such like were baits that blazed still
　　Before mine eye to feed my greedy will.

2. Before mine eye to feed my greedy will,
Gan muster eke mine old acquainted mates,
Who helped the dish (of vain delight) to fill
My empty mouth with dainty delicates:
And foolish boldness took the whip in hand,
To lash my life into this trustless trace,
Till all in haste I leaped a loof from land,
And hoist up sail to catch a courtly grace:

Each lingering day did seem a world of woe,
Till in that hapless haven my head was brought;
Waves of wanhope so tossed me to and fro,
In deep despair to drown my dreadful thought:
    Each hour a day, each day a year did seem,
    And every year a world my will did deem.

3. And every year a world my will did deem,
Till lo, at last, to Court now am I come,
A seemly swain, that might the place beseem,
A gladsome guest embraced of all and some:
. . . . .¹⁰

The enchaining strategy keeps these sonnets from running together, but none of them coheres internally. Instead of a fourteen-line complex we have a series of three quatrains of narration and description, followed by a couplet that pauses to comment on the stage the courtier has arrived at by the end of each series. The English sonnet inhibits the linear forward progress of the story less than the Italian form would have done: it is easier to disintegrate into two-line or four-line sentences, as Gascoigne does here.

The project of using autobiography to prove an adage is a metonymic one: the story of one man's coming to court distills its generalizable features, and gestures continually toward the larger social world in which his exemplary career unfolded—"embraced of all and some," egged on by "mine old acquainted mates." Such a project cannot use the sonnet in the way that, for example, an Elizabethan poet will use it to define love or to tell what happened when he looked into a lady's eyes.

Gascoigne's sonneteering has its own kind of strength and competence. He saw, for example, that the way to make his enchaining strategy really effective was to incorporate the repeated line into a new syntagma, using it not to say the same thing twice but to make a bridge between two different statements: "These . . . were baits that blazed still / Before mine eye to feed my greedy will"; "Before mine eye to feed my greedy will, / Gan muster eke mine old acquainted mates." In this particular instance the narrative moves forward a step from one sonnet to the next, but meanwhile the repeated phrase attests to the persistence of a certain attitude on the courtier's part —the "greedy will" that will cook his goose in the long run. Although the sonnets tend to break down into two-line or four-line sentences, the fit between the discourse and the rhyme scheme is precise and clear. Gascoigne used enjambment sparingly, and would never allow consecutive quatrains to melt together, as they do in this sonnet by a mid-century contemporary of his:

> To blame myself, or pinch me to the quick,
> To rub the bare, which fain would rankled lie,
> To raise the mire, within the water thick,
> Is all in vain; experience plainly try,
> To warn of that, as Horace did in Rome:
> Exhorting thee from that which I should use,
> That guerdon due unto my share would come
> Which for his hire Scylla could not refuse,
> Exhorting those which then in Rome did stay
> To sober life, when he a ruffian was:
> Lo everyone which ready tongue would say,
> Scylla, Scylla, seek to amend thy case:
>   Amend thy life: a good example give,
>   So we by thee shall better know to live.[11]

This writer has made no sense of the form at all. He breaks the fourteen lines up 5, 5, and 4; instead of rhetorically motivated enjambment there is just a kind of slopping over of the argument from one line to the next that ignores the units afforded by the rhyme scheme. The punchline of the anecdote about Scylla comes in line 12, so that the couplet is repetitious and anticlimactic.

Gascoigne saw how to use the sonnet to underwrite the syntagmatic configuration of his argument. He did not, however, allow the form to generate another kind of argument, whose coherence would be metaphoric rather than discursive or narrative. The Elizabethan poets had to reinvent the sonnet to turn it into what Petrarch's sonnets had been: a self-focused metaphoric complex.

As we have already seen, Spenser developed for his *Amoretti* sequence a rhyme scheme of his own that would increase the synchronic cohesiveness of the form by linking its quatrains together. When he uses the sonnet to mount a little allegorical narrative, as he quite often does, his rhyme scheme helps him to reduce and complicate its linear forward pressure: the narrative will change its pace, or pause and then shift direction, as the second rhyme of one quatrain becomes the first rhyme of the next:

> One day as I unwarily did gaze
>   on those fayre eyes, my love's immortall light:
>   the whiles my stonisht hart stood in amaze,
>   through sweet illusion of her look's delight;
> I mote perceive how in her glauncing sight,
>   legions of loves with little wings did fly:
>   darting their deadly arrowes fyry bright,

at every rash beholder passing by.
One of those archers closely I did spy,
   ayming his arrow at my very hart:
   when suddenly with twincle of her eye,
   the Damzell broke his misintended dart.
Had she not so doon, sure I had bene slayne,
   yet as it was, I hardly scap't with paine.

(Amoretti, 16)

This sonnet makes an allegorical anecdote out of an exchange of looks. Story-telling is finally not the purpose of the anecdote; it is the means of staging an encounter that is at once interpersonal and impersonal, slight and momentous.

The closer one looks at Spenser's narrative strategy the cleverer it appears, and an important part of it is the way in which the beginnings and ends of its three quatrains are synchronized. The first quatrain records and also dramatizes the lover's initial state of amazement, by allowing its third and fourth lines to double the clause of attendant circumstance: "the whiles my stonisht hart stood in amaze," the argument itself stands still. The first line of the second quatrain initiates a busy little scene, but it also reemphasizes the lover's posture of static contemplation, while at the same time it marks a change in that posture, from astonished "gaze" to a more active grasping of the object. The relation between the second quatrain and the first line of the third is similar but more complex. As the second rhyme of the second quatrain becomes the first rhyme of the third, the line itself picks up one of the second quatrain's little archers: "One of those archers closely I did spy." "I did spy" has a double relationship to what has gone before. It corresponds to "I did gaze" in line 1 and "I mote perceive" in line 5: the lover is looking more closely still. By doing so, ironically, he becomes eligible to be shot at: he is one of the "rash beholders" of the preceding, rhyme-linked line. In this way the ninth line effects a transition from the "I"-initiated perceptual activities of the first two quatrains to the climactic moment in lines 9 and 10, when the object of all this looking "suddenly" takes the initiative herself.

In this sonnet of Sidney's, from the Arcadia, narration is synchronized in a different way. It is an unusually complicated piece of "correlative" or "repeating" verse, a form that became very popular in England in the 1580s and 1590s.

```
      1         2          3        1       2       3
Virtue, beauty, and speech, did strike, wound, charm,
         1    2    3          1       2        3
My heart, eyes, ears, with wonder, love, delight:
```

```
     1     2     3        1     2         3
First, second, last, did bind, enforce, and arm,
         1     2     3        1   2              3
His works, shows, suits, with wit, grace, and vow's might.
```

```
            1       2       3     1    2      3
Thus honor, liking, trust, much, far, and deep,
     1         2           3           1        2         3
Held, pierced, possessed, my judgment, sense, and will,
         1       2          3      1     2      3
Till wrong, contempt, deceit, did grow, steal, creep,
      1       2      3      1        2          3
Bands, favor, faith, to break, defile, and kill.
```

```
         1          2              3     1       2       3
Then grief, unkindness, proof, took, kindled, taught,
     1                2       3    1     2       3
Well grounded, noble, due, spite, rage, disdain,
     1   2    3                  1     2         3
But ah, alas, in vain my mind, sight, thought,
         1       2            3        1     2      3
Doth him, his face, his words, leave, shun, refrain,
         1     2        3          1     2      3
For no thing, time, nor place, can loose, quench, ease,
       1       2         3       1    2      3
Mine own, embraced, sought, knot, fire, disease.[12]
```

In order to figure out what is being said by each of these sentences, we have to move back and forth between the correlated sets of subjects, verbs, objects, modifiers. What is conveyed by the arrangement is that at each stage of the love affair several things happened simultaneously, or in quick succession: virtue struck my heart with wonder, meanwhile speech charmed my ears with delight; honor held my judgment while liking pierced my sense. The correlative system is complex but not confusing, because the story is a simple, familiar one: attraction, courtship, betrayal, suffering. Narration and analysis proceed together, but the narrative syntagm is overpowered by the analytic structure, which transforms the chronological sequence into a paradigmatic series. The analytic structure is reinforced by the formal divisions of the sonnet, into whose three quatrains and a couplet it is symmetrically fitted, half-sentence by half-sentence, two three-term sets to a line.

Through being so highly patterned, the poem conveys Philoclea's sense of her own powerlessness as various parts of her capitulated programmatically, in unison, to Pyrocles' wooing. As Neil Rudenstine has pointed out in connection with another of her love laments, "there is no sense of Philoclea's controlling and directing her feelings; on the contrary, the feelings have an inflexible logic of their own, and seem to operate purely according to their own laws."[13] In his study of Sidney's early poetry, Rudenstine points out that the meanings of poems like this one "reside to a large extent in the shapes or patterns created on the page by syntax and rhetoric."[14] These shapes and patterns are themselves significant of what the experience of being in love is like. The intricate coherence they give to the lover's account of her or his feelings serves to lift the whole experience out of context. The poem is highly self-focused, and so is the predicament it dramatizes. In the couplet of this lament of Philoclea's, she explicitly says that she finds herself unable to use her faculties of "mind, sight, thought" to reattach her to the external world:

> For no thing, time, nor place, can loose, quench, ease,
> Mine own, embraced, sought, knot, fire, disease.

Sidney's early sonnets are not all as intricately patterned as this, but it is characteristic of them to use rhetorical schemes as figures for what it is like to be in love. Chiasmus and antimetabole convey the lover's sense of being immobilized by conflicting pressures:

> What medicine then, can such disease remove,
> Where love draws hate, and hate engendreth love?

> Let me be loved, or else not loved be.

Anaphora and other figures of repetition convey obsession. Anadiplosis, the repetition of the last word of one line or clause to begin the next, conveys the interdependence of successive stages in an escalating or circular process. Schemes like these are just as obtrusive as rhyme, and they have the same impact on the discourse: they project the principle of equivalence from the axis of substitution into the axis of combination in a radical and thorough-going way. Here is another example from the *Arcadia*, where the same syntactic structure is repeated three times, dividing the quatrains into antithetical halves, and is then reversed in the concluding couplet.

> In vain, mine eyes, you labor to amend
>   With flowing tears your fault of hasty sight:
> Since to my heart her shape you so did send,
>   That her I see, though you did lose your light.

> In vain, my heart, now you with sight are burn'd,
>   With sighs you seek to cool your hot desire:
> Since sighs (into mine inward furnace turn'd)
>   For bellows serve to kindle more the fire.
>
> Reason, in vain (now you have lost my heart)
>   My head you seek, as to your strongest fort:
> Since there mine eyes have played so false a part,
>   That to your strength your foes have sure resort.
>   And since in vain I find were all my strife,
>   To this strange death I vainly yield my life.
>
> (Poems, p. 38)

In this poem corresponding lines are as closely correlated at their beginnings by anaphora, and in the middle by parallel syntax, as they are by the pattern of line-ending rhyme words. This use of repetition makes the internal structure of the sonnet very obvious, and gives the poem a strong paradigmatic coherence. As David Kalstone points out, its argument has a sting in its tail, because of the way in which the repeated word "vain" has its impact reversed in line 14: " 'vain' connotes throughout the entire poem . . . the speaker's fruitless attempts to resist passion; now at the end of the sonnet he recognizes, with wry wit, that accepting passion is also vain and self-defeating."[15] In the *Astrophil and Stella* sonnets, where Sidney tends to work ironically against the sonnet form, the final line will often subvert or topple an argument he has used the first thirteen lines to develop. Here the ironic reversal has the effect, instead, of strengthening the sonnet's self-enclosure and the impression it creates of the lover's having been conquered, immobilized, caught within a vicious circle of self-betrayal from which there is no escape.

Fulke Greville was not as successful with the sonnet as Shakespeare or Spenser or his good friends Sidney and Daniel. His sonnets are notoriously crabbed and difficult, and that is usually because he has tried to say too much in fourteen lines and has not allowed the structure of the sonnet to help him say it effectively. The highly reiterative, metaphoric arguments that are typical of Elizabethan sonneteering may seem vapid by comparison with Greville's dense and complicated reasoning, but by the same token his sonnets are often structurally obscure. Here is a typical example:

> Caelica, you that excell in flesh and wit,
> In whose sweet heart Love doth both ebb and flow
> Returning faith more than it took from it,
> Whence doth the Change, the World thus speaks on, grow?

If Worthiness do joy to be admired,
My soul, you know, only be-wonders you;
If Beauty's glory be to be desired,
My heart is nothing else; What need you new?

If loving joy of worths beloved be,
And joys not simple, but still mutual,
Whom can you more love, than you have lov'd me?
Unless in your heart there be more than all;
    Since *Love* no dooms-day hath, where bodies change,
    Why should new be delight, not being strange?[16]

I think that in the first quatrain Caelica's lover is asking how such an essentially perfect creature as she is could possibly be unfaithful to him; but that is a guess. The syntax does not make it clear enough how the question addressed to Caelica in line 4 is related to the apostrophes that characterize her in the first three lines, and the description of her nature in the second and third lines is itself ambiguous. What is the antecedent of the first "it" in line 3: love, or faith? Is faith being cited as an imperative her nature acknowledges, or as the essence of his posture toward her? Does "thus" in the fourth line indicate that the World draws an obvious conclusion from her nature —from Love's "ebb and flow"—or does it invoke a rumor which has given rise to the poem, and which the lover finds incredible in view of her essential excellence?

The second quatrain is much clearer, with its parallel "if-then" clauses. But the third is overloaded again, this time with an elliptical syllogism; and then the couplet mounts a new piece of syllogistic reasoning that is even more compressed. By packing the poem so full of reasoning, Greville has failed to capitalize on the potentialities of the form; and he has also made the fulfilment of its fixed requirements too hard for himself. Instead of using the couplet to conclude the foregoing argument by topping off the metaphysical conundrum of the third quatrain or in some other way, he has used it to ask a fresh question that incorporates a new set of abstract metaphysical premises. The rhyme scheme does not assist the argument but seems partly responsible for its clumsiness, especially in line 3, with that ambiguous double "it."

Greville wrote a *Treatise Of Human Learning*, in which he takes a very pessimistic view of all the disciplines of human knowledge and all the arts with which we try to remedy our fallenness, including the arts of language. The view he takes there of language, especially of figurative language, is consistent with the structural obscurity of his sonnets, and probably accounts for it. Ideally, as he continually reiterates, language is transparent to thought. Properly used, words will expound Nature to us. Figurative uses of language are justifiable only on the grounds that they are often necessary, "Because no language in the earth affords / Sufficient characters to express all things." Lately, however, Rhetoric "plays the wanton with this need" (stanza 108), "Captiving reason, with the painted skin / Of many words; with empty sounds misleading / Us to false ends . . ." (stanza 107). She has alienated words from their proper or natural usage, violating the bonds that keep language truthful:

> Whereas those words in every tongue are best,
> Which do most properly express the thought;
> For as of pictures, which should manifest
> The life, we say not that is fineliest wrought,
>   Which fairest simply shows, but fair and like:
>   So *words must sparks be of those fires they strike.*
>
> For the true Art of *Eloquence* indeed
> Is not this craft of words, but forms of speech,
> Such as from living wisdoms do proceed;
> Whose ends are not to flatter, or beseech,
>   Insinuate, or persuade, but to declare
>   What things in Nature good, or evil are.[17]

(stanzas 109–10)

Greville has had to use figurative expressions himself to discuss these matters, and his choice of figures is revealing. The metonymic relation of sparks to fire, the iconic relation between a portrait and the person it depicts, the insistence that true eloquence is the reflex of living wisdoms, all privilege the message-to-context relation and suggest that it is a natural bond. Poetry, as he explains a little later in the treatise, should raise her creations "on lines of truth," and thereby " [teach] us order under pleasure's name" (stanza 114). The order poetry teaches would not be conferred or constituted by art but taken from Nature:

> Since, *if the matter be in Nature vile,*
> *How can it be made precious by a style?*

(stanza 112)

The other Elizabethan poets whose sonnets we have been looking at were more hospitable than this to the poetic function of language and the metaphoric way of conducting an argument. They allowed the sonnet form to produce a strongly self-focused message, whose paraphrasable argument is minimal but whose articulation of that argument is complex and rich. They allowed the sonnet to privilege synchrony over diachrony, metaphor over metonymy. What prompted them to approach the sonnet as they did was a shared conception of the status of lyric poetry and a collective attitude toward the poetic function of language that differed sharply from the view that Gascoigne and his contemporaries took of these matters.

Gascoigne's "Certain Notes of Instruction concerning the making of verse or ryme in English" is not a defense of poesy or a treatise about it, but just a few thoughts put in writing at a friend's request:[18]

> Signor Eduardo, since promise is debt, and you (by the law of friendship) do burden me with a promise that I should lend you instructions towards the making of English verse or rhyme, I will essay to discharge the same, though not so perfectly as I would, yet as readily as I may: and therewithall I pray you consider that *Quot homines, tot Sententiae*, especially in poetry, wherein (nevertheless) I dare not challenge any degree, and yet will I at your request adventure to set down my simple skill in such simple manner as I have used, referring the same hereafter to the correction of the *Laureate*.

Apparently Gascoigne just did not bother to work the ensuing notes up into a more formal treatise when he decided to include them in the second edition of his poetry. But their modesty, their casualness, their nuts-and-bolts practicality are perhaps not entirely accidental but partly strategic: they help to constitute the persona Gascoigne is at pains to project throughout the *Posies*, that of a virile and versatile man of action who has done more of his learning from experience than from books, for whom poetry has been a hobby and a dimension of social intercourse. Like the poems that were published along with them, these notes profess to have been socially motivated "(by the law of friendship)," and the status they attribute to the lyric is that of stylized social gesture:

> If I should undertake to write in praise of a gentlewoman, I would neither praise her crystal eye, nor her cherry lip, &c. For these things are *trita et obvia*. But I would either find some supernatural cause whereby my pen might walk in the superlative degree, or else I would undertake to answer for any imperfection that she hath, and thereupon raise the praise of her commendation. Likewise if I should disclose my pretence in love . . . (pp. 465–66)

He does no theorizing about what poetry is, or what it is good for; his objective is just to help his friend become a more accomplished courtier of ladies.

The *Posies* were published in 1675. Twenty-eight years later, in 1603, Daniel published a little discourse he too had originally written as a private letter to a gentleman friend of his (Fulke Greville, probably),[19] with a prefatory dedication which explains that he had "now given a greater body to the same argument" and decided to share it with "all the worthy lovers and learned professors of Rhyme within his Majesty's Dominions." It was the accession of King James, who was known to be favorably disposed toward the arts, that emboldened him to do this: "the complexion of the times," as he puts it, is such as to make the profession of Rhyme an honorable one. It is in any case the profession he has chosen for himself, for better or for worse, with the encouragement of Greville and the Countess of Pembroke, to whose son the treatise is addressed. Daniel's willingness to claim for himself the status of a professional man of letters is a sign of the times; and so are his expansive, idealistic generalizations about the cultural function and value of poetry:

> I stand forth only to make good the place we [professors of Rhyme] have thus taken up, and to defend the sacred monuments erected therein, which contain the honor of the dead, the fame of the living, the glory of peace, and the best power of our speech, and wherein so many honorable spirits have sacrificed to Memory their dearest passions, showing by what divine influence they have been moved, and under what stars they lived.[20]

This is the Sidneian vein of defense: poetry is being represented as a national institution. Thomas Campion's disparagement of rhyme and his advocacy of quantitative meter are tantamount, Daniel implies, to treason. Campion does

> wrong to the honor of the dead, wrong to the fame of the living, and wrong to *England*, in seeking to lay reproach upon her native ornaments, and to turn the fair stream and full course of her accents, into the shallow current of a loose uncertainty, clean out of the way of her known delight. (p. 153)

The subject of Gascoigne's "Notes" and Daniel's *Defense of Rhyme* is really the same: it is the poetic function of language; but we can more easily recognize that this is Daniel's subject because he theorizes about it. Principles of versification, he argues, are generated from within each language according to its own acoustic properties: Latin is a quantitative language, English is not. Gascoigne's notes are full of sound advice about how to capitalize on the acoustic properties of his native language, but his knowledge is held and shared on a practical rather than a theoretical level. It is possible nevertheless to derive Gascoigne's attitude toward the poetic function of language from his remarks about invention, especially his warning about the kind of trouble that rhyme can get you into with your invention:

> 6. I would exhort you also to beware of rhyme
> without reason: my meaning is hereby that your
> rhyme lead you not from your first invention,
> for many writers when they have laid the platform
> of their invention, are yet drawn sometimes (by
> rhyme) to forget it or at least to alter it, as
> when they cannot readily find out a word which may
> rhyme to the first (and yet continue their
> determinate invention) they do then either botch
> it up with a word that will rhyme (how small
> reason soever it carry with it) or else they alter
> their first word and so percase decline or trouble
> their former invention: But do you always hold
> your first determined invention, and do rather
> search the bottom of your brains for apt words,
> than change good reason for rumbling rhyme.
>
> (*The Posies*, p. 469)

The assumption Gascoigne is making here is that rhyme and meter are what you do to a message to turn it into a poem. Your choice of verse form ought, he suggests, to be directed by the genre of your message: "as this riding rhyme serveth most aptly to write a merry tale, so Rhythm royal is fittest for a grave discourse. Ballads are best of matters of love, and roundelets most apt for the beating or handling of an adage or common proverb: Sonnets serve as well in matters of love as of discourse" (p. 473). Why you would bother to cast your merry tale or your grave discourse into "rumbling rhyme" is a question he scarcely addresses. "Let your poem be such as may both delight and draw attentive reading," he says at one point, but all of his advice presupposes that verse at its best just enhances, and at its worst detracts, from the virtues the discourse should have regardless of whether its medium be verse or prose: economy, perspicuity, "matter . . . worth the marking."

Daniel's notion of what good poetry is, and what poetry is good for, seems at first to be quite similar: "All verse," he explains, "is but a frame of words confined within certain measure; differing from the ordinary speech, and introduced, the better to express men's conceits, both for delight and memory" (p. 131). But as he warms to his project, we can begin to see that he thinks very differently from Gascoigne about the relation between "conceit" or "invention" and the poetic function of language. Conveniently enough, the passage that expresses this most clearly is a discussion of the sonnet. "And indeed," he begins,

> I have wished there were not that multiplicity of rhymes, as is used by many in sonnets, which yet we see in some so happily to succeed, and hath been so far from hindering their inventions, as it hath begot conceit beyond expectation, and comparable to the best inventions of the world: for sure in an eminent spirit whom Nature hath fitted for that mystery, rhyme is no impediment to his conceit, but rather gives him wings to mount and carries him, not out of his course, but as it were beyond his power to a far happier flight (*Defense*, pp. 137–38).[21]

Rhyme is here being allowed to play a constitutive role in the invention itself. Instead of having to be careful not to let the demands of the rhyme scheme interfere with the message or the rhetorical objective one has in mind, it seems one ought to let the sonnet structure transform that original conception, taking one's imagination beyond what would have been conceivable in ordinary speech.

"Nor is this certain limit observed in sonnets, any tyrannical bounding of the conceit," Daniel continues, "but rather a reducing it *in girum*, and a just form, neither too long for the shortest project, nor too short for the longest, being but only employed for a present passion." Daniel appreciates that the sonnet is self-focused and synchronistic, that what it is therefore best suited to do is to depict "a present passion." He sees that the sonneteer should not be trying to tell a story, and that he need not have very much of an argument. What counts is not how much or how little he has to say, but how he lays it out within the given dimensions.

Gascoigne was aware that stanzas of various kinds are structural units to be exploited in some way by the argument. He advises, for instance, that you "do finish the sentence and meaning at the end of every staff when you write staves, and at the end of every two lines where you write by couplets or poulter's measure." But the reason he gives for this is to "eschew prolixity" and to reinforce the syntactic structure of the poem's discourse: "for I see many writers which draw their sentences in length, and make an end at latter

Lammas: for commonly before they end, the Reader hath forgot where he begun" (p. 472). The function of poetic structures, as far as he knows, is to reinforce and clarify discursive structures. Neither in his own sonnets nor in the "Notes" does he show any awareness of the sonnet's potential to hold its argument together as one integral, synchronized complex of meaning.

As Daniel proceeds with his defense of the way that a sonnet bounds in the writer's conceit, he uses a metaphor which confirms that he thinks of poetic structures not as vehicles for one kind of message or another, one sort of discursive project or another, but as being radically constitutive of the poetic invention itself:

> For the body of our imagination, being as an unformed chaos without fashion, without day, if by the divine power of the spirit it be wrought into an orb of order and form, is it not more pleasing to Nature, that desires a certainty, and comports not with that which is infinite, to have these closes, rather than not to know where to end, or how far to go, especially seeing our passions are often without measure. (p. 138)

In his poetic treatise "Musophilus," a more generalized defense of arts and letters, he draws the same analogy between the poetic function of language and the form-giving activity of God. Musophilus explains to his interlocutor, Philocosmos, that poetry is with good reason said to be "the speech of heaven."

> Those numbers wherewith heaven and earth are mov'd,
> Show, weakness speaks in prose, but power in verse.[22]

The analogy between musical or poetic "numbers" and the divine mathematics of the cosmos makes both God's and the poet's creations out to be essentially synchronic structures. Right on the heels of this passage, Musophilus makes the further claim that verse is the best possible way to memorialize a man's glorious deeds after his death.[23] He is crediting poetry with a power of "monumentality" that is a function of its synchronicity.

The literary theorist Michael Riffaterre has used the term "monumentality" to emphasize that a poem "is so well built and rests upon so many intricate relationships that it is relatively impervious to change and deterioration of the linguistic code." A word in a poem can be obsolete, or it can be a neologism, but its meaning will be recoverable from the poem itself, because it is overdetermined by cooperating structures. Riffaterre defines monumentality as an inherent property or essential predicate of all literary texts; but a poem, and especially a fixed form like the sonnet, possesses this property to the highest degree, because of being, as Riffatere puts it, "a closed entity."[24] A poem carries its meaning not just as a signified message but as a configuration of the signifier. It possesses monumentality by virtue of the way in which it synchronizes its message and lifts it out of context. This is what Daniel, Spenser, and Shakespeare are getting at also when they refer to poems as monuments. The word is carried over from sculpture and architecture, and is metaphorically suggestive both about the function or purpose of poetry—as a monument it memorializes a person's or a nation's greatness —and about its special properties as a configuration of the signifier. As to these, the word suggests that the shape and coherence of a poem are synchronic, that we apprehend its structure as a simultaneous unity; and also, that poems promote the materiality of the signifier to maximum perceptibility. Shakespeare's argument that his "powerful rhyme" would outlive "the gilded monuments of princes" is one that claims for poems the solid materiality of sculptured stone, the difference being that poems are materialized by successive generations of readers:

> Your monument shall be my gentle verse,
> Which eyes not yet created shall o'er-read,
> And tongues to be your being shall rehearse,
> When all the breathers of this world are dead,
>   You still shall live—such virtue hath my pen—
>   Where breath most breathes, ev'n in the mouths of men.
>
> (Sonnet 81)

The Elizabethan poet who most consistently and often cites monumentalizing as the function of poetry is Spenser, and he is also the one whose poetic practice was most thoroughly informed by this notion of what a poem is. In "The Ruines of Time," where the passing of the greatness of ancient Britain is lamented, along with the recent deaths of Leicester and Sidney, it is explained that

> deeds doe die, how ever noblie donne,
> And thoughts of men do as themselves decay,
> But wise wordes taught in numbers for to runne,
> Recorded by the Muses, live for ay.[25]

In "The Teares of the Muses," where each of the Muses complains in her turn about the literary barbarism of the present time, the last one to speak, Polyhymnia, makes one exception:

> One onelie lives, her ages ornament,
> And myrrour of her Makers majestie;

> That with rich bountie and deare cherishment,
> Supports the praise of noble Poesie:
> Ne onelie favours them which it professe,
> But is her selfe a peereless Poetresse.
>
> Most peereles Prince, most peereles Poetresse,
> The true *Pandora* of all heavenly graces,
> Divine *Elisa*, sacred Emperesse:
> Live she for ever, and her royall P'laces
> Be fild with praises of divinest wits,
> That her eternize with their heavenlie writs.[26]

In both these poems, the importance of the claim that is made about poetry is political, and it is motivated by personal ambition: Spenser aspired to be England's poet laureate. But it is not just something Spenser said about poetry; he had a fully developed conception, which he put into practice in all of his poems, of the kind of verbal construct a poem needed to be in order to have this kind of staying power. That conception is manifest at the level of syntax and lexicon. He developed a special vocabulary, full of archaisms and archaizing coinages, that would put the language of his poems at a distance from the language of every day. As for syntax, J. W. Lever has observed that for poetic purposes Spenser "virtually discarded the word-order of his own language."[27] By doing this he allowed the Spenserian stanza, or the form of the sonnet that he invented, to control the discourse in a very obvious way and to lift it out of context. To promote this configuration of the signifier to maximum perceptibility, he used alliteration to reinforce the metric pattern and make it more obvious. With his special vocabulary he gave the verbal signifier a certain opacity, and with alliteration he maximized its acoustic materiality.

The opacity of the signifier is differently manifest in the highly reiterative arguments of Shakespeare's sonnets. Often a single word has two completely different meanings: overdetermination produces what Renaissance rhetoricians called "syllepsis," "the figure of double supply."[28] In the following example, from his sonnet 3, the word "husbandry" has two different meanings activated, partly by the rhyme scheme and partly by the agricultural metaphor that is introduced as the second quatrain repeats the argument of the first:

> Look in thy glass, and tell the face thou viewest
> Now is the time that face should form another,
> Whose fresh repair if now thou not renewest,
> Thou dost beguile the world, unlesse some mother.

> For where is she so fair whose uneared womb
> Disdains the tillage of thy husbandry?
> Or who is he so fond will be the tomb
> Of his self-love to stop posterity?
> Thou art thy mother's glass, . . .
>
> (Sonnet 3, 11.1–9)

The tenor of lines 5 and 6 is something like "What potential mother would not be glad to have you for her husband?" The agricultural metaphor is introduced by the words "uneared" and "tillage." "Husbandry" participates in this metaphor, but it also brings the noun "husband" to mind because of the metaphor's partly explicit tenor: "where is she . . . whose . . . womb . . ." Because it includes "womb" and "posterity," the paradigm of line-ending words ensures that "performing the office of a husband" will surface as a meaning for "husbandry" along with the more common sense of "careful management." The rhyme scheme also helps to establish a metaphoric equation between the two senses of the word: "husbandry" acts on behalf of the womb against the tomb.

In another of the sonnets that urge the beloved young man to marry, several words have more than one meaning activated—either simultaneously, as in the interesting case of the word "contracted," or retroactively, as a newly introduced metaphor claims some part of the language of the metaphor it displaces:

> From fairest creatures we desire increase,
> That thereby beauty's rose might never die,
> But as the riper should by time decease
> His tender heir might bear his memory:
> But thou, contracted to thine own bright eyes,
> Feed'st thy light's flame with self-substantial fuel,
> Making a famine where abundance lies—
> Thyself thy foe, to thy sweet self too cruel.
>
> (Sonnet 1, 11.1–8)

In line 1, "increase" means "offspring" or "harvest." In line 3, the rhyme-word "decease," a synonym for "die," brings legal language into play, and in a legal context "contracted" means "bound by a contract" or "betrothed." At the same time, however, the first quatrain sets up an opposition between "fairest creatures" and "thou," which puts "contracted" in opposition to "increase": "From fairest creatures we desire increase . . . But thou, contracted . . ." The poetic structure thus enables the poet to accuse the young man of being perversely self-betrothed, and thereby diminished. In line 6, a fire metaphor comes into play which claims the brightness of "thine own bright eyes" retroactively, and takes it literally: thus we are invited to picture a wasted face from which the young man's eyes blaze with the unhealthy brightness of fever. Then in line 7 "Feed'st," which is a dead metaphor in connection with "thy light's flame" in the previous line, is brought to life by a feast-famine oxymoron, which in turn harks back with the word "abundance" to the harvest metaphor of line 1. Borrowing the sonnet's own initial metaphor, we could say that its metaphors breed with each other in a quite uncanny way, from one line to the next.

Where Shakespeare's sonnets are at their most self-focused, synchronistic and metaphoric, syllepsis gives them the haunting richness that has earned Shakespeare his preeminence among English practitioners of the sonnet. The sonnets whose project is to be "all in war with time for love of you"[29] are the most hospitable of all to this trope, because their arguments are reiterative, shifting from one metaphoric vehicle to another as the same tenor is repeated again and again.

Whereas the sonnet itself is synchronistic, the sonnet sequence harbors a diachronic potential of a special sort. Robert Durling follows C. S. Lewis in citing Petrarch as the first poet to disclose that potential by arranging his *Rime sparse* chronologically but without the prose narrative that holds Dante's *Vita nuova* together. Each individual sonnet of Petrarch's is a distinct, self-focused unit, and in many of them Laura's presence to her poet's imagination seems to suspend time for a moment. And yet, as Durling points out, "the poems are arranged as if deposited by the passage of time."[30] At intervals, the poet reflects explicitly about the way in which his love persists and even intensifies, whereas the rest of his experience as he grows older is of losses and changes and endings. By means of the relationship between synchrony and diachrony that is established in this way, the poems present themselves as islands of time-transcendence within a natural time-continuum.

Gascoigne and his contemporaries did experiment with "sonnets in sequence"—two or three or seven sonnets linked together by external tag lines or by repetition of the last line of one as the first line of the next. But this kind of "sequence" is not a series of "present passions" spaced apart in time; it is a series of stanzas, affording the opportunity for a more extended piece of narration or argumentation than a single sonnet could manage. Its enchaining strategy may have been copied from the Italian *corona di sonnetti*, which enchains a series of sonnets in a circle so that the last line of the last one repeats the opening line of the first; but William Harris found that none of these mid-Tudor poets sought "the characteristically circular effect obtained by the Italians." Theirs is a "purely linear design."[31] The coherence of this kind of sequence is syntagmatic—it is a matter of narrative or discursive continuity, whereas the coherence of both the corona and the looser, more extended Petrarchan sequence is paradigmatic—a matter of arriving back at the beginning, or continuing to reiterate the same argument over and over again.

Some of the mid-Tudor poets published groups of love poems arranged in their ostensible order of composition at different stages of a love affair, whose changing moods reflect its ups and downs. It is here, perhaps, that we should locate the English vernacular ancestry of the Elizabethan sonnet sequence. But just as these poets failed to appreciate the sonnet's potentiality to be a self-focused semantic complex, so they show no signs of having understood that a group of poems might constitute the record of a subjective state that endures while time passes. Instead, they represent the lover's experience as a melodramatic story. At the beginning there are petitions, complaints, and other poems to woo the lady *comme il faut*. In the middle, there may be a brief period of happy consummation to celebrate; but in the end, the lady proves faithless and the lover grows suicidal or cynical. These poets often invoke Troilus as the archetype of the lover, and they have probably taken this story line from Chaucer's *Troilus and Criseyde*.[32] If we turn from *Master F.J.*, or *Dan Bartholmewe's Dolorous Discourses*, to Daniel's *Delia* and the sonnet sequences of Spenser and Shakespeare, we can see that the Elizabethan poets not only had a different conception of the form-to-content relation within a single poem but also that they had a different notion of what the project of writing a series of love poems was all about.

In Daniel's sequence, there is no story at all. Delia remains aloof and impervious to entreaty from first to last, and we know that she will, because the first four sonnets presuppose that the rest of the sequence has already been written:

> Go wailing verse, the infants of my love,
> *Minerva*-like, brought forth without a mother:
> Present the image of the cares I prove,
> Witness your father's grief exceeds all other.
>   Sigh out a story of her cruel deeds,
> With interrupted accents of despair:
> A monument that whosoever reads
> May justly praise, and blame my loveless Fair.[33]

This sonnet is prospective in a double sense: it refers to the already-written sonnets we have not read yet, and it looks beyond the end of the sequence, hoping that as a completed "monument" it may have more power to move Delia than any of the individual poems had, along the way:

> Knock at that hard heart, beg till you have mov'd her;
> And tell th'unkind, how dearly I have lov'd her.

After the first four poems, which are also the last four poems of the sequence, each individual sonnet speaks in the present tense of the poet's admiration and desire. Sonnet after sonnet accumulates, each the discrete embodiment of a fresh complaint; meanwhile time passes, as we must suppose, in the spaces between them. Many of them, from sonnet 5 onward, speak of the lover's weariness, as if he had been in love with Delia for a long time already. In this way the temporal perspective of the sequence is lengthened into the past, just as the introductory sonnets project the lover's predicament beyond the end of the sequence into the foreseeable future.

Around the middle of the sequence of fifty sonnets, the poet begins to remind the lady that Time will eventually take her beauty away, and to suggest that she should value his poems because they will preserve it for posterity. It seems that these new topics have been generated by the internal diachronic dimension of the sequence: the lady is older than when he began to write poems to her; the "eternizing" argument is made on the strength of his already-written tributes. It was probably from Ronsard that Daniel learned to regard "eternizing" as a generic project for sonnets, but Petrarch is the poet he cites in connection with it:

> Thou canst not die whilst any zeal abound
> In feeling hearts, that can conceive these lines:
> Though thou a *Laura* hast no *Petrarch* found,
> In base attire, yet clearly Beauty shines.
>   And I, though born in a colder clime,
> Do feel mine inward heat as great, I know it:
> He never had more faith, although more rhyme,
> I love as well, though he could better show it.
>   But I may add one feather to my fame,
> To help her flight throughout the fairest Isle:
> And if my pen could more enlarge thy name,
> Then shouldst thou live in an immortal style.
>   But though that *Laura* better limned be,
> Suffice, thou shalt be lov'd as well as she.

>   (35)

In the first of his "eternizing" sonnets, sonnet 30, Daniel actually uses the Italian sonnet form, and that is probably an act of homage to Petrarch, because it is an unusual departure for Daniel from the English sonnet, with its less demanding rhyme scheme. When he credits Petrarch in sonnet 35 with "more rhyme" than himself, he means either that Petrarch managed to write sonnets in which more of the line-ending words rhyme with each other, or else—more likely—that Petrarch's love had more poems to show for it than he can boast as yet. If the latter reading is the correct one, it confirms that for Daniel the length of a sonnet sequence counts as proof of the poet-lover's "faith," by testifying to the duration and persistence of his love. At the same time, the sequence as a whole is conceived of synchronically. It is a monument which every sonnet makes larger, as well as being a record of faithful love which every sonnet lengthens.

Spenser's and Shakespeare's sequences also take on a diachronic dimension synchronically, as it were. In Spenser's *Amoretti* there is less narrative interest than we might expect from his having published "Epithalamion" along with it: for upward of sixty sonnets the lady spurns her suitor, and then rather abruptly, with the beginning of a new year, his poems begin to convey that she has accepted him, although she still holds back out of virgin modesty. That the beloved's posture changes so little is discouraging, during the first year of the courtship, but her suitor also admires her for it: if at times it seems "she is no woman, but a senseless stone," at other times it seems a man could not do better than to love one who is so "assured to herself." Constancy is also a central value in Shakespeare's sequence, but it is the poet himself who exemplifies it, as he continues to love the young man in the face of every conceivable discouragement. In Shakespeare's sequence more seems to happen than in Spenser's or Daniel's: there is a love triangle, a rival poet, the beloved young man falls into ill repute or bad company, and so apparently does the poet at one point. But their relationship keeps renewing itself, and the sequence is punctuated at intervals with poems that celebrate its immunity to change: "love is not love, / Which alters when it alteration finds." What the sequence seems to give us, instead of the history of a relationship, is a paradigm of every conceivable threat to love's persistence, every conceivable pretext of estrangement, presupposed and overcome.

If Troilus stands behind the love story depicted by the mid-century poets, the archetype that is implicit in these Elizabethan sequences is Narcissus, the lover who will never possess the object of his love, nor ever leave off loving. The poet of the *Amoretti* likens himself to Narcissus even after the lady has begun to favor him:

> My hungry eyes, through greedy covetize
>   still to behold the object of their paine,
>   with no contentment can themselves suffize:
> but having pine, and having not complaine.
> For lacking it they cannot lyfe sustayne,

and having it they gaze on it the more:
in their amazement lyke *Narcissus* vaine
whose eyes him starv'd: so plenty makes me poore.[34]

Shakespeare invokes Narcissus's predicament, without actually naming him,
in a sonnet that pauses over halfway through the sonnets to the young man
to generalize about what it is like to be in love with him:

So are you to my thoughts as food to life,
Or as sweet seasoned show'rs are to the ground;
And for the peace of you I hold such strife,
As 'twixt a miser and his wealth is found;
Now proud as an enjoyer, and anon
Doubting the filching age will steal his treasure;
Now counting best to be with you alone,
Then bettered that the world may see my pleasure;
Sometime all full with feasting on your sight,
And by and by clean starved for a look,
Possessing or pursuing no delight
Save what is had or must from you be took.
    Thus do I pine and surfeit day by day,
    Or gluttoning on all, or all away.

(75)

For the reader, this account of the lover's subjective experience, "day by day,"
corresponds to the rhythm of the sequence, sonnet by sonnet.

In both Spenser's and Shakespeare's sequences, seasonal references inter-
mittently help, as they did in Petrarch's *Canzoniere*, to register the passage of
time. In Spenser's sequence the time-frame that is provided in this way is
schematic and symbolic. The sixtieth sonnet explains that a year has passed
since he began to be in love:

They that in course of heavenly spheares are skild,
To every planet point his sundry yeare:
in which her circles voyage is fulfild,
as Mars in three score yeares doth run his spheare.
So since the winged God his planet cleare,
began in me to move, one yeare is spent:
the which doth longer unto me appeare,
then al those fourty which my life outwent.
Then by that count, which lovers books invent,
the spheare of Cupid fourty yeares containes:
which I have wasted in long languishment,

that seemd the longer for my greater paines.
But let thy loves fayre Planet short her wayes
this year ensuing, or else short my dayes.

Spenser probably was forty or thereabouts when he wrote this sonnet, but
the number forty has symbolic significance too, as the number of Christ's
nights and days in the wilderness. The new year brings the lover's period of
probation to an end: in sonnet 63 he begins to "descry the happy shore,"
and the first line of 64 is "Comming to kisse her lyps, (such grace I found)."
The temporal order that is invoked by his references to cosmic cycles and
Christian numerology is synchronic, finally: it subsumes the lover's experience of protracted frustration and suspense into a providential order that
appoints to every phase of a relationship its due season.[35] In Shakespeare's
sequence, the seasonal cycle is more haphazardly invoked, partly to confer
upon the vicissitudes of an ongoing relationship the rhythm of seasonal
change, and partly to call attention to its "unnatural" persistence:

To me, fair friend, you never can be old,
For as you were when first your eye I eyed,
Such seems your beauty still. Three winters cold
Have from the forests shook three summers' pride,
Three beauteous springs to yellow autumn turned
In process of the seasons have I seen,
Three April perfumes in three hot Junes burned,
Since first I saw you fresh, which yet are green.

(104)

Here again, the periodic seasonal references are diachronic markers, but the
temporal order they invoke is synchronic—a self-renewing cycle.

In all three of these sequences—Shakespeare's, Spenser's, and Daniel's—we
can speak of a recuperation or sublimation of diachrony into synchrony at
the level of the individual sonnet, and again at the level of the sequence as a
whole. At the level of the individual sonnet, the line of argument or story
line is transformed into a synchronic configuration with strong internal
cohesion that lifts its message out of context. As we have seen, all three of
these poets tended to collaborate with the inherent bias of the sonnet form,
producing self-focused, metaphoric arguments that dramatize the mind's
capacity either for reflective detachment, as in "That time of year thou mayst
in me behold," or, as in Spenser's Anacreontic fable about a moment of eye
contact, for subjective expansion of a moment in the lover's emotional life.
At the level of the sequence as a whole, time is supposed to pass in the spaces
between the sonnets, and the lover will occasionally pause to take an

overview that lengthens or deepens the temporal distance he has "tr<
since he first caught sight of the beloved. His persistence in love is
strated by its reiteration and renewal in one sonnet after another. _____
while, however, the diachronic lifeline or story line is subsumed into a
synchronic perspective. The ways this is done and the perspective invoked
are different from one sonneteer to another. In *Delia*, Daniel invokes the
"monumentality" of art, which is the theme of particular sonnets in all three
sequences, to confer synchronic coherence on the sequence as a whole. In
the *Amoretti*, Spenser uses Christian numerology to give the lady's constancy
to herself, and his to her, a higher sanction. In Shakespeare's sequence
alienation and estrangement are continually reinstantiated and overcome, so
that finally the rhythm of loss and recovery seems to express the essential
nature of human erotic love.

In his discussion of *Astrophil and Stella*, David Kalstone remarks that "Sidney's sonnets noticeably lack a sense of time and the bearing of time upon
love, a characteristic that distinguishes them from the sonnets of
Shakespeare and other Elizabethans. He chooses to ride on the dial's point of
the moment."[36] It could also be argued, however, that there is a stronger
sense of time in *Astrophil and Stella* than in any of the other Elizabethan
sequences. What Sidney does not do in his sequence—or rather, what Astrophil never does—is take up an extratemporal vantage point from which he
might consider the bearing of time upon love in the abstract, or claim that
his love for Stella "was builded far from accident," or promise that his poems
will give their relationship an "endless monument." Astrophil does not pull
himself out of context in this way; he speaks out of the mood of the moment;
and so for the reader there is a very strong sense of the passage of time, as
successive sonnets afford access to successive moments in his emotional and
interpersonal life. From time to time Astrophil takes stock of his situation, or
explains what has become of him since he fell in love with Stella, but his
synopsis is itself a projection of the moment, to be suspended by the next
sonnet's here and now.

Sidney creates this sense of time for the reader by using a number of
devices, including deictic presuppisal, to contextualize each sonnet from
within. Sonnet 47 is contextualized more strongly and elaborately than most
of them, but the ways in which that has been managed are by no means
unusual for the *Astrophil and Stella* sonnets:

> What, have I thus betrayed my liberty?
>   Can those black beams such burning marks engrave
>   In my free side? or am I born a slave,
> Whose neck becomes such yoke of tyranny?

Or want I sense to feel my misery?
Or sprite, disdain of such disdain to have?
Who for long faith, though daily help I crave,
May get no alms but scorn of beggary.
Virtue awake, Beauty but beauty is,
I may, I must, I can, I will, I do
Leave following that, which it is gain to miss.
Let her go. Soft, but here she comes. Go to,
Unkind, I love you not: O me, that eye
Doth make my heart give to my tongue the lie.

In the first eight lines, Astrophil's rhetorical questions have the force of metonymy: they explicate his predicament just enough for us to know what it is, but not so fully as to detach him from it, which a full-blown past-tense narrative would do. At first it is not clear whether "*have* I *thus* betrayed," "*those* black beams," "*such* burning marks," are retrospective, reflecting Astrophil's awareness that he has been Stella's slave for some time now, or whether they are meant to indicate that he has just now caught sight of her coming toward him. Either or both, as it turns out, would be appropriate readings. The subordinate clause that elaborates upon these deictic references in lines 7 and 8 gives them a relatively deep perspective into past time; then the last few lines of the sonnet presuppose that even as he speaks, Stella passes by him close enough for a fresh instance of eye contact to renew his enslavement to "those black beams."

Whereas the first eight lines are metonymically retrospective, the last six are firmly situated in the immediate present, and set toward the immediate future also, by a number of cooperating strategies: the performative assertion in which Astrophil's self-exhortation culminates in line 11 ("I . . . do leave following"); the imperative "let her go"; the interjection "Soft," which cooperates with the deictic adverb "here" to herald the advent of Stella herself; the shift from third-person "her" to second-person "you" in lines 12–13. The reversion to talking *about* Stella ("that eye") in lines 13–14 is assisted by a second interjection, "O me," and by the modal auxiliary "doth" to emphasize that what the verb refers to is happening simultaneously with the utterance itself.

Many of the *Astrophil and Stella* sonnets use these same devices for situating Astrophil's utterances in the immediate present. Interjections and performatives are frequent. A perspective into past time will often be rendered by subordinate clauses, while the main clause holds to the present tense and deictic adverbs attach it to the here and now. Often the structural divisions of the sonnet, with its modified Petrarchan rhyme scheme, assist the argument to "ride the dial's point of the moment," as in this case where the octave is retrospective and the last six lines more strongly set toward the immediate present and future. Several of the sonnets are addressed to an interlocutor who is supposed to have just said or done something to provoke Astrophil into speech. Others stage their own writing as an immediate, self-reflexive event.

Astrophil's sense of time is different from the synchronistic Petrarchan time-sense of the one who says "I" in Daniel's or Shakespeare's sequence. We can see this if we compare a sonnet of Sidney's whose contextualizing deixis is mostly temporal, and is mostly in the verbs, with a sonnet of Shakespeare's whose argument is comparable but differently oriented:

> *Stella* oft sees the very face of woe
>> Painted in my beclouded stormy face:
>> But cannot skill to pity my disgrace,
> Not though thereof the cause herself she know:
> Yet hearing late a fable, which did show
>> Of lovers never known, a grievous case,
>> Pity thereof gat in her breast such place
> That, from that sea deriv'd, tears' spring did flow.
>> Alas, if Fancy drawn by imag'd things,
> Though false, yet with free scope more grace doth breed
> Than servant's wrack, where new doubts honor brings;
> Then think my dear, that you in me do read
>> Of lover's ruin some sad tragedy:
>> I am not I, pity the tale of me.
>
> (45)

> When to the sessions of sweet silent thought
> I summon up remembrance of things past,
> I sigh the lack of many a thing I sought,
> And with old woes new wail my dear time's waste.
> Then can I drown an eye, unused to flow,
> For precious friends hid in death's dateless night,
> And weep afresh love's long since cancelled woe,
> And moan th'expense of many a vanished sight.
> Then can I grieve at grievances foregone,
> And heavily from woe to woe tell o'er
> The sad account of fore-bemoaned moan,
> Which I new pay as if not paid before.
>> But if the while I think on thee, dear friend,
>> All losses are restored, and sorrows end.
>
> (30)

The argument of both these sonnets turns on an opposition between what usually happens and what happens under certain special circumstances. But in Sidney's sonnet, the opposition is put to use by an argument that is strongly situated, both temporally and interpersonally, in Astrophil's ongoing social life. Sidney's first quatrain uses a frequentative present tense, which subsumes the moment of the utterance itself but remains unlocalized. The second quatrain is a past-tense narrative, which is put into relation with the immediate present by the deictic adverb "late." In the last six lines, Astrophil addresses Stella directly, referring in the same complex sentence to the recent event of the second quatrain, the more enduring status quo described in the first, and the immediate present, in which he urges her to begin to pity him. Shakespeare keeps his argument in a frequentative present tense: this is what happens every time he summons up remembrance of things past, except on those occasions when he happens to "think on thee, dear friend." The poem's perspective into past time is indefinitely deep, whereas in Sidney's poem it is rendered finite by the deictic adverb "late" and the specificity of the second quatrain's little narrative. Astrophil's set toward the future is also finite, insofar as his optatives ask for a response from Stella. Shakespeare's poem takes no initiative toward the future, but we may suppose that its present tense subsumes an indefinitely extensive future as well as an indefinitely long past. Occasionally one of Astrophil's sonnets is like this, but usually his sense of time is finite: he remembers something that happened recently, and explains what it was; he uses an imperative or optative mode to try to control the immediate future.

Sidney's sequence has a much more fully realized social context than the other Elizabethan sonnet sequences, as well as a different time sense. Astrophil's affair with Stella is almost as well elaborated, in terms of both setting and story line, as *The Adventures of Master F.J.*, but without a narrative framework to carry it. We piece the story together from the occasional anecdote, from soliloquies in which Astrophil takes stock of his situation, and from things we overhear him say to other people. We also draw inferences about how his courtship is going from the different kinds of situations that are presupposed at different points in the sequence by deictic and topical references. A diachronic dimension accrues to the sequence as a whole from the way in which Sidney uses these metonymic strategies to give fullness and immediacy to the situations that are presupposed by the individual sonnets, one at a time.

In sonnet 30, for example, Astrophil addresses Stella directly for the first time, and it is as if a new chapter in the relationship had suddenly begun:

> Whether the Turkish new moon minded be
> To fill his horns this year on Christian coast;

How Poles' right king means, without leave of host,
To warm with ill-made fire cold Moscovy;
If French can yet three parts in one agree;
  What now the Dutch in their full diets boast;
  How Holland hearts, now so good towns be lost,
Trust in the shade of pleasing Orange tree;
  How Ulster likes of that same golden bit,
Wherewith my father once made it half tame;
If in the Scottish court be weltering yet;
These questions busy wits to me do frame;
  I, cumbered with good manners, answer do,
  But know not how, for still I think of you.

Up until this point, Astrophil had been publishing his infatuation for Stella in a flamboyant, high-spirited way, with Anacreontic fables and the like. Stella had been in the audience, presumably, and so had we. Suddenly in the last line of this sonnet her status changes from "she" to "you," and we are put in the position of overhearing a message that was not, as we suddenly realize, addressed to us. It seems there is a prior understanding of some kind between this "I" and the "you" of whom he "still" thinks. Meanwhile the riddling allusions to current events produce a social background that is vivid and detailed. They give us a great deal of information, without detracting from the immediacy of the foreground action, the conversation Astrophil is using the sonnet to have with Stella.

As the sequence continues, new levels of intimacy and depths of feeling continue to be established metonymically in this way, by the kinds of things Astrophil says to other people and the social contexts that are presupposed by the things he says. In sonnet 51, he scornfully dismisses the kind of conversation he had been willing to go along with in sonnet 30 for politeness's sake. In sonnet 59, he has been watching Stella play with her lapdog; in sonnet 83, he puts himself on terms of bold familiarity with her pet sparrow. After he has kissed her their physical intimacy goes no further, apparently, and by the end of the sequence there are some indications that the affair is cooling: in sonnet 91, he protests to Stella that if he has been enjoying the company of other women lately that is only because they remind him of her; in sonnet 107 he asks her for permission to devote himself to a public career again. Toward the end of the sequence there are a few sonnets, including the very last one, sonnet 108, that pull themselves out of context to speak of a deep and seemingly endless state of inner darkness and pain, but meanwhile neighboring sonnets continue to give Astrophil's desire for Stella more finite circumstances. Whereas the other sonneteers we have looked at shared an inclination to recuperate diachrony into synchrony and to pull the sequence as a whole out of context, Sidney shows the reverse inclination, right through to the end of the sequence.

I have already suggested, in connection with Gascoigne's use of the sonnet to do autobiographical narration, that this is not what a fixed form whose rhyme scheme gives it a strongly metaphoric bias should be used to do. But many of the *Astrophil and Stella* sonnets do narration, both in Anacreontic fables and in anecdotes like the one that is incorporated into sonnet 45. I have used Greville's difficulty with the sonnet to suggest that complex reasoning should also be eschewed, in favor of arguments that are reiterative, metaphoric, and self-focused. But these sonnets of Sidney's demonstrate that a sonnet's argument can instead be metonymic, strongly set toward the context, highly compressed, and tightly reasoned. Sidney works against the form's inherent bias. The secret of his success is that the internal structure of the sonnet is always made to count, even as he works his argument against it.

The sonnets I have already cited are all good examples of this. In sonnet 47, the argument of the octave is continuous through eight lines; in sonnet 45, it is split into opposed quatrains; but in both, the integrative rhyme scheme functions ironically. The irony in sonnet 47 is at Astrophil's expense: the rhyme scheme assists the comically protracted spate of questions to convey that despite his vigorous efforts to talk himself out of his infatuation, he is stuck. In sonnet 45, the rhyme scheme assists Astrophil himself to set up an irony: the lovers in the tale Stella wept over recently are in no more grievous case than he is, and the rhyme scheme helps to convey this by synchronizing the two scenarios he is playing off against each other. In sonnet 30, a list of questions about current events is made to overrun the octave, which is nevertheless perceptible because of the shift in line 9 from Europe at large to Britain, and to problems of really pressing interest for Astrophil himself. Our awareness that the octave has been overrun enhances the impact of the sudden twist at the end of the poem whereby foreground becomes background, and background foreground. In both sonnets 45 and 47, the argument has a final twist or punchline that is strengthened by the couplet rhyme, but at the same time the last six lines are deployed as two tercets, composing a sestet that takes a new initiative based on the evidence adduced by the octave. The cohesiveness of the Italian sonnet has been regained, in these sonnets, but to very different effect.

By making these poems self-focused, but also conspicuously and intricately context-embedded, Sidney has produced a tension between the poem as poem and the poem as message-in-context that is always potentially ironic. "Let her go," says Astrophil to himself, in the context of an obsessively self-focused soliloquy—"soft, but here she comes," as Stella turns up in his immediate neighborhood. "I am not I," he urges, "pity the tale of me," offering to take up residence in one of his own poems so that she will give his predicament a more sympathetic reading: the deictic conundrum he uses to make the offer gets its cutting edge from the fact that the rest of the poem has given this "I" not a tale but an immediate, ongoing situation from which to speak.

As we have already seen, Sidney's earliest work with the sonnet was very different from this. In the *Arcadia* sonnets, and also in the group that was published as "Certain Sonnets" and were probably written somewhat later, he worked with the inherent bias of the form rather than against it, and produced metaphoric, synchronistic, self-focused poems. From a technical standpoint, what he achieved in the *Astrophil and Stella* sonnets could only have been managed on the strength of a very thorough understanding of the form: he could only work against it successfully after he had learned to work successfully with it. But Spenser also had a long apprenticeship to the sonnet form, before he produced the *Amoretti* sequence, and the direction Spenser's innovation took was toward enhancement of the sonnet's synchronistic, metaphoric bias. Both Daniel and Shakespeare took that direction also, whereas they might have followed in Sidney's footsteps; and so did the other sonneteers of the 1590s, except for Michael Drayton, whose stance is often more like Astrophil's. Sidney's sequence was influential in fomenting the sonneteering vogue of the 1590s, but it was not very influential from a generic and technical point of view: other practitioners of the sonnet tended to take the line of least resistance with the form.

In *Astrophil and Stella* 90, Astrophil dissociates himself from the kind of project that became closely associated with the sonnet, and was consistent with its synchronistic bias—the project of giving his homage to the beloved a lasting poetic monument:

> *Stella* think not that I by verse seek fame,
> Who seek, who hope, who love, who live but thee;
> Thine eyes my pride, thy lips my history:
> If thou praise not, all other praise is shame.
> Nor so ambitious am I, as to frame
> A nest for my young praise in laurel tree:
> In truth I swear, I wish not there should be
> Graved in mine epitaph a Poet's name:

This stance is consistent with the context-embeddedness of Astrophil's courtship. Ostensibly, the love lyric has the same status for him that it had for Wyatt and Surrey. But Sidney, if not Astrophil, knows that some have laurels thrust upon them—just as Sidney knows, and keeps us aware even when Astrophil is at his most spontaneous, that he is speaking sonnets.

6 "Happy ye leaves": Metaphor, Metonymy, and the Phases of English Petrarchism

In the world as language ordinarily represents it to us, eyes and stars or leaves of a book and prisoners of war belong to different spheres of activity or being. Metaphor proposes that the one be taken for an instance of the other. It follows that whereas the orientation of metonymy is worldward, metaphor tends to pull the external world into the mind. Metonymy presupposes a contiguous, extrinsic field of reference that is in some sense already given. Metaphor pulls its terms out of context: the metaphorist, whom Sidney called "the poet" in his *Defense of Poesy*, creates "forms such as never were in Nature," forms that call attention to their status as mental constructs.

This sonnet of Shakespeare's not only illustrates but also talks about how metaphorizing promotes introspection.

> When I consider everything that grows
> Holds in perfection but a little moment,
> That this huge stage presenteth naught but shows
> Whereon the stars in secret influence comment;
> When I perceive that men as plants increase,
> Cheered and checked ev'n by the self-same sky,
> Vaunt in their youthful sap, at height decrease,
> And wear their brave state out of memory;
> Then the conceit of this inconstant stay
> Sets you most rich in youth before my sight,
> Where wasteful time debateth with decay
> To change your day of youth to sullied night;

> And all in war with time for love of you,
> As he takes from you, I ingraft you new.
>
> (Sonnet 15)

At the outset, the speaker portrays himself mentally generalizing about what the world is like. His attention is outwardly oriented, but he "sees" the world in metaphorical terms. Natural process seems to behave like an art form—a play. Then this kind of thinking—"the conceit of this inconstant stay"— triggers a shift toward an entirely mental experience. Time, which had been discernible as the rhythm of natural process out there in the world, is hypostatized and encountered on the stage of the mind. The mind has become an independent realm where things may happen such as never were in Nature: in particular, the rescue of the beloved from his fate as part of the natural order.

The sonnet promotes this sort of enterprise. Because it is self-focused by its high degree of internal organization, and because it fosters the kind of argument that progresses by reiterative reformulation of one idea, it promotes the display of ideation *per se*: consideration, meditation, reflection. Petrarch's sonnets, which are more profoundly introspective than any sonnets in English except Shakespeare's, will continually seize upon the very smallest occurrence—the smaller the better, it seems—and use metaphor to give it a subjective elaboration that astonishes with its complexity relative to the external stimulus. Here, for example, is how one of Laura's glances struck the poet:

> Quel vago impallidir, che'l dolce riso
> d'un'amorosa nebbia ricoperse,
> con tanta maiestade al cor s'offerse
> che li si fece incontr' a mezzo 'l viso.
>
> Conobbi allor si come in paradiso
> vede l'un l'altro; in tal guisa s'aperse
> quel pietoso penser ch'altri non scerse,
> ma vidil io, ch'altrove non m'affiso.
>
> Ogni angelica vista, ogni atto umile
> che giamai in donna ov' amor fosse apparve,
> fora uno sdegno a lato a quel chi'io dico.
>
> Chinava a terra il bel guardo gentile
> et tacendo dicea, come a me parve:
> "Chi m'allontana il mio fedele amico?"

That lovely pallor, which covered her sweet smile with a cloud of love, with so much majesty presented itself to my heart that he went to meet it in the midst of my face.

I learned then how they see each other in Paradise; so clearly did that merciful thought open itself, which no one else perceived, but I saw it, for I fix myself nowhere else.

Every angelic expression, every humble gesture that ever appeared in a lady who harbored love, would be scorn beside what I speak of.

She bent to earth her lovely noble glance and in her silence said, as it seemed to me: "Who sends away from me my faithful friend?"[1]

The sonnet form itself gives the moment of eye contact its temporal structure: the lover's heart is summoned to attention in the first four lines, held by her look through seven lines of subjective elaboration, then released in the final tercet as she lowers her eyes once more. The sonnet seems to catch and hold her glance while he unpacks its significance with his metaphors. His comparisons are full and leisurely. They help to lift the moment out of time, onto a transcendent plane which is also the plane of exclusively mental life: this "pietoso penser" that opens itself up to him as they hold each other's eyes, this look of hers "ch'altri non scerse / ma vidil io"—this is how the angels communicate with one another in Paradise.

Wyatt and Surrey read and translated and imitated Italian poetry, and their depiction of love is recognizably Petrarchan, in the sense that they took on the oxymoronic fire-in-ice paradigm and the masochistic passivity of the lover enthralled to a proud fair lady. And yet we do not find them depicting love as an epiphanic transcendence of temporality, or as aesthetic contemplation of the beloved. It is as if they had not noticed this dimension of Petrarchan erotic experience. In the Elizabethan phase of Petrarchan imitation, this is precisely the dimension that emerged as most important, not only in the sonnet but in lyric poetry generally, and also in chivalric romance, where heroic action takes the form of Eros-inspired homage.

As poetry became caught up in the Elizabethan ideological program, there was a double incentive for Spenser's and Shakespeare's generation of writers to take this erotic paradigm over from the Italian tradition. The status of lyric poetry changed, from stylized social gesture to enduring literary "monument," and this was an inducement to cooperate with the inherent bias of fixed forms like the sonnet and thereby to create a special, self-focused realm for the beloved to inhabit. A related inducement to this way of using the lyric, as I have already explained in chapter 2, was the cult of Elizabeth itself as an ideological project: the Petrarchan paradigm could be used interchangeably for private courtship and for depiction of the ruler-to-subject relation.

Whereas the Petrarchan originals of their poems represent the object of desire as a figment of the poet-lover's imagination, Wyatt's and Surrey's translations depict him reaching out toward an object in the world external to the mind. In keeping with this shift, the dreamlike allegorical scenes envisioned by Petrarch get renegotiated in Wyatt's and Surrey's translations. In Petrarch's poems, the ordinary logic of spatiotemporal experience is suspended. In Wyatt's and Surrey's, Petrarch's atemporal, metaphoric narrative becomes amatory "histoire," and the lover's special realm, with its paradoxical laws of life, fails to be constituted.[2]

Here, for example, with a prose translation of their Petrarchan original, are the first eight lines of a poem I have already cited in chapter 3 to illustrate the metonymic bias of early Tudor lyric:

> Such vain thought as wonted to mislead me,
> In desert hope, by well assured moan,
> Maketh me from company to live alone
> In following her whom reason bid me flee.
> She fleeth as fast by gentle cruelty,
> And after her my heart would fain be gone,
> But armed sighs my way do stop anon,
> 'Twixt hope and dread locking my liberty.

> Full of a yearning thought that makes me stray away from all
> others and go alone in the world, from time to time I steal
> myself away from myself, still seeking only her whom I should flee;

> and I see her pass so sweet and cruel that my soul trembles to
> rise in flight, such a crowd of armed sighs she leads,
> this lovely enemy of Love and me.

> (*Rime*, 169; Durling, p. 314)

In Petrarch's poem, alienation from the world has two stages or levels. He lives habitually apart from society; but on top of that, there is what he calls "stealing myself away from myself" ("a me stesso m'involo"): alienation from an ordinary state of consciousness. On this second level, "seeking" is a purely subjective, mental activity. This is emphasized by the way in which Laura is introduced into the poem: not as an object to be attained by pursuit but as a vision that comes when a certain posture is adopted. By metaphorically

transforming the lover's sighs into the lady's retinue, Petrarch makes it
impossible to keep the one who is desired distinct from the one who desires:
she is not just the object but also in part the figment of his seeking. In
Wyatt's translation, the lover's preoccupation has alienated him "from company," but there is no mention of self-alienation. The lady Wyatt's speaker
pursues is an elusive prey at large in the world.

   In another sonnet, one of his most famous, Petrarch lifts the experience of
falling in love with Laura out of ordinary space-time completely:

> Una candida cerva sopra l'erba
> verde m'apparve con duo corna d'oro,
> fra due riviere all'ombra d'un alloro,
> levando 'l sole a la stagione acerba.
>
> Era sua vista si dolce superba
> ch'i' lasciai per seguirla ogni lavoro,
> come l'avaro che 'n cercar tesoro
> con diletto l'affanno disacerba.
>
> "Nessun mi tocchi," al bel collo d'intorno
> scritto avea di diamanti et di topazi.
> "Libera farmi al mio Cesare parve."
>
> Et era 'l sol gia volto al mezzo giorno,
> gli occhi miei stanchi di mirar, non sazi,
> quand'io caddi ne l'acqua et ella sparve.
>
> (Rime, 190)

A white doe on the green grass appeared to me, with
two golden horns, between two rivers, in the shade of
a laurel, when the sun was rising in the unripe season.

Her look was so sweet and proud that to follow her I
left every task, like the miser who as he seeks
treasure sweetens his trouble with delight.

"Let no one touch me," she bore written with diamonds
and topazes around her lovely neck. "It has pleased
my Caesar to make me free."

And the sun had already turned at midday; my eyes
were tired by looking but not sated, when I fell into
the water, and she disappeared.

(Durling, p. 336)

This is not an account of "what happens to me from time to time," like the other poem, but the record of a singular event. But if it were to be asked when this happened to the speaker, the answer would have to be tautological: it happened whenever Laura appeared to him in the guise of a white doe with two golden horns. He might by then have known her for a long time, or he might here be recalling their very first meeting. The poem is not patient of such a question, because its narrative is a metaphor, whose tenor is the imaginative experience of Laura's worth, her desirability, her untouchability. The landscape, the references to sunrise and midday, the preterit narrative sequence, are metaphorical instruments. The place helps to furnish an otherworldly context for the experience; "the unripe season," to characterize it as an initiation; the temporal sequence, to give it a certain trajectory—it begins, it flowers into meaning, it is over. The speaker's actions must also be understood metaphorically: he says that "to follow her I left every task," but we do not therefore envision him working somewhere near this place where the doe appeared.

I say "we" euphemistically: one of Petrarch's earliest commentators, according to Patricia Thomson, interpreted the last line of the poem to mean that Laura had gone off home.[3] An early reading modern commentators find more acceptable has this poem presaging Laura's death, "in spite of the fact," as Thomson points out, "that it occurs rather too early in the sequence." Oddly enough, neither reading addresses itself to the event in the poem that immediately precedes or perhaps coincides with Laura's disappearance: "quand'io caddi ne l'acqua et ella sparve." Surely Petrarch is here alluding to Narcissus, so as to frame the vision and to confirm that it is an imaginative projection.

Petrarch often used the sonnet in this way, to represent an imaginative experience that flowers into synchronic fullness within strict boundaries. By exploiting the synchronicity of the sonnet form, while his sequence reflects and responds to the passage of time in various ways, he enabled the *Rime* to acknowledge that the lover is Time's creature, but also to harbor his soul's intermittent need to spread its wings. It is this need that Laura triggers, again and again.

This is how Wyatt adapted Petrarch's allegory of the elusive "candida cerva":

> Whoso list to hunt: I know where is an hind.
> But as for me, alas I may no more:
> The vain travail hath wearied me so sore,
> I am of them that farthest cometh behind.
> Yet may I by no means my wearied mind

> Draw from the deer, but as she fleeth afore
> Fainting I follow. I leave off therefore,
> Sithens in a net I seek to hold the wind.
> Who list her hunt, I put him out of doubt,
> As well as I may spend his time in vain,
> And graven with diamonds in letters plain
> There is written her fair neck round about:
>   'Noli me tangere, for Caesar's I am,
>   And wild for to hold, though I seem tame.'[4]

Instead of projecting an imaginative vision, Wyatt's metaphor puts a certain construction upon a social situation in which the speaker, the lady, and "whoso list to hunt" are all implicated. Instead of Petrarch's allegorical preterit, we have a sequence of tenses from perfect ("hath wearied") through frequentative present ("as she fleeth afore, fainting I follow") to a performative assertion that takes effect as of the moment of utterance: "I leave off therefore." The poem is firmly anchored by its deictics to a particular occasion: "Whoso list . . . may . . . but as for me, I may no more." The hind conceit itself takes on a deictic function, and the inscription round her neck becomes a form of deictic innuendo: "You'll know her when you see her: she's the one who belongs to you know who."

A poem of Petrarch's that Surrey translated does anchor the lover's meditation to an external situation: "Now, while heaven and earth and wind keep silence, and the beasts and birds are sleeping, [and so on] I am awake." What this seems at first to be is a paradox grounded in the contiguity-relation between the "I" who thinks, burns, and weeps and the tranquil landscape around him:

> Or che 'l ciel et la terra e 'l vento tace
> et le fere e gli augelli il sonno affrena,
> notte il carro stellato in giro mena
> et nel suo letto il mar senz'onda giace,
>
> vegghio, penso, ardo, piango; et chi mi sface
> sempre m'e inanzi per mia dolce pena:
> guerra e 'l mio stato, d'ira e di duol piena,
> et sol di lei pensando o qualche pace.
>
> Cosi sol d'una chiara fonte viva
> move 'l dolce et l'amaro ond'io mi pasco,
> una man sola mi risana et punge;

> et perche 'l mio martir non giunga a riva,
> mille volte il di moro et mille nasco,
> tanto da la salute mia son lunge.
>
> (*Rime*, 164)

But almost as soon as this "I" comes into the poem, he begins to be resituated in a different world, where life is sustained by a paradoxical fountain whose waters are sweet and bitter at once, and where he dies and is reborn a thousand times a day, under the aegis of a goddess who heals and wounds with the same hand. Having thus resituated its speaker, the poem concludes by reassessing his relationship to the original night scene, in metaphoric terms: "tanto da la salute mia son lunge." The contiguity-relation of immediate neighborhood turns out to have no force: the lover is really, the poem suggests, as distant from all of that as war is from tranquillity, sleep from waking, self-division from wholeness.

Surrey's translation keeps roughly the same proportions as the original between description of the night scene and analysis of the lover's emotional situation. But he turns Petrarch's metaphoric distance between different realms of experience into what it had at first seemed to be, an anomalous contiguity-relation.

> Alas! so all things now do hold their peace:
> Heaven and earth disturbed in nothing;
> The beasts, the air, the birds their song do cease;
> The nightës chair the stars about doth bring.
> Calm is the sea, the waves work less and less;
> So am not I, whom love, alas! doth wring,
> Bringing before my face the great increase
> Of my desires, whereat I weep and sing
> In joy and woe as in a doubtful ease:
> For my sweet thoughts sometime do pleasure bring,
> But, by and by, the cause of my disease
> Gives me a pang that inwardly doth sting,
> When that I think what grief it is again
> To live and lack the thing should rid my pain.[5]

The poem takes the paradoxical conjunction of opposites, the irreducible structure of experience in the realm to which Petrarch's lover is exiled, and unpacks it along a narrative axis. What it comes down to, Surrey explains, is joy and woe in quick succession. Sweet thoughts trigger pleasurable feelings, but "by and by" the cause of these original thoughts begets another sort of thought, which yields different feelings altogether. For Petrarch's lover, the laws of ordinary temporal experience no longer obtain: "mille volte il di moro et mille nasco." As far as he knows, his suffering will never come to an end. Surrey represents the inner life as a chronological procedure in the ordinary sense: tomorrow, his speaker may have the thing he lacks tonight.

Another of the *Rime* that Surrey translated will help us to compare the first and second phases of English Petrarchism, because it was also translated in the 1590s.

> Zefiro torna e 'l bel tempo rimena
> e i fiori et l'erbe, sua dolce famiglia,
> et garrir Progne et pianger Filomena,
> et Primavera candida et vermiglia;
>
> ridono i prati e'l ciel si rasserena,
> Giove s'allegra di mirar sua figlia,
> l'aria et l'acqua et la terra e d'amor piena,
> ogni animal d'amar si riconsiglia.
>
> Ma per me, lasso, tornano i piu gravi
> sospiri che del cor profondo tragge
> quella ch'al Ciel se ne porto le chiavi;
>
> et cantar augelletti, et fiorir piagge,
> e 'n belle donne oneste atti soavi
> sono un deserto et fere aspre et selvagge.

(*Rime*, 310)

> The soote season, that bud and bloom forth brings,
> With green hath clad the hill and eke the vale:
> The nightingale with feathers new she sings:
> The turtle to her make* hath told her tale:
> Summer is come, for every spray now springs,
> The hart hath hung his old head on the pale:
> The buck in brake his winter coat he flings:
> The fishes float with new repaired scale:
> The adder all her slough away she slings:
> The swift swallow pursueth the flies small:
> The busy bee her honey now she mings:
> Winter is worn that was the flowers' bale:
> And thus I see among these pleasant things
> Each care decays, and yet my sorrow springs.
> *mate

(Surrey, poem 2)

As J. W. Lever pointed out when he compared these two poems in *The Elizabethan Love Sonnet*,[6] Surrey has demythologized Petrarch's returning spring. In Surrey's poem, says Lever, spring is objectively observed, whereas Petrarch's spring is imaginatively envisioned. This is a slightly misleading way to put the difference, because it implies that Surrey just recorded what he saw around him on a spring day. His poem does pretend that its speaker is doing this, but the description itself is quite conventional. "The hill and eke the vale" is a formula for "everywhere you look." The nightingale, turtle dove and busy bee, Surrey had probably observed more often in literary texts than in the English countryside. The difference between the two poems is really a matter of figurative strategy. Surrey's representation of spring is a metonymic catalogue, and metonymy creates the illusion of objective description, whereas metaphor calls attention to subjective fabrication. F. M. Padelford, in his edition of Surrey's poems, reacted tellingly because naively to this difference between the two kinds of writing:

> Petrarch's spring is typically Italian with its smiling plains and serene sky, and Zephyrus and Venus are introduced as in the beautiful spring pieces of Botticelli. Surrey's sonnet is as typically English with its green-clad hills and dales, its blossoming hedgerows and shady streams.[7]

Petrarch's metaphoric description, although Padelford calls it "typically Italian," actually reminds him of spring as it has been represented in other works of art. Surrey's metonymic description prompts him to fill in the rest of a conventionally English scene from nature, by allowing the metonymies to summon appropriate contexts: sprays beget hedgerows, and fishes, shady streams.

Another reason, no doubt, why Lever stresses that Surrey's spring scene is objectively observed is that the poem explicitly positions its speaker vis-à-vis "these pleasant things," thereby giving his observations a particular occasion. There is a good deal of unobtrusive deictic anchorage in the Surrey poem: the adverb "now," the demonstrative "these," the admixture of perfect tenses with the predominating present tense ("With green hath clad . . ."). The original does not anchor the lover's account of the returning spring to a particular instance of observation, in this way. Just as in "Alas so all things now do hold their peace," Surrey has taken the paradox Petrarch produced by substitution and regrounded it in a contiguity-relation.

Somewhere around 1590, Thomas Watson translated the first eight lines of "Zephira torna . . ." for a madrigal setting,[8] and Nicholas Young translated the whole thing. Both of them reproduced the metaphorically envisioned landscape of the original:

Zephirus brings the time that sweetly senteth
  with flowers and herbs, which Winter's frost exileth:
Progne now chirpeth, Philomel lamenteth,
  Flora the garlands white and red compileth:
Fields do rejoice, the frowning sky relenteth,
  Love to behold his dearest daughter smileth:
The air, the water, the earth to joy consenteth,
  each creature now to love him reconcileth.
But with me wretch, the storms of woe persever,
  and heavy sighs which from my heart she straineth
That took the key thereof to heaven forever,
  so that singing of birds, and spring-time's flowering,
And ladies' love, that men's affection gaineth,
  are like a desert, and cruel beasts devouring.

This is Young's version, which eventually found its way into *England's Heli-con* as a shepherd's complaint.[9] It is more faithful to the original than Sur-rey's not only insofar as Young has reinstated Zephirus, Procne, and Philomel, but also because he has restored the Petrarchan conceit whereby the external world is said to have been transformed for the lover by his inner condition. (Young weakens its force a little by turning Petrarch's metaphoric equation—"sono un deserto. . ."—into a simile, "are *like* a desert.") Surrey's pun on "springs" is alive to the possibility of a metaphoric correspondence between outer and inner climate, but uses irony to keep them distinct:

> And thus I see among these pleasant things
> Each care decays, and yet my sorrow springs.

A more powerful and impressive version of the original Petrarchan conceit is to be found in the double sestina from Sidney's *Arcadia*,[10] which was also gathered into *England's Helicon*:

> I that was once free-burgess of the forests,
> Where shade from sun, and sports I sought at evening,
> I that was once esteem'd for pleasant music,
> Am banish'd now among the monstrous mountains
> Of huge despair, and foul affliction's valleys,
> Am grown a screech-owl to myself each morning.
>
> I that was once delighted every morning,
> Hunting the wild inhabiters of forests,
> I that was once the music of these valleys,
> So darkened am, that all my day is evening,

> Heart-broken so, that molehills seem high mountains,
> And fill the vales with cries instead of music.

In both of these stanzas, and for ten more as well, the lover's message is essentially the same: that his once idyllic relationship to the world around him has been transformed into its opposite by his longing for the absent beloved.

The sestina, like the sonnet, is a highly self-focused structure. The message it carries must be highly reiterative, because in order to fill its formal requirements, six line-ending words must be repeated according to a fixed permutation: 1 2 3 4 5 6; 6 1 5 2 4 3; 3 6 4 1 2 5; etc. In his double sestina, Sidney does this twice over with the same set of six words: mountains, valleys, forests, morning, evening, music. This is an astonishing tour de force, and he has managed it by achieving a perfect fit between the demands of the form and the erotic predicament it dramatizes.[11] These six line-ending words are the crucial terms of the shepherd's existential situation. Mountains, valleys, forests together epitomize its physical setting; morning-evening, its temporal structure. Music, the final term, is the one that mediates between this external setting and the shepherd/lover's inner condition, making inner harmony or disharmony outwardly manifest. The sestina's permutation of these six words seems to take the measure of the pastoral estate again and again, while at the same time it serves to outpicture an inner landscape. In the final stanza, the cause of the lover's suffering is finally disclosed:

> For she, to whom compar'd, the alps are valleys,
> She, whose least word brings from the spheres their music,
> At whose approach the sun rose in the evening,
> Who, where she went, bare in her forehead morning,
> Is gone, is gone from these our spoiled forests,
> Turning to deserts our best pastured mountains.

The absent beloved is cited as the center of coherence for the outer and the inner world. In this way, the poem becomes a "total metaphor"[12] for the human condition as the shepherd is forced by love to experience it. The form itself has been used to say that love is an utterly consuming and transformative experience. Sidney assists the form to say this by giving the sestina a pair of authors, whose perfect cooperation is another of Urania's miraculous works.

When he revised the *Arcadia*, Sidney used these two shepherds as an introductory framing device. He had begun the original version of the work with a brief account of recent events in Arcadia, an introduction to his two young heroes, the princes Pyrocles and Musidorus, and an explanation of how they came to be there. That is a conventionally metonymic way to begin a narrative work: the narrator lets the reader know that he is picking up the lives of some particular few people at some particular juncture in their lives; their past, and a larger geographical purview or social network, could in principle have been elaborated but are only briefly epitomized for reader orientation. In the "New" *Arcadia*, instead of beginning with an introduction to his chief protagonists or a scene-setting account of the political situation into which they will be thrown, Sidney casts them up on shore in the midst of the shepherds' "rite of remembrance" in honor of the absent Urania. In this way he establishes what season it is, in a literal but also in a metaphorical sense, and foregrounds love as the theme of the work as a whole.

> It was in the time that the earth begins to put on her new apparel against the approach of her lover, and that the Sun running a most even course becomes an indifferent arbiter between the night and the day, when the hopeless shepherd Strephon was come to the sands which lie against the island of Cithera; where viewing the place with a heavy kind of delight, and sometimes casting his eyes to the isleward, he called his friendly rival, the pastor Claius unto him, and setting first down in his darkened countenance a doleful copy of what he would speak:
>
> "O my Claius," said he, "hither we are now come to pay the rent, for which we are so called unto by over-busy Remembrance, Remembrance, restless Remembrance, which claims not only this duty of us, but for it will have us forget ourselves." (p. 5)

As the shepherds work together to recall how Urania spent her last few moments on shore, the reader may well be reminded of an Italian painting, just as Padelford was by Petrarch's "Zephira torna . . ." Urania departed at the same time of year, and in the same way, as Venus Pandemos arrives to bring spring to the earth in Botticelli's *Birth of Venus*. Her name suggests, of course, that she is a human avatar of the other, the "heavenly" Venus:

> "Yonder, my Claius, Urania lighted, the very horse (methought) bewailed to be so disburdened. . . . There she sat, vouchsafing my cloak (then most gorgeous) under her: at yonder rising of the ground she turned herself, looking back toward her wonted abode. . . . And here she laid her hand over thine eyes, when she

saw the tears springing in them, as if she would conceal them from other, and yet herself feel some of thy sorrow: But woe is me, yonder, yonder, did she put her foot into the boat, at that instant, as it were dividing her heavenly beauty, between the earth and the sea." (p. 6)

Here are all the ingredients of the Petrarchan situation: the paradoxes attendant on the beloved's every gesture; the mythologically animated landscape; the lover's condition of introspective self-forgetfulness; the subjective status of the entire scene of departure. It is never explained to us why Urania left, but it is obviously best that she did, so that the shepherds' love for her could continue the ennobling work they describe to each other:

> ". . . hath not the only love of her made us (being silly ignorant shepherds) raise up our thoughts above the ordinary level of the world, so as great clerks do not disdain our conference? hath not the desire to seem worthy in her eyes made us when others were sleeping, to sit viewing the course of the heavens? when others were running at base, to run over learned writings? when other mark their sheep, we to mark our selves?" (pp. 7–8)

Love has given them an incentive toward abstract thinking and introspection that sets them apart from their fellow shepherds. If not for Urania, they would never have had an inner life.

The fictional lives of Strephon and Claius are asyntagmatic. While the princes and princesses are having and recounting adventures, and moving toward consummation of their loves, the shepherds are simply commemorating Urania, with joyful sorrowfulness. In the "Old" *Arcadia* they figure only as participants in the pastoral interludes between the work's five books or "acts." By using their rite of remembrance to begin the revised *Arcadia*, Sidney was apparently trying to render the work as a whole more seriously and thoroughly "poetic." It is one of a number of changes that work together to establish the land of Arcadia as a world unto itself, where the princes are forced not only to suspend their heroic careers but to give up being Pyrocles and Musidorus, while love transforms them from within. Love is a more introspective and a more radically transformative experience than in the original version. Strephon and Claius's rite of remembrance is a paradigm or abstract model or highest type of that experience, which is then circumstanced, "narratized," in the fictional lives of the princes and princesses.

In a prefatory letter to his sister the Countess of Pembroke, Sidney describes the original romance as "a trifle, and that triflingly handled." His revision is obviously an effort to transform this elegant toy into a piece of heroic poesy, according to the specifications of his own *Defense*. Though dates of composition cannot be precisely fixed, he must have been working on both simultaneously, or within the same two-year period.[13] This coincidence enables us to watch the metaphoric bias of Elizabethan poetry being produced in theory and in practice simultaneously, as the *Arcadia* becomes self-focused and thereby takes on the status of total metaphor.

In the "New" *Arcadia*, just as in the Elizabethan love sonnet, a certain way of being in love comes along with, and is fostered by, a change in the status of "poesy." The poetic work becomes a self-focused, synchronic gestalt, an enduring monument for the beloved or a total metaphor for the human condition; and love correspondingly becomes an experience that pulls the lover out of context and suspends or violates the chronologic of ordinary social life.

One of the most powerful accounts in English of this way of being in love is a poem that has come down to us perplexingly entitled "The 21th: and laste booke of the Ocean to Scynthia."[14] Apparently it was written by Sir Walter Ralegh in a desperate attempt to regain the favor of the queen, whom he had displeased by secretly marrying one of her ladies-in-waiting. Its title and its apparently fragmentary state in the Hatfield manuscript suggest that there was, or was to have been, much more to the poem than we have. "As often happens in the work of an amateur," remarks C. S. Lewis, "what is unfinished is more impressive, certainly more exciting, than what is finished ."[15] But how could so structurally amorphous a piece of writing ever have been finished? It is more likely, as Stephen Greenblatt suggests, that Ralegh used the title "to create the aura of an immensely long poem, suggesting to the queen—and to himself, perhaps—an almost boundless suffering immortalized in verse."[16]

The poem has no narrative backbone, nor any logically developed argument, nor even the kind of emotional sequence that shapes the greater ode and the pastoral elegy. Near the beginning, and again as he prepares to end both his poem and his life, the speaker invokes the conventions of pastoral, but in the interim the pastoral landscape does not persist as a setting for his complaint, nor does he continue to represent himself as a shepherd. If he is to be taken also to be speaking as the ocean to the moon, his persona is a mixed metaphor. The poem refuses to allow any situation, even a fictive one, to coalesce as ground or context for the complaint. And yet the complaint itself is powerfully coherent, in terms of its speaker's obsessive vacillation between what was once and what is now, between repudiation and acknowledgment of his love for Cynthia, between loss and recuperation of her presence to his imagination. "She is gone, she is lost, she is found, she is ever fair": occurring toward the end of the poem as we have it, this line epitomizes the movement of the whole.

The emotional relationship memorialized in "The Ocean to Cynthia" has no history, only a persistent rhythm of favor and disfavor, alienation and reconciliation. "Cynthia" is paradoxically immune to the passage of time, but in her behavior changeable, fickle. In her service, the speaker has experienced temporality as insubstantial and illogical:

> of long erections such the sudden fall
> one hour diverts, one instant overthrows
> for which our lives, for which our fortune's thrall
>
> so many years those joys have dearly bought
>
> (11.230–33)

What was will not stay in the past: memories invade the present as he speaks, and more than once he turns around on one of his own statements to identify it as a line from a poem of his own, written long ago. For the most part his vantage point is at one or two removes from external reality. He dwells obsessively, not on things that once happened, but on former states of mind:

> sometime I died sometime I was distract,
> my soul the stage of fancy's tragedy
> then furious madness where true reason lacked
>
> wrate what it would, and scourged mine own conceit.
>
> (11.143–46)

These lines are doubly self-reflexive. They use a metaphor of writing to explain that the speaker was continually forced by unrequited love for Cynthia to behave in his own worst interests; and the metaphor calls attention to the way in which this very piece of writing is itself continually getting out of hand.

In the sonnet and the sestina, selection and substitution, comparison and contrast, are fostered by the fixed form itself, to whose system of repetitions or equivalences the discursive syntagma must be accommodated. This is what it means to say that the forms themselves have a metaphoric bias. But it is also possible to give the axis of selection and substitution free rein to generate a train of thought, and this is what Ralegh has done in "The Ocean to Cynthia." Stylistically this poem is very different from the short lyrics, all of a magisterial simplicity and well-formedness, that were certainly or probably Ralegh's. It is syntagmatically incoherent at two different levels: macrostructural and syntactic.

Editors have disagreed as to whether to break up what Greenblatt calls "the troubled flow of the original" into quatrains.[17] Sometimes the utterance will lend itself to the units demarcated by the rhyme scheme, but more often it spills over into great sweeping paragraphs of uneven length. Each sentence seems indefinitely extensible at the whim of the speaker, and it is not just their length that makes them amorphous. Here, for contrast, is the stanza of a syntagmatic master-craftsman:

> Considering that, all hatred driven hence,
> The soul recovers radical innocence
> And learns at last that it is self-delighting,
> Self-appeasing, self-affrighting,
> And that its own sweet will is Heaven's will;
> She can, though every face should scowl
> And every windy quarter howl
> Or every bellows burst, be happy still.

This stanza from Yeats's "Prayer for My Daughter" is one sentence, with a hypotactic structure that establishes firm logical relationships among its members:

> Considering that . . . .
> . . . .
> She can, [though . . . .
> . . . .], be happy still.

Each of the subordinate units can be considerably expanded, paratactically (as in the "though" clause) or hypotactically (as in the initial phrase, with its embedded absolute construction), without unsettling or obscuring the super-structure, whose cornerstones occur at pivotal points in the stanza. Now here are the same number of lines from Ralegh's poem:

> Lost in the mud of those high-flowing streams
> which through more fairer fields their courses bend,
> slain with self-thoughts, amazed in fearful dreams,
> woes without date, discomforts without end,
>
> from fruitful trees I gather withered leaves
> and glean the broken ears with miser's hands,
> who sometime did enjoy the weighty sheaves
> I seek fair flowers amid the brinish sand. . . .

(11.17–24)

We must anticipate the main clause of this sentence through four and one-half lines, but when it comes, it changes the metaphor to repeat what has already been said in subordinate phrases. The grammatical structure whereby a main clause governs subordinate units is thus rendered inoperative, whereas in the Yeats stanza it is used to establish a logical relationship between two premises. In the second of Ralegh's two quatrains, the third and fourth lines set up an antithesis between what used to be and what is now, but the metaphors themselves link the second and third lines instead: the utterance slides from one metaphor to another, to the undoing of its own syntactic structure.

At the level of the sentence, the poem's discourse is forwarded almost exclusively by similarity-relations: synonymy or even tautology; analogy and similitude; repetition with change of metaphoric vehicle. The following sentence will serve to illustrate them all. It begins with three consecutive similes, each developed into a metaphoric conceit to represent the same paradoxical condition. The series performs an iconic imitation of that condition, as each conceit subsides into antithesis at roughly the same point in its quatrain.

> But as a body violently slain
> retaineth warmth although the spirit be gone,
> and by a power in nature moves again
> till it be laid below the fatal stone
>
> Or as the earth even in cold winter days,
> left for a time by her life-giving sun,
> doth by the power remaining of his rays
> produce some green, though not as it hath done,
>
> Or as a wheel forced by the falling stream
> although the course be turned some other way
> doth for a time go round upon the beam
> till wanting strength to move, it stands at stay,
>
> So my forsaken heart, my withered mind
> widow of all the joys it once possessed
> my hopes clean out of sight with forced wind
> to kingdoms strange, to lands far-off addressed
>
> Alone, forsaken, friendless on the shore
> with many wounds, with death's cold pangs embraced,
> writes in the dust, as one that could no more
> whom love, and time, and fortune had defaced,
>
> Of things so great, so long, so manifold
> with means so weak, the soul even then departing,

the weal, the woe, the passages of old
and worlds of thoughts describ'd by one last sighing.

(11.73–96)

The syntax of this passage is typical of the entire poem in being powerfully and variously rhythmic. The same thought recurs at first with monotonous insistence ("Or as the earth . . . / Or as a wheel . . ."), then with increasing intensity (the third, fourth, and fifth stanzas are full of pairs and trios of antithetical or synonymous words), and finally culminates in a slowly-building, expansive paraphrase:

> as if when after Phoebus is descended
> and leaves a light much like the past day's dawning,
> and every toil and labor wholly ended
> each living creature draweth to his resting
>
> we should begin by such a parting light
> to write the story of all ages past
> and end the same before th' approaching night.

(11.97–103)

These are the rhythms of a self-focused consciousness, disengaged from practical verbal behavior—the delivery of a message, the prosecution of an argument. The sentence itself comments on the distance between discourse that acquiesces in the achronic, obsessively cyclical rhythm of the inner life and the sort of discourse that would be needed to produce "the story of all ages past." For that kind of discourse, syntagmatic combination and linear chronology would of course be crucial; this kind of discourse is the province of binary opposition, selection and substitution—of the metaphoric way.

As a piece of love poetry, "The Ocean to Cynthia" is extreme; but as political rhetoric, it is really bizarre. The discourse is so self-focused, so obsessive and incoherent, that its speaker seems unable or unwilling to make himself minimally intelligible. He is his own interlocutor: his "wasted mind" seems to have turned completely in upon itself. Yet we know that the poem was a device to ingratiate Ralegh with the queen; and Ralegh's fellow poet Spenser seems to have admired it as such.[18] Its incoherence may even have given him a hint toward his rendition of the predicament of Timias, in the fourth book of The Faerie Queene. Banished from the service of his beloved Belphoebe, the faithful squire degenerates into a "salvage man," to the point where he loses human speech. And Spenser was not the only admirer of Ralegh's poem: it made a reputation for him among his contemporaries as the most eloquent of the royal Cynthia's disappointed lovers.[19] Paradoxically, a discourse that borders on aphasia through its refusal of syntagmatic coherence was fashioned as an instrument for improving Ralegh's political fortunes, and regarded as an appropriate instrument for such a purpose by contemporary readers.

It was an appropriate instrument for such a purpose because its discourse assisted its central metaphor to depict Ralegh's political predicament as a natural state of affairs. The poem's rhetoric and its rhythms enable the frustrated courtier to present himself as a frustrated "Petrarchan" lover. At the same time, they seem to render the natural speech of the Ocean. "The Ocean to Cynthia" may be said to have personified the Ocean, but it can equally be said to have "oceanified" the lover. The central metaphor is a strategy for conveying the extremity of despair into which the queen's disfavor has cast her servant, and also for justifying her power over him in terms of the divinely sanctioned order of things. She is depicted not as a political actor but as the center or source of his life's coherence on the personal and the cosmic level.

In his study of the court of Elizabeth, G. K. Hunter explains that appeals on which her courtiers' livelihood depended were likeliest to succeed with the queen if they were made "without political overtones." He cites the case of Sir Edward Dyer, who got himself restored to favor by having it rumored about that his near-fatal illness had been brought on by the queen's displeasure. As part of the Woodstock entertainment of 1575, Dyer sang a complaint of his own composition from inside a hollow tree.[20] Here we have a way to understand why Ralegh had recourse to a pastoral figure for his predicament at the beginning and again at the end of his poem. Both the pastoral metaphor and the discourse of the Ocean assimilate contemporary political events and persons to a transhistorical frame of reference, and explain Tudor despotism as a natural law.[21] As a figment of the Elizabethan ideological program, Ralegh's poem demonstrates that the erotic ideology of Elizabethan love poetry is not only congruent but interconvertible with the political ideology of the Elizabethan regime.

In 1611, the year in which Donne's *First Anniversary* was published, Lord Thomas Howard noted in a letter to Sir John Harington that whereas "your Queen did talk of her subjects' love and good affections, . . . our King talketh of his subjects' fear and subjection."[22] The language that Howard attributes to James is partly a symptom, and partly a contributing cause, of his alienation from his subjects and the breakdown under the Stuart rulers of the Elizabethan centripetal kingdom. A great deal of artistic activity continued to be invested in promoting the vision of a unified kingdom with the sovereign as its transcendent center or life-giving sun. Court entertainments became more costly and spectacular under the Stuarts, and Inigo Jones evolved a mode of illusionistic staging for them that turned the whole performance into an act of homage to the king, he being the only member of the audience for whom the visual spectacle was perfectly in perspective. The staging of these masques, as Stephen Orgel and Roy Strong have explained it, transformed the audience into "a living and visible emblem of the aristo-cratic hierarchy: the closer one sat to the King, the 'better' one's place was."[23] The masques themselves paid elaborate homage to the sovereign's power of transforming night into day, or bringing peace and order out of strife and disorder. For twenty years, as Inigo Jones's collaborator, Ben Jonson was directly involved in the production of these images of royal power. John Donne made his contribution from the pulpit, where James saw to it that eloquent clergymen were placed to sustain his authority as head of the English Church and speak out strongly against the dissident puritan faction.[24]

Meanwhile, however, James neglected the business of government, and refused to be held accountable to the people for the ways in which he chose to spend his time and their tax money,[25] invoking instead the inscrutable privilege of kingship. He had no taste or aptitude for civic pageantry, and when he visited the country estates of the nobility, he went not to show himself to the people and receive the symbolic tribute of pastoral shows but to indulge his passion for hunting and be lavishly feasted at his hosts' expense.[26] His foreign policy was unacceptable to a powerful faction of the nobility who wanted a military commitment to the cause of Protestantism in Europe, and it had the effect of reducing the external pressure that had kept internal differences from dividing England against itself in the 1580s and 1590s: James dreamed of becoming the peacemaker of Europe by forging dynastic alliances with the European Catholic powers. After the death of his oldest son, Prince Henry, from whom more active and charismatic leadership had been hoped for, the aristocracy became increasingly factionalized. Mean-while the court turned in upon itself, and was more and more out of touch with the nation at large.[27]

Although Donne and Jonson became directly involved in sustaining the royalist vision, Jonson in his texts for the court masques and Donne in his sermons,[28] they both express in their "occasional" poetry—Donne more obviously than Jonson—an impulse to pull away and establish provisional centers of coherence elsewhere, in the lives of virtuous individuals and in the private sphere of personal relationships. It is not surprising that Donne wished to repudiate his secular lyrics after he became an apologist for the authority of the king and the English Church: the stance of many of them is overtly iconoclastic. Jonson's poems are not, but in the aggregate they imply that a virtuous man or woman must become his or her own firm center, whereas the rest of the world no longer has any.

" 'Tis all in pieces, all coherence gone," asserted Donne with prophetic urgency in 1611. As harbingers of the end of the world, he cites traumatic dislocations at every level of the universal order of things. The structure of the physical universe is being very differently mapped by "the new philosophy"; the patriarchal family is losing its viability as an economic/political structure; and the prince-to-subject relation, like the father-son relation to which it corresponds at another level, is also now a "thing forgot." The epideictic project of the *First* and *Second Anniversaries*, which is to claim that a public nonentity, a fifteen-year-old girl named Elizabeth Drury, had been the true magnetic center or soul of the world, is a symptomatic by-product of the very condition that is being so forcefully deplored by these poems.

In her book-length study of the *Anniversaries*, Barbara Kiefer Lewalski put her finger on the problem that they make for the reader when she took issue with O. B. Hardison's attempt to assimilate their claims on Elizabeth Drury's behalf to the conventions of Petrarchan elegy. Even though this may be the most eligible generic category for the *Anniversaries*,

> neither the conventional funeral elegy nor Petrarch's *Canzoniere* seem to provide a basis for the kind of praise Donne's speaker accords Elizabeth Drury. . . . In Petrarch the dramatic situation of the speaker as lover qualifies the hyperbole: it is the speaker's world (not the real world) that has been destroyed by Laura's death; it is to and for him that she is a *donna angelicata*, a sun, a phoenix, a miracle, the cause and symbol of spiritual transformation, the image of the divine. . . . In the *Anniversaries*, the speaker is not a lover: he professes to speak of the real world and for us all.[29]

Lewalski points out that Elizabeth Drury is by no means the only person Donne saw fit to honor with fantastically hyperbolical claims. Whereas Jonson's epideictic poems will focus on the specific virtues and characteristics of the person he is praising, Donne's will typically urge that virtue or goodness or divinity itself is incarnate in the individual who is being praised or mourned. "The 'All,' " as Lewalski puts it, "is persistently epitomized in the particular example."[30]

In his verse letter to the Countess of Salisbury, Donne acknowledges that his strategy of compliment is problematic, and justifies it in the following way:

> And if things like these, have been said by me
> Of others, call not that idolatry.
> For had God made man first, and man had seen

The third day's fruits, and flowers, and various green,
He might have said the best that he could say
Of those fair creatures, which were made that day;
And when next day he had admir'd the birth
Of sun, moon, stars, fairer than late-prais'd earth,
He might have said the best that he could say,
And not be chid for praising yesterday;
So though some things are not together true
As, that another 'is worthiest, and that you:
Yet, to say so, doth not condemn a man,
If when he spoke them, they were both true then.[31]

(11.37–50)

What is striking about the conceit Donne uses here to explain his epideictic stance is that it insists on the unavailability of a total perspective or synchronic overview of the human condition. If God had made man first, he must have relied on the partial, limited view of reality afforded him by his own experience from one day to the next; and from one day to the next he must continually, of necessity, have revised his estimate of the relative worth of things.

Lewalski explains Donne's epideictic strategy in terms of contemporary trends in Protestant hermeneutics. There had been a shift of emphasis away from the medieval Catholic emphasis on Christ as the anti-type to which all Old Testament types refer, and to which the experience of the individual Christian was also assimilated, toward a focus on the individual Christian him/herself as anti-type. Donne, Lewalski suggests, carried this tendency "much further still, developing from it an all-encompassing 'incarnational' symbolism whose focus is the individual."[32] It is God's prerogative to invest any particular individual—Elizabeth Drury, for instance—with the merits of Christ, not in response to her own deserts but as a free and arbitrary gift. The eulogist who discovers them in her is responding to the Protestant injunction to find occasions for meditation not only in the life of Christ, and other traditional *topoi*, but in his own immediate environment.

Lewalski's account of Donne's epideictic strategy will be misleading if it convinces us that the eulogist's stance in these poems is not really problematic after all.[33] Instead, it should prompt us to recognize the subversiveness of a radically Protestant posture. A little further on in his verse letter to the Countess of Salisbury, Donne argues that even if his eulogies are not consistent with each other, this should not put his own integrity in question:

I adore
The same things now, which I adored before,

The subject changed, and measure; the same thing
In a low constable, and in the King
I reverence; His power to work on me:

(11.57–61)

Donne's insistence on the radical importance of his own personal experience
is at the same time a refusal to give the existing political order any authority
to structure his priorities.

His stance is subversive, finally, of the very possibility of ideological consensus or community. The more willing that one is to grant Elizabeth Drury's
or the Countess of Salisbury's eulogist the right to make the claims that he
does, the more pessimistic one must be about the availability of a shared
perspective on the human condition. For all I know, Elizabeth Drury may
have been the soul of the world, as her eulogist claims, but as far as I know,
she was not. And if I recognize that she is only provisionally the magnetic
center that brings the world coherent and whole, only until such time as his
personal experience may produce a recentering somewhere else, then I must
relinquish the supposition that the world has any coherence except as a
projection from the vantage point of each individual, subject to continual
revision from moment to moment of his life.

If we introduce synecdoche as a mediating third term between metonymy
and metaphor, then Jakobson's bipolar model affords a way to understand
Donne's "anatomy of the world" as a deconstruction of the static, synchronistic, Elizabethan World Picture. The relation between synecdoche and
metonymy is worth developing for theoretical reasons also: Jakobson's model
has been disparaged as a basis for literary stylistics on the grounds that it
collapses synecdoche and metonymy together, whereas they have different
cognitive implications. Jakobson himself has acknowledged that they do, but
insists that the difference between both of them and metaphor is more
fundamental. Both metonymy and synecdoche presuppose a relationship of
contiguity between the explicit and the implicit term of the figure. The
difference between them, Jakobson suggests, is that whereas for metonymy
the contiguity-relation is "external," for synecdoche it is "internal." Synecdoche refers to part of an entity as a way to signify the whole.[34]

We can improve this explanation and take it further on the strength of one
of the basic axioms of Prague School linguistics: language is a hierarchical
structure such that combination on any level produces not just a linear
collocation or "string" at that level but a higher-level gestalt. The explicit
and the implicit term of a metonymy are not just contiguous but in some
sense functionally interdependent: the one is the cause of the other, or its
container, and so forth. Metonymy does invoke a higher-level gestalt,

whether it be an entity, a situation, or a temporal sequence. Synecdoche is a special case of metonymy, in which the relationship between the metonym and the higher-level gestalt it invokes has certain limiting features. With metonymy, we need not suppose the higher-level gestalt to be capable of totalization: it might be open-ended, as temporal processes are, and it need not have definite boundaries. Synecdoche presupposes a distinct entity, usu- ally an organism or a system to which organic unity is attributed. For synecdoche, the contiguity-relation is always synchronic. And the most important limitation of all is that in a synecdoche the part is supposed to epitomize the larger whole. Synecdoche turns metonymic contiguity into metaphoric correspondence: it metaphorizes metonymy.

Insofar as the cognitive implications of synecdoche and metonymy are different, so are their ideological uses. When, for example, a fiction such as *The Shepheardes Calender* is proffered as a total metaphor for the human condition, the passage of life it depicts is being presented as a synecdoche: not just part of a larger field of events and social relations but an epitome or truly representative sample. It can be taken for this only insofar as certain assumptions are made about the larger field. It must in principle be a coher- ent whole, and its wholeness must be graspable synchronically, as if it were an organism or a functioning system of some kind. The Elizabethan World Picture is such a construct, and it is therefore hospitable to the status of total metaphor that Elizabethan fictions tended to claim for themselves. Met- onymic fictions allow for the possibility that the big picture cannot be synchronically totalized, or that there is no such thing. Both Donne and Jonson are metonymic poets, and Donne will very often call attention to the ideological implications of a metonymic stance by using it to proffer a meta- phoric vision that is patently outlandish or self-subverting.

In the *First Anniversary,* for example, the medical metaphor he uses to name his project is one which presupposes that the world is an organism and that he, as its "anatomist," is in a position to apprehend its totality and articulate its structure. But then his conduct of the anatomy, and the kinds of things he says about the world, belies this. For one thing, the project has to stop arbitrarily, at some point short of completeness:

> But as in cutting up a man that's dead,
> The body will not last out to have read
> On every part, and therefore men direct
> Their speech to parts, that are of most effect;
> So the world's carcase would not last, if I
> Were punctual in this Anatomy.
> Nor smells it well to hearers, if one tell

> Them their disease, who fain would think they're well.
> Here therefore be the end:[35]

(11.435–43)

This announcement, which heralds the end of the *First Anniversary*, keeps the poem itself from coming across as an "organic whole." Meanwhile the corpse itself turns out to be amorphous—" 'Tis all in pieces, all coherence gone"—and its incoherence forces the anatomist to be continually undercutting his own generalizations and sabotaging his own metalanguage. "We kill ourselves, to propagate our kind," he announces; but then just as the reader is rising to the challenge of this paradox, he withdraws its premise:

> And yet we do not that; we are not men:
> There is not now that mankind which was then

(11.111–12)

After he has argued at length that the world is no longer in proportion, he invokes the notion he has just discredited, as a condition contrary to fact, so that beauty's other aspect, color, can be forcefully regretted also:

> But beauty's other second element,
> Color, and luster now, is as near spent.
> And had the world his just proportion,
> Were it a ring still, yet the stone is gone.

(11.339–42)

These rhetorical strategies bring it home to us that, the world's condition being what it is, the only way it can be described is by invoking the wholeness, the coherence, the beauty it does *not* have. Coherence and totality are not in the world: they are thought-paradigms which the anatomist uses deconstructively in the *First Anniversary*, and in the *Second* as a springboard upward, to heaven.

One of these poems' most obsessive themes is novelty. The very structure of the cosmos has apparently changed over the centuries, and is changing. In the heavens themselves "arise

> New stars, and old do vanish from our eyes:
> As though heaven suffered earthquakes, peace or war,
> When new towers rise, and old demolished are.

(11.259–62)

These changes may be symptoms of the world's decay, or they may be figments of our inability to come up with an adequate cosmology—it is difficult to tell which. In the *Second Anniversary*, the claim is made that on earth "essential joy" is impossible because of the radical transitoriness of everything:

> Dost thou love
> Beauty? (and beauty worthiest is to move)
> Poor cozened cozener, that she, and that thou,
> Which did begin to love, are neither now.
> You are both fluid, changed since yesterday;
> Next day repairs, (but ill) last day's decay.
> Nor are (although the river keep the name)
> Yesterday's waters, and today's the same.[36]
>
> (11.389–96)

The insoluble problem novelty poses for the anatomist is that a synchronic overview or "total picture" of the world is never actually available for dissection.

The claims that both the *Anniversaries* make on behalf of Elizabeth Drury are at once a symptom and a solution to the problems the anatomist's self-appointed task presents him with. They are symptomatically disproportionate claims, as he admits at one point:

> And, oh, it can no more be questioned,
> That beauty's best, proportion, is dead,
> Since even grief itself, which now alone
> Is left us, is without proportion.
>
> (*First Anniversary*, 11.305–8)

But they enable him to construct a thought-model whose improvisatory status is patent because of its "occasional" nature.

Donne is making the same kind of move in several of the *Songs and Sonets* where he playfully invests metonymic associations with magical or sacramental efficacy. In "Witchcraft by a Picture," he plays with the superstition that his mistress knows how to murder a man by destroying a picture of him; in "The Funeral" he pretends that a bracelet of her hair, "which crowns my arm," has usurped the brain's prerogative to control his body. In one of his valedictions the ruling conceit is that the lover can leave himself in his signature, engraved in her window. The hair-bracelet reappears in "The Relic,"[37] where it becomes a device to reunite the lovers on Judgment Day:

> When my grave is broke up again
> Some second guest to entertain
>
> . . . .
>
> And he that digs it spies
> A bracelet of bright hair about the bone,
>   Will he not let us alone,
> And think that there a loving couple lies,
> Who hop'd that this device might be some way
> To make their souls, at the last busy day,
> Meet at this grave, and make a little stay?

In the second stanza of this poem, he entertains the fancy that the bone and the bracelet of hair will be worshipped as relics by a future generation:

> Thou shalt be a Mary Magdalen, and I
> A something else thereby.

The rhetorical context of these conceits always motivates them as playful or fanciful or love-desperate, but they have religious/political importance nevertheless, because they arrogate to private individuals the prerogative of church and state to authorize symbols for collective worship.

The poem of Donne's that does this most explicitly and knowingly is "The Canonization," which proffers the vantage point of a private individual as a privileged locus from which the rest of the world is to derive its importance *and* take its bearings, henceforth:

> And by these hymns, all shall approve
> Us *canoniz'd* for Love:
>
> And thus invoke us: 'You, whom reverend love
>   Made one another's hermitage;
> You, to whom love was peace, that now is rage;
>   Who did the whole world's soul extract, and drove
>   Into the glasses of your eyes
>   (So made such mirrors, and such spies,
>   That they did all to you epitomize)
>   Countries, towns, courts: beg from above
>   A pattern of your love!'

The speaker and his beloved, self-canonized by this very poem, are to perform the office that had traditionally belonged to the saints of the Catholic Church—intercession with the deity.

> And if no piece of chronicle we prove,
>   We'll build in sonnets pretty rooms;

A "piece of chronicle" records events that have been significant for the nation as a whole, such as wars, outbreaks of the plague, and the accessions and deaths of kings. The chronicler is as far as possible from taking an interest in the private individual as such, and this lack of interest extends to himself as well: the status of chronicle as a nation's official record is a function of its impersonality. This poem challenges the authority of chronicle by proposing to commemorate a merely private, personal relationship as a point of reference, henceforth, for "all." Against the paratactic preterit of chronicle, its narrative without a narrator, "The Canonization" asserts the value of a representation that is tied to the vantage point of the one who here and now says "I": the vantage point of the private individual *as such*.

The strategy of this poem is iconoclastic not only in relation to the authority of the Church and the king but also in relation to the institution of "poesy." With his "pretty rooms" and his well-wrought-urn metaphor Donne invokes the poetic function of language and its power to create timeless literary monuments. Meanwhile, however, he exploits its deictic function to give the lover's performance a very specific occasion: "For God's sake, hold your tongue. . . ." We have already found the same kind of thing going on in Sidney's *Astrophil and Stella* sequence, where the sonnet form is fulfilled yet resisted by the seeming spontaneity and immediacy of the lover's rhetoric. This could only have been managed in reaction to an earlier phase of self-focused, metaphoric writing: iconoclasm presupposes icons. Sidney, as we have seen, was himself part of that earlier phase in which the "monumentality" of the lyric, especially of fixed forms like the sonnet, was discovered by a whole generation of poets. Donne and Jonson took their achievement for granted, and reasserted the importance of the poem-to-context relation.

7 "This bed thy center is": The Metonymic Poetry of Donne and Jonson

Donne's lyric poetry is very different from Jonson's, and yet they were kindred members of the same post-Elizabethan generation. Douglas Bush groups them together, in the *Oxford History of English Literature*, as having both rebelled against the "half-medieval idealism" of the Elizabethan poets and the "decorative rhetorical patterns" that went along with it, and cultivated "a new realism of style . . . , fitted for the intellectual and critical realism of their thought."[1] Joseph Summers explains, in *The Heirs of Donne and Jonson*, that "one is tempted to characterize the poetry of Donne and Jonson in terms of a whole series of seemingly opposed ideals and practices," but he agrees with Bush that their difference from the Elizabethan poets is more fundamental than their differences from each other.[2] As recently as 1983, Richard Helgerson has again cited Bush approvingly, and reasserted the claim that Donne and Jonson belong to "a single literary generation, a generation that defined itself in opposition to the generation of Sidney and Spenser."[3] Whereas for Bush the hallmark of this generation is "realism," for Helgerson it is satire, which emerged as a dominant literary mode in the late 1590s, and was used to debunk both Petrarchan eroticism and heroic romance.

Helgerson argues that this change in orientation is sufficiently explained by "the historical dynamic that opposes generation to generation and the literary system that sets genre against genre."

> Jonson and his immediate contemporaries could not do what Spenser had done because Spenser had so recently done it. . . . The pastoral, the sonnet sequence, the chivalric, Arcadian, and amorous romance, the long nationalistic poem, perhaps even the epic had been exhausted, and along with them the mellifluous,

ornamented style and the aureate attitude that had been their
body and soul. (p. 123; pp. 104–5)

In my introductory chapter I took the position that this way of explaining
shifts in literary fashion is not sufficient, and that we also need to look
toward ideological shifts whose basis is extraliterary. Even where a poet
explicitly claims that a certain genre of writing has been "exhausted" by his
immediate precursors,[4] it is equally likely that he is not using it because the
political assumptions that had promoted and informed that kind of work are
in the process of being superseded. As for this particular change in orientation, I have used Donne's *Anniversaries* and some of his *Songs and Sonets* to
argue that it was closely related to the demise of the cult of Elizabeth and the
synchronistic, centripetal vision that had informed it. Donne's and Jonson's
lyrics bear witness to the emergence of a polity that was, and was experienced
as being, more atomistic and incoherent.

And yet it *is* appropriate also, at this juncture in literary history, to have
recourse to the notion of a generational dynamic internal to the literary
system. In fact, this is the first time in the history of English literature that it
does become appropriate to speak of reaction and innovation within the
literary system itself. English poesy is a late sixteenth-century invention: it
was in Sidney's and Spenser's generation that it began to be articulated, both
synchronically and diachronically, as an autonomous cultural institution.
Jonson and Donne reacted against the prevailing bias of Elizabethan poetry
in both its ideological and its formal aspect: their poetry supersedes the
Elizabethan cultural moment from within the institution of English poesy.

We have seen how a generation of self-focused, metaphoric writing developed the potential of the lyric to be a space apart, where inner states and
mental images are sustained against the passage of time and the pressure of
immediate circumstances. Donne's and Jonson's poetry reasserts the poem-
to-context relation: it is metonymic, in the sense of adhering to particular
contexts and reacting to particular situations. At the same time, however,
these poets were in a position, as their predecessors had not been, to take the
autonomy and prestige of the lyric for granted, and thus they both also claim
to be producing "well-wrought urns," lasting monuments in words. There is
a tension in their poems between "monumentality" and topicality or timeli-
ness, which is sometimes ironic and which always calls attention to the
eccentricity of the poet's vantage point.

This is much less obviously true of Jonson's lyrics than of Donne's, and so
I will use a poem of Jonson's for a brief preliminary demonstration. Jonson's
epigram to William, Lord Mounteagle,[5] offers quite literally to be the monument that Mounteagle deserves, but has not otherwise received, for service
to his country:

Lo, what my country should have done (have raised
An obelisk, or column to thy name,
Or, if she would but modestly have praised
Thy fact, in brass or marble writ the same)
I, that am glad of thy great chance, here do!
And proud, my work shall outlast common deeds,
Durst think it great, and worthy wonder too,
But thine, for which I do it, so much exceeds!
My country's parents I have many known;
But saver of my country thee alone.

(*Epigrams*, no. 60)

This poem itself, with its ten lines of equal length, makes a memorial "column" of print on the page. It is highly self-focused, by virtue of its compactness, by the way that its rhyme words highlight references to the act of praise and the person to be praised—his name and deeds, his uniqueness and "exceedingness"—and finally also by the relationship of symmetrical opposition that obtains between its first and last lines, the first referring to what "my country" should have done for Mounteagle and the last to what he has done for "my country." What he had done a contemporary reader would either have known or been challenged by the poem to find out: Mounteagle had informed the government about the Gunpowder Plot in time for it to be quashed.[6] Since he was a Roman Catholic, it is easy to see why Jonson found his patriotism remarkable; but this is not the kind of deed that obelisks and columns have traditionally been raised to honor. Implicit in the poet's assertion of pride in his own "work" is a claim to be redefining heroism and patriotism, in terms of contemporary political realities. This poem highlights what Jonson was doing in all of the encomiastic epigrams he wrote for particular contemporaries: he put the monumentality of the lyric in the service of timely, topical discriminations of his own, striking a carefully calculated balance between self-focus and set toward the context.

Donne, as we have already seen, was more subversive and iconoclastic. His encomiastic rhetoric is patently outlandish; his poetic monuments, unstable. In his love poems, he typically asserts that the here and now of a private, personal relationship is a privileged locus from which the rest of the world must derive its importance, and take its bearings, henceforth.

The *Songs and Sonets* insist harder on their occasions than any other poems written in English, and the occasions they presuppose are complex and volatile. Often the first line of the poem objects to what its addressee must have been saying or doing, or takes a bold new initiative with respect to their mutual situation:

> For God's sake hold your tongue, . . .
>
> Mark but this flea, and mark in this
> How little that which thou deny'st me is;
>
> So, so, break off this last lamenting kiss,
>
> I'll tell thee now, dear love, what thou shalt do
> to anger destiny, as she doth us;[7]

These poems' set toward particular occasions is enhanced still further by their imitation of the idiom, syntax, and speech rhythms of spontaneous conversational utterance. We are very much aware of reading a poem, because the stanza format is usually complex and the line-ending rhymes are often obtrusive and witty:

> Take you a course, get you a place,
> Observe his Honor, or his Grace,
> And the King's real, or his stamped face
> Contémplate; . . .

At the same time, however, we seem to be hearing what a man might actually say under the pressure of his immediate circumstances.

Often what he is saying belongs to the class of utterances that are called "performatives" in speech-act theory: greeting, valediction, promise, insult, curse, prediction.[8] This kind of utterance does not just talk about what its speaker wants, or has experienced: it is itself an action taken, an event in the relationship. Typically the performatives in Donne's poems have complicated settings. In one of them, a lover tries without success to keep his lady from killing a flea. In the second stanza he enjoins her to spare the creature's life—"Oh stay, three lives in one flea spare"— and then the third stanza begins with a rhetorical question which lets the reader know that she has killed it. In Donne's valedictions it is not just a question of bidding goodbye, but also of coping with the emotions the moment of parting has aroused in both parties. Often in these poems performative utterances are accompanied by nonverbal gestures (mutual tears, for example, in "A Valediction: of weeping"), or presuppose nonverbal gestures, as in the first line of "The Expiration" ("So, so, break off this last lamenting kiss"), or try to fend off such manifestations of feeling, as in "A Valediction: forbidding mourning." As we move from poem to poem, each depicts a slightly different set of immediate circumstances for its speaker: no two occasions of parting are quite the same, and the lover's performative strategy changes accordingly, from one set of circumstances to the next.

In chapter 3, I used "The Sun Rising" to show how temporal, spatial, and social deixis will enable a poem to function as a metonymy for the entire situation in which we must suppose its speaker's utterance to be embedded. In order to highlight the metonymic function of deixis, that discussion told only half the story of the poem-to-context relation in Donne's poetry. The other half concerns his use of metaphor as a strategy for transforming a poem's occasion in terms of its speaker's feelings. In "The Good Morrow," it is maintained that "love, all love of other sights controls, / And makes one little room, an everywhere." The mode in which this transformative power is exercised is linguistic, of course: specifically, its instrument is metaphor. But in order for an impressive demonstration of the power of metaphor to occur, the poem's setting, its "one little room," needs to be well realized. Metaphor and metonymy work together in Donne's poems by working against each other, as metonymy creates a resistance for metaphor to overcome.

In "The Sun Rising," the metaphor that comes into play is personification, which is undertaken by the lover as an act of aggression toward the situation in which he unwillingly finds himself. He personifies the sun in order to be able to order it around:

> Busy old fool, unruly Sun,
>   Why dost thou thus,
> Through windows, and through curtains, call on us?
> Must to thy motions lovers' seasons run?
>   Saucy pedantic wretch, go chide
>   Late schoolboys. . . .

Meanwhile, however, the poem's deictics keep us in touch with what is literally happening, which is that the sun is quite imperviously rising higher, even as he speaks. The first stanza presupposes that it is just beginning to poke its rays through the bed curtains. By the beginning of the second stanza, its rays are stronger, and fresh tactics must be improvised to dismiss them:

> Thy beams, so reverend and strong
>   Why shouldst thou think?
> I could eclipse and cloud them with a wink,
> But that I would not lose her sight so long:

Closing his eyes is a gesture the lover could literally make, to fend off the sunlight. "Eclipse" and "cloud" are metaphors which transform this defensive gesture into an act of aggression, one that is commensurate with the status and power of the adversary; he has only to close his eyes to eclipse the sun. His final move, in the third stanza, is to extend to the sun, which has by that time fully risen, a lordly invitation to do what it is already doing without his permission: "Shine here to us, and thou art everywhere." It is because he has been using conceits to stay on top of a rapidly changing situation that his rhetorical ingenuity seems so impressive.

Donne's poems are exceptionally time-sensitive. Like most of Wyatt's lyrics, most of them are situated at a temporal crisis-point. Twelve out of fifty-five are aubades and valedictions; seven more anticipate or react to a death; and in almost all the ones that have specific occasions, the speaker is looking backward and forward from the midst of a relationship whose time-shape is at issue for him somehow:

> I wonder, by my troth, what thou and I
> Did, till we lov'd;
>
> Now thou hast lov'd me one whole day,
> Tomorrow when thou leav'st, what wilt thou say?[9]

Only a few of the *Songs and Sonets* are cast in the achronic present tense of generalization about "the life of man" or the frequentative present tense of "how it is with me these days." More typically, Donne uses verbal, pronominal, and adverbial deixis to situate the present moment of his speaker's utterance in a diachronic continuum. Where he uses a narrative preterit, he tends to play games with it, foregrounding and subverting the discontinuity it produces between past events and the vantage point from which they are being cited in the present.

The most interesting case of his subversion of the preterit is in "The Ecstasy," where the lovers' "dialogue of one" is made to swallow its own narrative frame. The poem begins by using a preterit narrative to situate them on "a pregnant bank" where they are said to have been together "all the day," without speaking or moving, while their souls came forth and spoke as one. As a pretext for quoting what was said, a hypothetical observer is invoked—not just any passerby, but only an observer "so by love refin'd / That he souls' language understood, / And by good love were grown all mind," so that his presence would not violate their privacy. Then in the last stanza of the poem, the lovers invoke this hypothetical observer from within the quoted "dialogue," and the vantage point from which it had originally been situated and quoted is never reasserted. By transgressing its own frame in this way, the ecstatic dialogue refuses to stay in the past, and the possibility arises that we the reader are the one who has stood "within convenient distance" to overhear it.

Several of the *Songs and Sonets* begin with a deictical conundrum that puts temporal and interpersonal shifters at odds with each other, or with nondeictic elements of the speaker's message.

> For the first twenty years, since yesterday,
> I scarce believ'd thou could'st be gone away;
>
> Twice or thrice had I loved thee,
> Before I knew thy face or name;
>
> When I died last. . . .[10]

In each of these cases the temporal dimension of the speaker's relationship to his addressee is all-important, and is sharply in focus, but in each case the only way to make sense of what he is saying is to give it a metaphoric reading. In "The Computation," from which the first example is taken, what the speaker really means is that although the woman he addresses as "thou" has only been gone since yesterday, he has been forced by his love for her to experience the intervening time as if it were thousands of years, many lifetimes, ages and ages. In the second example, from "Air and Angels," he is explaining that although he had been in love with others before he met "thee," now that he has met her he realizes that those others did not really count: she is the one his soul had all along been seeking. In the third he is again giving a hyperbolical account of how much he has missed her since they parted: he goes on to explain that he dies "as often as from thee I go." In all three cases, the deictical conundrum is a metaphoric conceit: metaphor overcomes metonymy as a way to insist on the unusual strength of the speaker's feelings.

Many of Donne's poems have a physical location that is quite specific and detailed, and the speaker will often pick up one of its elements, some item whose physical contiguity to himself and his addressee the poem presupposes, and use metaphor to give it unusual prominence in his discourse. In both "A Valediction: of weeping" and "The Flea," for example, an entire poem is built from conceits that give a very small part of the speaker's physical situation—a tear, the flea—a hugely disproportionate share of his attention. In "The Flea," this is being done to show a resistant lady that he too can make a big fuss about a small matter:

> Mark but this flea, and mark in this,
> How little that which thou deny'st me is;

In "A Valediction: of weeping," ingenuity is lavished on a token of their presence to each other (only "whilst I stay here" could his tear conceivably reflect her face), as if to stave off impending absence for just a few moments longer. The ingenious conceits are also being used to suggest that although lovers very often cry at parting, on *this* occasion, whereas it is *you* being left and *I* leaving, crying is a very special business. In both poems the whole situation is put in perspective by an outlandish metaphorical treatment of the part. Metonymy furnishes the vehicles for metaphor, and then metaphor is used to master the poem's occasion in terms of the lover's feelings.

We have encountered a partly similar strategy among the mid-Tudor poets, who also tended to derive their metaphoric vehicles from the poem's contextualizing occasion. Gascoigne, who did more interesting things with the poem-to-context relation than any of the others, would often use an allegory or an extended similitude to turn an originally unpromising situation to advantage, by shifting the perspective from which it is viewed. As we saw in chapter 4, this is a way to insist that a poem be implicated in, and have an impact on, the given world of human social relations. But Gascoigne's metaphors are less ingenious than Donne's, he introduces them less peremptorily, and he develops them more slowly and carefully. The rhetorical strength of the "woodmanship" metaphor, or of the extended similitude in "Gascoigne's Good Morrow," is achieved by its explicitness and its predictability. The allegorist enlists the reader's acquiescence in his application of the figure by reassuring us that he has no surprises in store for us—nothing up his sleeve. By the same token, Gascoigne's claims on behalf of fictions and imaginative constructs are far more guarded and modest than Donne's. Donne uses metaphor to assert the uniqueness of a private relationship or to privilege an idiosyncratic perspective, whereas Gascoigne sought to avoid an open challenge to common sense.

A certain kind of transaction is typical of Donne's most often anthologized lyrics, taken as wholes: "The Sun Rising," "A Valediction: of weeping," "A Fever," "The Relic," "Twickenham Garden," "The Canonization." To begin with, a particular situation is emphatically presupposed by metonymic deixis, and the speaker makes an idiosyncratic bid for mastery of that situation, by violating grammatical and social conventions ("Oh do not die") or by using a flamboyant, outrageous metaphor ("Blasted with sighs, and surrounded with tears, / Hither I come . . ."). His attitude is opposed, by verbal gestures of this kind, to what ordinary people would make of such an occasion. In the middle of the poem, his distance from the world at large is consolidated by further conceits, and his discourse may turn away from the particular situation in which it had originated and become self-focused. Finally, however, it will turn back, inviting the world to take its bearings henceforth from the perspective, the behavior, the writings of the one who says "I"—or asserts that "they" are already doing so:

Hither with crystal vials, lovers, come,
  And take my tears, which are love's wine,
And try your mistress' tears at home,
For all are false, that taste not just like mine;
          ("Twickenham Garden")

And, since at such times miracles are sought,
I would have that age by this paper taught
What miracles we harmless lovers wrought.
          ("The Relic")

Weep me not dead, in thine arms, but forbear
To teach the sea, what it may do too soon;
       ("A Valediction: of weeping")

Shine here to us, and thou art everywhere;
This bed thy center is, these walls, thy sphere.
       ("The Sun Rising")

A situation gives rise to a poem, but the poem asserts its transformative power with respect to that situation, and finally there is a move to reverse the priority of context over poem, putting the world in the poem's jurisdiction.

The single poem that best illustrates all the linguistic strategies involved in this transaction is "The Canonization." In the first two stanzas of this poem, the argument is vigorously addressee-oriented, by its exclamations, its rhetorical questions, its hyperbolical sarcasm. Its set toward the context is further strengthened by offhanded references to the speaker's situation in life and by a conspectus of his society's most important institutions: the royal court, the university, the lawcourts, the marketplace. The speaker refers to all of these things in order to reject their claims upon him, in favor of a private attachment:

For God's sake hold your tongue, and let me love,
  Or chide my palsy, or my gout,
My five gray hairs, or ruin'd fortune flout,
  With wealth your state, your mind with arts improve,
    Take you a course, get you a place,
    Observe his Honor, or his Grace,
And the King's real, or his stamped face
  Contemplate; what you will, approve,
  So you will let me love.

Alas, alas, who's injured by my love?

What merchant's ships have my sighs drown'd?
Who says my tears have overflow'd his ground?
When did my colds a forward spring remove?
When did those heats which my veins fill
Add one man to the plaguey bill?
Soldiers find wars, and lawyers find out still
Litigious men, which quarrels move,
Though she and I do love.

In the next two stanzas, the speaker turns away from his interlocutor and
the world he represents. He signals this maneuver by guessing in the first line
of each stanza what kind of thing "they" might have to say about "us," then
taking up that very saying and authorizing it himself as a way to get at the
true nature and value of the relationship. Rhetorical posturing gives way to
explanation, the interlocutory situation becomes less important, and the
speaker's conceits no longer deal in metonymies of that situation or of the
world at large, but reach instead for mythical paradoxes, things that never
were in Nature: the Phoenix riddle; the mystery of androgyny. In this way the
contextual anchorage of the utterance is loosened and the message becomes
more self-focused:

Call us what you will, we are made such by love;
Call her one, me another fly,
We are tapers too, and at our own cost die,
And we in us find the Eagle and the Dove.
The Phoenix riddle hath more wit
By us; we two being one, are it.
So to one neutral thing both sexes fit,
We die, and rise the same, and prove
Mysterious by this love.

We can die by it, if not live by love,
And if unfit for tombs and hearse
Our legend be, it will be fit for verse;
And if no piece of chronicle we prove,
We'll build in sonnets pretty rooms;
As well a well-wrought urn becomes
The greatest ashes, as half-acre tombs,
And by these hymns, all shall approve
Us *canoniz'd* for Love:

Paradox is obviously the dominant figure in stanza three. In stanza four, not so obviously perhaps, syllepsis is crucial. "Die" and "live" both have two different meanings activated by the discourse, where talk of ordinary life and death, of living in the sense of livelihood, and of death in the sense of sexual orgasm, are all going on together. "Legend" means "inscription" where tombs are concerned and "marvellous story" insofar as "ours" will be "fit for verse." As one of Donne's editors noticed, poems are "pretty rooms" not just metaphorically but also by virtue of an interlingual pun: the Italian word for "room" is "stanza."[11] Paradoxes use the linguistic code against itself; puns call attention to arbitrariness in the relation between signifier and signified. Both devices assist the poetic function of language to become predominant in these two stanzas.[12]

At the same time, the poem takes up the question of what poetry is good for, so that its message is not only self-focused but self-referential. We are reading a poem which says that a poem is where the speaker and his love will be by the time future readers make their acquaintance. And in the last stanza, we find ourselves preemptively quoted:

> all shall approve
> Us *canoniz'd* for Love:
>
> And thus invoke us: 'You, whom reverend love
> Made one another's hermitage;
> You, to whom love was peace, that now is rage;
> Who did the whole world's soul extract, and drove
> Into the glasses of your eyes
> (So made such mirrors, and such spies,
> That they did all to you epitomize)
> Countries, towns, courts: beg from above
> A pattern of your love!'

Whereas at the outset the speaker had taken his rhetorical bearings from the chiding of a spokesman for the world's values, now the world is put in the position of taking its bearings from his poems. This is a highly eccentric move, and the one who makes it calls attention to his alienation from a common center.

Jonson professed admiration for Donne's poetry, but he objected strongly to its extravagance, its obscurity, and its violations of decorum.[13] His own poems are urbane, concise, perspicuous, elegantly "plain." In his elegies, epigrams, and verse epistles we seem to see a reversion to the plain-style poetics of Gascoigne's generation.[14] Metonymy is the all-pervasive trope in Jonson's poetry; metaphor comes into play quite inconspicuously, to reinforce the metonymic strategies that give his poems a firm, decisive grip on the "facts" of contemporary social life.

He established his credentials as a "realist" partly by way of the image of himself that his poems consistently put forth. "No other English Renaissance poet so intrudes on his work," exclaims Richard Helgerson (p. 185). "No other makes so much of his physical appearance, of his illness and poverty, of his quarrels, friendships, defeats, triumphs, likes, and dislikes, of his very name."[15] He emerges from his poems as a sociable, quarrelsome middle-aged man whose pleasure in eating and drinking has made him fat, and who is therefore appropriately pessimistic about his chances of succeeding with ladies. Jonson's poetic persona is very different from Donne's, but they are alike in being very much aware of the passage of time and very firmly situated, always, in contemporary social settings.

Especially in his short satiric epigrams, Jonson used metonymic devices to give his poems the status of personal observations in particular contexts. Such devices create the illusion of spontaneous incidental witticisms, caught and preserved in his couplets like flies in amber:

On Reformed Gamester

Lord, how is gamester changed! His hair close cut!
His neck fenced round with ruff! His eyes half shut!
His clothes two fashions off, and poor! His sword
Forbid' his side! And nothing, but the Word
Quick in his lips! Who hath this wonder wrought?
The late ta'en bastinado. So I thought.
What several ways men to their calling have!
The body's stripes, I see, the soul may save.

(Epigrams, no. 21)

The effectiveness of a poem like this comes partly from its elliptical brevity, which enhances the impression of witty ad lib. The supposition is that we are already familiar with the larger social world to which a metonymic phrase like "the late ta'en bastinado" refers, and if the epigrammatist need not labor to put us in the picture, he can chat all the more offhandedly and spontaneously with us. He begins with a series of vigorous exclamations, ostensibly prompted by surprise at the sudden change they describe, but prolonged to the point where surprise can be detected to be a rhetorical pretext for the satiric description itself. A perfect balance is struck in this poem between the topicality of its message, an effect created by its exclamations and metonymies, and the monumentality that accrues to its shapely couplets. A man who could toss off couplets like these impromptu would be a rare companion indeed—one whose observations you'd want to record and publish!

Even where this kind of balance needed not to be struck, where the occasion called for a more formal poetic performance, Jonson tended to give his poems relatively well-developed vantage points. In his birthday ode to Sir William Sidney, he places himself at the birthday feast and pretends to derive his inspiration from the festive activity that is going on all around him:

> Now that the hearth is crowned with smiling fire,
> And some do drink, and some do dance,
>   Some ring,
>   Some sing,
> And all do strive to advance
> The gladness higher:
>   Wherefore should I
>   Stand silent by,
>   Who not the least,
> Both love the cause, and authors of the feast?
>
> (*The Forest*, no. 14)

To pay a clever compliment to the Countess of Bedford in another poem, he pretends that "this morning" he made a deliberate effort to invent an ideal beloved for himself, and his act of imagination was climaxed by a sudden intuition:

> Such when I meant to feign, and wished to see,
> My muse bad, *Bedford* write, and that was she.

In this latter instance of the strategy, it is especially obvious that it constitutes a reaction against the synchronistic, metaphoric bias of Elizabethan poetry, because Jonson first invents the beloved as a purely mental construct, and then discovers that she is a particular, proper-named individual after all.

Jonson's *Epigrams* are like the mid-Tudor auto-anthologies, in the sense of creating "a cultured social world which the reader can join for the price of the book."[16] In fact they do this more successfully than the auto-anthologies: Jonson was more skillful at using deixis to give his poems particular vantage points; he imitated the rhetoric of letter writing and familiar conversation more skillfully; and his references to contemporary social life—its settings, its furniture, its customary rituals and pastimes—are more specific and detailed. In all of these ways, his poems are more vividly metonymic than Googe's, Turberville's, or Gascoigne's. To find this true, we need only to think, for example, of "Inviting a Friend to Supper," with its exuberantly detailed catalogue of anticipated pleasures, the air of easy familiarity that its discourse establishes between the writer and his friends even though he is speaking couplets, and the use that is made of a particular social occasion to epitomize "the good life." Jonson's poems are so dexterously self-contextualizing that they do not need elaborate headnotes. As we read through the collection, it has a cumulative effect: we become gradually acquainted not only with all the different people who are named or whose behavior is epitomized but with a whole society and its "custom," by way of all the different kinds of relationship and degrees of intimacy that obtain between these individuals and the epigrammatist himself.

Often instead of depicting oral speech, a poem of his will call attention to the material conditions that belong to written communication: the distance in both space and time between its production and its reception, the paper it is written on, and so forth. Oddly enough, this has the effect of enhancing the poem's immediacy: by acknowledging its condition of being a published written message, it acquires social currency as such, and seems to speak from the page:

> Would God, my Burges, I could think
> Thoughts worthy of thy gift, this ink,
> Then would I promise here to give
> Verse, that should thee, and me outlive.
> But since the wine hath steeped my brain,
> I only can the paper stain;
> Yet with a dye, that fears no moth,
> But scarlet-like outlasts the cloth.
>
> (*Underwoods*, no. 55)

It is also clear from poems like this that Jonson took the dissemination of the lyric by way of the printed book very much for granted, both in the sense that he expected his poems to reach a contemporary audience beyond his immediate circle of friends and patrons, and in the sense that he expected them to "outlive" that original audience. His poems claim the status of social gestures in particular contexts which had belonged to the poems of Gascoigne and his contemporaries, along with the monumentality that had accrued to the lyric in the hands of Elizabethan writers like Spenser, Shakespeare, and Daniel. So confident is he of producing verbal monuments, "verse that should thee and me outlive," that he can afford to joke about his inability to produce any message worthy of being preserved.

Jonson "cursed Petrarch," says Drummond, "for redacting verses to sonnets, which he said were like that tyrant's bed, where some who were too short were racked, others too long cut short." He professed to detest all other rhymes but couplets, and "said he had written a discourse of poesy both against Campion and Daniel, especially this last, where he proves couplets to

be the bravest sort of verses . . . . and that cross-rhymes and stanzas (because
the purpose would lead him beyond eight lines to conclude) were all
forced."[17] These are the prejudices that a poet could be expected to have who
wrote all his poems in prose first, as on another occasion he told Drummond
that "his master Camden" had taught him to do. Whether or not this is how
he wrote his poems, the remark expresses a pronounced bias in favor of the
sentence as the controlling armature of a poem's discourse.[18] Couplets make
it possible to compose an indefinitely extensible argument and shape it
sentence by sentence. Such an argument can be firmly self-enclosed or
self-focused—Jonson's epigrams always are—provided that the last of its
couplet-sentences sums up or clinches its argument. Cross-rhymes and stanzas and intricate fixed forms like the sonnet cannot be assimilated, in the way
that couplets can, to a discourse that privileges the axis of combination.

Wesley Trimpi has pointed out that Jonson's curse on Petrarch had been
anticipated by the satirists of the 1590s, who had accused the Elizabethan
sonneteers of vapid, effeminate writing that rhymed without really having an
argument. Even Sidney had made a similar objection to the writing of many
of his contemporaries, in his Defense of Poesy: if you were to paraphrase their
poems, he remarks, "and then ask the meaning, . . . it will be found that one
verse did but beget another, without ordering at the first, what should be at
the last; which becomes a confused mass of words, with a tingling sound of
rhyme, barely accompanied with reason."[19] But for all his impatience with
writers who had caught the trick of the rhyme scheme but could not use it to
structure an argument, Sidney had himself thoroughly mastered both the
sonnet and the sestina, as vehicles for the kind of argument that is metaphoric, synchronistic, and self-focused. With the Astrophil and Stella
sequence, he began, as we have seen, to work against the inherent bias of the
sonnet, and in many of the sonnets in that sequence there is an ironic
tension between the poem as poem—self-focused, synchronistic, monumental—and the poem as message-in-context, an urgent, spontaneous, of-this-
moment outburst. This kind of tension is characteristic of Donne's poetry
also, as we have seen. Jonson reacted against the bias of Elizabethan poetry
not by contesting or subverting it in his poems but by favoring poetic forms
that are compatible with "the metonymic way" of developing a discourse.

His couplets are syntactically very sophisticated. He varies the caesura
within the line and makes strategic use of runovers to give himself a four-line
sentence, or three lines with a one-line afterthought, and so forth. His
syntactic repertory is greater and he exploits it more deftly by far than the
mid-Tudor poets, who also favored metric forms that would allow them to
put a discursive argument into verse without having to "change good reason
for rumbling rhyme." His syntax is capable of every degree of formality, from
the colloquial informality of a seemingly haphazard run-on—

I'll tell you of more, and lie, so you will come:
Of partridge, pheasant, woodcock, of which some
May yet be there; and godwit, if we can:
Knat, rail, and ruff too. Howsoe'er, my man
Shall read a piece of Vergil, Tacitus,
Livy, or of some better book to us,
Of which we'll speak our minds, amidst our meat;
And I'll profess no verses to repeat:

(*Epigrams*, no. 101)

to the sculptured elegance of a balanced antithesis—

I do but name thee Pembroke, and I find
It is an epigram, on all mankind;
Against the bad, but of, and to the good:
Both which are asked, to have thee understood.

(*Epigrams*, no. 102)

In the first of these two passages,[20] the couplets enhance the comically haphazard effect of the syntax, calling attention to the absence of balance or parallelism between the syntactic units they tie together. In the second passage, the line-ending rhymes help to increase the rhetorical force and gravity of the speaker's pronouncement by emphasizing its most important terms: Pembroke's goodness, and the discernment it challenges from all mankind, which is modeled by the epigrammatist himself as he takes the measure of Pembroke's "name." In both passages, the couplet enhances the work that the syntax is doing to turn the poem's message into a social or moral gesture, a speech act of a certain kind.

"Pure and neat language I love, yet plain and customary":[21] in this piece of *Timber*, Jonson has paraphrased Quintilian, but they are qualities he often cites approvingly in other men's writing, and that his own possesses also. The one that is the least self-explanatory, but also the most important as an index of his difference in orientation from the Elizabethan poets, is "customary." "Custom," he explains (again making direct use of Quintilian), "is the most certain mistress of language, as the public stamp makes the current money."[22] The coinage analogy suggests that by "custom" he would be understood to mean not only "common practice," what is usually done by most people, but also business dealings, "commerce." Custom in the first sense is what makes custom in the second sense possible. Language, like money, is a medium of exchange that assigns "customary" values to things.

The analogy with money, and the meaning it lends to the idea of customary usage, makes it seem quite pointless and wrongheaded to "affect the ancients," as Spenser did in the language of his poems: "for what was the ancient language, which some men so dote upon, but the ancient custom?"[23] When Jonson accused Spenser to Drummond of having "writ no language," this was not just a dismissive hyperbole; it reflects the importance Jonson seems to have attached to the contextual orientation of language, what Jakobson calls its "metonymic" aspect. Spenser's hybrid amalgam of archaic and current usage pulls both its archaic and its modern elements out of context. In doing so, it helps to establish the status of Faeryland, or the pastoral setting of *The Shepheardes Calender*, as a world unto itself—a world that metaphorically reflects, but refuses to be assimilated, either to the contemporary context of its author and readers or to any particular moment in past history. Clearly Jonson was unsympathetic to such a project. As far as he was concerned, the language of poems should have just the same "currency" as the language people use to do their business with one another outside of poems.

This attitude emerges even more clearly from his discussion of metaphor, and we can also see how he differs from Donne, who used outlandish metaphors to transcend or else transform the contexts to which his poems assimilate themselves. Metaphors should only be used, Jonson argues, to serve necessity—"or commodity, which is a kind of necessity." Necessity is when we have no other word; "commodity" is when "we have not so fit a word." Like the word "custom," Jonson's word "commodity" implies that what words are fit for is to do people's business with each other in particular settings. "Farfetched" metaphors should be avoided because they keep the discourse from being transparently perspicuous, by importing their vehicles from out of context—"from a wrong place," is how Jonson puts it:

> As if a privy councillor should at the table take his metaphor from a dicing house, or ordinary, or a vintner's vault; or a justice of peace, draw his similitudes from the mathematics; or a divine from a bawdy-house, or taverns; or a gentleman of Northamptonshire, Warwickshire, or the midland, should fetch all his illustrations to his country neighbors from shipping, and tell them of the main sheet, and the boulin.[24]

Taken as a whole, the list of examples registers a quite literal-minded concern for the actual setting in which a person's business lies, and which has occasioned his speech: no use talking of bowlines and mainsheets to people who live inland. The privy councillor's metaphor and the divine's also violate social and professional decorum: they are taken from places that such persons are not accustomed to frequent. The metonymic aspect of language, its attachment to particular speech situations and social settings, is the dimension that Jonson has chosen to emphasize here, and in his poems also. The discourse of Jonson's poems is urbane and sociable, whereas Donne's lyrics come across, by way of a different use of metaphor, as iconoclastic, elitist, and subversive.

Metonymy is everywhere you look in Jonson's epigrams, elegies, and verse epistles. What is most obviously gained from the figure, especially in his epigrams, is conciseness and pointedness:[25] a setting or a person's behavior is epitomized where a more detailed or circumstantial account might have been given. But metonymy is also, in Jonson's poems, a moral action taken by the poet: it is his principal means of asserting his authority as a moralist and social critic.[26] It is a device which conveys to us that he has not made anything up, or substituted anything else for the data given to him by his own experience, but has used his powers of discrimination to determine which of the "facts" at his disposal is truly noteworthy or significant. He is never just describing, but always discriminating or passing judgment, as he chooses a part to epitomize a larger whole.

In order, for example, to praise Sir Robert Wroth for preferring to make his home in the country, Jonson describes him as

> Free from proud porches, or their gilded roofs,
> 'Mongst lowing herds, and solid hoofs:[27]

Metonymies have here produced a highly condensed antithesis that uses the form of the couplet to advantage. They express the difference between country and city living in terms of the relationship that obtains, in either place, between the part and the whole, and by extension, between the place of residence and the one who lives there. A porch with a gilded roof is not essential to the townhouse it decorates or the livelihood of the house's owner, as hoofs are to Sir Robert's cattle and the cattle to Sir Robert himself. The choice of a part to represent the whole is itself a means of conveying that the city dweller is oppressed by the otiose structures his own pride has built, whereas the country dweller has his feet solidly planted on the ground.

"To Penshurst" begins with a similar use of contrastive epitomes, and here the difference between the two metonymies helps to establish a pretext for the detailed survey of the Sidneys' estate that is to come:

> Thou art not, Penshurst, built to envious show,
> Of touch,* or marble; nor canst boast a row
> Of polished pillars, or a roof of gold:
> Thou hast no lanthern, whereof tales are told;
> Or stair, or courts; but stand'st an ancient pile,
> And these grudged at, art reverenced the while.
> *touchstone

Thou joy'st in better marks, of soil, of air,
Of wood, of water: therein thou art fair.

(The Forest, no. 2)

The metonymy that expresses Penshurst's "fairness" highlights its intrinsic, natural endowments, but does not help us to visualize the house and grounds. The other kind of house, the kind that is "built to envious show," has been made much easier to visualize by the metonymic representation it is given. Penshurst must be more deeply explored and experienced to be fully appreciated—just what the poem will enable the reader to do.

A metonymy that is also a metaphor will deliver a positive or a negative judgment with even greater force than these metonymic epitomes do. Here, for example, is Jonson's admonition to himself to stop writing for the stage:

And since our dainty age
    Cannot endure reproof,
Make not thyself a page,
To that strumpet the stage,
    But sing high and aloof,
Safe from the wolf's black jaw, and the
            dull ass's hoof.[28]

The wolf's black jaw and the ass's hoof are metaphoric substitutions that not only distill the vicious stupidity of theater audiences but demote them on the scale of being. Jonson does not do this very often; usually, metaphor comes into play in his poems as a way to reinforce metonymic associations, like the one that obtains between "solid" Sir Robert Wroth and his livestock.

The extended apostrophe in "To Penshurst" is another good example of the use of metaphor to strengthen metonymy.[29] Throughout the poem, this device affords a pretext for giving to physical contiguity, the relation that obtains between a house and its environs and appurtenances, the character of a social relation. Penshurst's ponds "pay thee tribute fish"; "each bank doth yield thee conies," while the woods and copses "provide / The purpled pheasant with the speckled side." And Penshurst requites these tributes, like a bountiful landlord whose proprietorship is not begrudged because it is expressed as hospitality:

The blushing apricot, and woolly peach
Hang on thy walls, that every child may reach.

Here it is easy to see how Jonson's use of metaphor differs from Donne's. In "The Sun Rising," personification is also used to give physical contiguity the character of a social relation, but Donne takes much greater liberties with metaphor, so that his personification is far more obvious and domineering than Jonson's: the sun is an old fool, a "saucy pedantic wretch," and finally a dutiful servant of the sovereign lovers.

Jonson's epitaphs are an interesting special case of his use of metaphor to enhance metonymic associations. Most of them are inscriptions for tombstones, based on the traditional *Hic jacet* and the *Siste viator* formula that beckons passersby to pause and read. But Jonson's inscriptions often establish a personal relationship between the gravestone and the corpse underneath it. Here, for example, instead of the stiff, marmoreal remoteness of the traditional formulas we encounter socially viable speech acts that are decorously formal but simple and direct:

> Epitaph on Elizabeth, L.H.
>
> Wouldst thou hear, what man can say
> In a little? Reader, stay.
> Underneath this stone doth lie
> As much beauty, as could die:
> Which in life did harbour give
> To more virtue, than doth live.
> If, at all, she had a fault,
> Leave it buried in this vault.
> One name was Elizabeth,
> The other let it sleep with death:
> Fitter, where it died, to tell,
> Than that it lived at all. Farewell.
>
> (*Epigrams*, no. 124)

The difference between the inscription that does not appear and the words that do produces an effect of unconventional, even uncanny, intimacy. By refusing to give us all the usual information about the deceased, the gravestone seems actively to cherish and protect the remains entrusted to it. Another of Jonson's epitaphs is an acrostic poem whose lines have been generated from the letters of the dead woman's name:

> M   arble, weep, for thou dost cover
> A   dead beauty underneath thee,
> R   ich, as nature could bequeath thee:
> G   rant then, no rude hand remove her.
> A   ll the gazers on the skies
> R   ead not in fair heaven's story,
> E   xpresser truth, or truer glory,
> T   han they might in her bright eyes.

R   are, as wonder, was her wit;
A   nd like nectar ever flowing:
T   ill time, strong by her bestowing,
C   onquered hath both life and it.
L   ife, whose grief was out of fashion,
I   n these times. Few so have rued
F   ate, in a brother. To conclude,
F   or wit, feature, and true passion,
E   arth, thou hast not such another.

(*Epigrams*, no. 90)

Here it is as if the inscription itself had acquired an autonomous power of admonition. A marble headstone cannot really be expected to weep for the lady, nor the earth to appreciate her irreplaceable uniqueness, but at least the words of the inscription have given the name of Margaret Ratcliffe a certain limited power of continuing social life.

Proper-naming is a poetic device of considerable importance in Jonson's poetry, and in the *Epigrams* he makes the reader very much aware of it *as* a device. Edward Partridge points out, in his valuable study of the *Epigrams*, that "Jonson directly and deliberately refers to naming in at least thirty-five [of these] poems," and that it is one of his most frequent rhyme words.[30] He begins to call attention to the significance of names and naming in the prefatory dedication, where he explains the project of the volume as a whole.

TO THE GREAT EXAMPLE OF HONOR AND VIRTUE, THE MOST NOBLE WILLIAM, EARL OF PEMBROKE, LORD CHAMBERLAIN, ETC.

My lord. While you cannot change your merit, I dare not change your title: it was that made it, and not I. Under which name, I here offer to your lordship the ripest of my studies, my *Epigrams*. . . .

If, as he has reason to expect, the majority of his readers discover their own likeness in his satiric epigrams, and find it more convenient to accuse him of libel than to bring his criticisms home to themselves, he will need the protection of a man like Pembroke, who both is and has the reputation for being "constant to your own goodness":

In thanks whereof, I return you the honor of leading forth so many good, and great names (as my verses mention on the better part) to their remembrance with posterity.

The convention of dedicating a published volume of poetry to an influential member of the aristocracy was by now well established. By calling attention in this way to his own use of Pembroke's name, Jonson has turned that convention into a special device for announcing the somewhat unusual character of his own undertaking. Whereas traditionally the epigram had been a vehicle for satire, he means to use it also for encomiastic memorials to particular men and women.

Often he makes the proper name the central focus of the epigram. Early in the volume, in the epigram to his teacher, William Camden, he does this in a very literal way:

> Camden, most reverend head, to whom I owe
> All that I am in arts, all that I know,
> (How nothing's that?) to whom my country owes
> The great renown, and name wherewith she goes.
> Than thee the age sees not that thing more grave,
> More high, more holy, that she more would crave.
>
> (*Epigrams*, no. 14)

Not only is Camden's name the first word of the poem; it is also the headword of a long first sentence whose structure reinforces its message by performing an iconic imitation of the claim that it makes about Camden's importance. Although there is a period at line 4, the sentence is really six lines long. Camden's name, and the honorific epithet[31] that calls attention to its position in the sentence and the poem, is followed by parallel clauses that put under its aegis both the identity of the epigrammatist himself, as a man of letters, and that of the British nation: the "name wherewith she goes" is a reference to Camden's historical work, *Britannia*. The fifth and sixth lines use an awkward inversion of normal English word order to give precedence to the object-pronoun "thee," which continues the apostrophe to Camden, over the sentence subject, "the age" personified.

At the beginning of the seventh line, where Camden's virtues as a historian begin to be cited, the word "name" occurs for the second time in the poem: "What name, what skill, what faith hast thou in things!" This is a reference both to Camden's own reputation and to his power of authoritative naming.[32] What he has done for his country, this poem would do for him, even in the face of his characteristic personal modesty:

> Pardon free truth, and let thy modesty,
> Which conquers all, be once overcome by thee.
> Many of thine this better could, than I,
> But for their powers, accept my piety.

The poem's final couplet is strongly closural. All the important words in its first line are references to the encomiastic project, to Camden, and to the poet, who had referred to himself also in the very first line. The deictic pronoun "I" is rhymed with "piety," which defines his purpose and refers back through the poem to his very first act of verbal homage, the pious epithet in line one.[33] The relationship between the opening couplet, which derives "all that I am" from Camden, and the last, which asks him to accept "this" from "me" in return, renders the poem very highly self-focused. It is a verbal monument to Camden in the sense that it praises him, and also in the more literal sense that it sits on the page, a self-enclosed verbal icon, bearing his name at its "head."

The most conspicuous difference between the encomiastic and the satiric epigrams is that to designate the subjects of the satiric ones Jonson used metonymic type-classifications instead of proper names. His reason for doing this, ostensibly, is that he did not want to mock or shame anyone in particular, but to scourge the vice that is illustrated by a particular person's behavior. In the dedication he claims to have avoided not only proper names in these poems but "all particulars"—any piece of information that might serve as a clue to a proper name. Occasionally also, as Edward Partridge points out (pp. 191–92), he claims to be doing this to "kill" the name of a person who does not deserve a lasting memorial. But the difference between the two groups of epigrams is more than just a matter of our knowing or not knowing who the person actually was. It is a question of two very different ways of giving particulars.

The satiric epigrams are much more adherent to particular social contexts. Jonson achieves this, as we have seen, through metonymic description of the contemporary social scene, and also by a strategic use of questions, indirect quotation, deictic presupposal, and other devices for creating the impression that the epigrammatist has just met his target on the street, as in the case of "Sir Cod the Perfumed" ("That Cod can get no widow, yet a knight, I scent the cause. . . ."),[34] or is passing on a piece of current gossip (". . . he will not tarry / Longer a day, but with his Mill will marry");[35] or that he is giving us the background we need to be able to read the person's recent behavior correctly, as in the case of Captain Hazard, the Cheater—

> Touched with the sin of false play, in his punk,
> Hazard a month foreswore his; and grew drunk,
> Each night, to drown his cares: but when the gain
> Of what she had wrought came in, and waked his brain,
> Upon the account, hers grew the quicker trade.
> Since when he's sober again, and all play's made.
>
> (*Epigrams*, no. 87)

The encomiastic epigrams are not embedded in this way in current events. Insofar as they deal in behavior, the particulars they refer to are "facts"— by which Jonson usually means achievements, things made or done by the person he is praising—that have mattered to the nation as a whole: Camden's history of England, Mounteagle's exposure of the Gunpowder Plot, Sir Horace Vere's military performance in the Netherlands.

More often, however, the encomiastic epigrams make a more abstract claim: that the proper-named individual possesses certain virtues, which he or she has demonstrated not by any particular achievement, but just by the way he or she has characteristically behaved. That it is possible to describe a man or woman in terms of characteristic behavior is itself a kind of tribute: constancy to one's own goodness, the virtue that is attributed to the Earl of Pembroke in the dedication, is as important as any of the virtues in Jonson's moral lexicon. What gives most of these epigrams particular contexts is just the proper name itself, and this tends to be true even of the ones that commemorate particular achievements. Except for Mounteagle's name in its headnote, the epigram that offers to commemorate his patriotic "fact" makes no allusion whatsoever to the particulars of what he did to earn the honorific epithet "saver of my country." The encomium lifts him out of context, while its headnote enables the reader to put him back again.

Like personal pronouns and other deictic words, proper names help to locate a discourse in time and space, to signify that it has a particular context. They are even more strongly "indexical" than personal pronouns, because they are understood to have particular referents but no general meanings. Other words can be defined in terms of synonymous expressions that might be substituted for them; proper names cannot. They can only be defined in a circular way: a name "means" the person or animal or place whose name it is. Jakobson, in a paper on "duplex" structures in language, uses the name "Fido" to illustrate the difference between proper names and ordinary nouns:

> The appellative *pup* means a young dog, *mongrel* means a dog of mixed breed, *hound* is a dog used in hunting, while *Fido* means nothing more than a dog whose name is *Fido*. The general meaning of such words as *pup*, *mongrel*, or *hound*, could be indicated by abstractions like puppihood, mongrelness, or houndness, but the general meaning of *Fido* cannot be qualified in this way. To paraphrase Bertrand Russell, there are many dogs called *Fido*, but they do not share any property of "Fidoness."[36] (p.131)

Even though there are many dogs called Fido, each one's name seems to belong to him as an individual more than any other word or phrase we might use to refer to him, such as "the pup," or "my dog." This is an even more powerful impression where people are concerned, and people whose name is Smith or Jones—the human counterpart of Fido—will very often call them-selves, or their children, by a distinctive or unusual first name: Benjamin Franklin Smith, Perdita Jones. Precisely because it has no general meaning, because it signifies nothing about a person except that it is his or her name, the name becomes the sign of her or his distinctiveness: it is his own, her *proper* name.

In his encomiastic epigrams the proper names of Jonson's contemporaries give abstractions like honor, virtue, or constancy particular contemporary settings. The virtues an epigram attributes to Sir Ralph Shelton or Sir Henry Savile or Susan, Countess of Montgomery, become his or her personal "property," along with the name that designates him or her alone. At the same time, Jonson's avoidance of circumstantial descriptions of behavior in these poems and the high degree of self-focus or "closure" that he gives them have the effect of detaching their addressees or dedicatees from particular settings and circumstances. The project of these poems is to *illustrate* virtue, but not in the way the satiric epigrams illustrate vice, by depicting exemplary behavior: they illustrate virtue by rendering particular men and women "illustrious."

The epigram to Sir Horace Vere is an interesting case of this, because Jonson has turned his proper name into a metaphoric conceit by means of an interlingual pun. "Vere" sounds like "vir," which signifies "man" in Latin and is the root of the Latin *virtus*, virtue.[37] The poem uses this coincidence to suggest that Vere's name is proper to him not just in the usual sense but also in the sense that it signifies what the man himself is really like:

> Which of thy names I take, not only bears
> A Roman sound, but Roman virtue wears,
> Illustrious Vere, or Horace; fit to be
> Sung by a Horace, or a muse as free;
> Which thou art to thyself: . . .
>
> (*Epigrams*, no. 91)

His first name, as it happens, can be made to reinforce the pun because it is the name of a Latin poet who also wrote epigrams and was an exponent of "Roman virtue." "Bears a Roman sound" is both a literal reference to the interlingual pun and a metaphoric reference to the fame that Vere's charac-teristically *vir*tuous deeds have won for him. In this way, his name is made to signify not just "man of virtue" but something more like "true Roman." His virtue, the poem goes on to explain, consists not only in military prowess but also in the less ostentatious but equally "Roman" virtues of humanity and piety.[38] Jonson has enlisted the prestige of Latin, the language of Horace, to lift Sir Horace Vere out of context into an atemporal present of eternal fame, while at the same time his proper name, as it appears in the headnote, keeps him tied to England and the immediate present.

The reference to Horace is used not only to reinforce the Roman sound of "Vere" but also to suggest that Sir Horace's deeds are self-celebrating: he is his own "Horace." This is a version of the claim that Jonson makes in several of the epigrams, that he cannot add to the luster the name Cecil, or Overbury, or Sidney or Pembroke already has without any assistance from a poem of his. This claim is important for the collection as a whole, because it is an acknowledgment that a poet's authority to confer distinction upon a particular man or woman is not absolute or unlimited. It is based on the prestige that certain names already carry in the society to which he belongs, and appeals to a social consensus about the achievements and attributes—the "facts"—that properly merit distinction. It is important for a Cecil and an Overbury to bring their own reputations with them into the collection, to provide a gold standard, as it were, for the reputations Jonson coins himself. The distaste he expressed to Drummond for Donne's *Anniversaries* is consistent with his own unwillingness to be perceived as quixotic or politically subversive, either as satirist or as encomiast. The first of his encomiastic epigrams, the fourth poem in the collection, is addressed to King James, whom he credits with being the "best of poets" as well as "best of kings."

And yet, Donne's contention that the world is "crumbled out again to his atomies" is implicit in the way that the *Epigrams* single out particular, proper-named individuals for special distinction, in poems that are highly self-focused and "monumental." Drummond reports that Jonson had had the intention of writing "an epic poem entitled *Herologia*, of the worthies of his country, roused by fame."[39] He did not do this, and if the encomiastic lyrics are what he produced instead, it is possible to understand why. A *Herologia* would have to have demonstrated its heroes' worthiness by means of one collective national project, and it would have had to represent their society as a coherent whole. From the *Epigrams*, as Don Wayne points out, society emerges instead as an aggregation of self-sufficient monads.[40]

The impression that this was indeed how Jonson saw it is strengthened by the frequency with which he praises both men and women for possessing virtues that render them self-sufficient, self-centered in a positive way: integrity, chastity, constancy.[41] He invents for the ideal woman, whose name turns out to be Lucy, Countess of Bedford, "a manly soul . . . that should, with even powers, / The rock, the spindle, and the shears control / Of destiny, and spin her own free hours." "Be always to thy gathered self the same," he urges Sir Thomas Roe. As his friend William Roe departs for Europe, he counsels him to "extract and choose the best" of all that he experiences, "And those to turn to blood, and make thine own." In one of the satiric epigrams, he ridicules an "English Monsieur" who has done just the opposite, and turned himself into a walking dressmaker's dummy, by affecting the latest fashions of a country he has never visited. His "Farewell [to the World] for a Gentlewoman, Virtuous and Noble" concludes with her resolve not to seek abroad for "my peace,"

> As wanderers do, that still do roam,
> But make my strengths, such as they are,
> Here in my bosom, and at home.
>
> (*The Forest*, no. 4)

The capacity to dwell successfully at home is also the main theme of "To Penshurst," where the country house itself is represented to be a self-sufficient center that does not compete with the court, but is able to flourish independently, and to produce just as warm a welcome for Ben himself as for the king.

The conception of personal identity that is suggested by all of this is one that privileges the contiguity-relation: selfhood consists, apparently, in being firmly grounded and having one's own things around one. Jonson's stance was not eccentric or "absolutist,"[42] like Donne's, but the lyrics of both of them advocate a posture of self-centered individualism. As they brought metaphor back under the aegis of metonymy, they were both giving expression to a post-Elizabethan sense of political and social fragmentation.

Postscript: The Metaphysical Conceit

In chapter 6, the metaphysical conceit is explained as a strategy for transforming a poem's occasion in terms of its speaker's feelings. It is argued that in order for the transformation to be maximally impressive, the poem's occasion needs to be pretty fully realized by means of deictic presupposal and other metonymic strategies. But there is more than this to be said about the way that metonymy comes to the aid of metaphor in Donne's conceits. I propose now to look more closely at how they are constructed, as a final demonstration of the usefulness of Jakobson's linguistic model for the analysis of poetic figuration.

In terms of the linguistic and cultural code, the "metaphysical conceit" is a highly aberrant substitution which, in order to be intelligible, stands very much in need of syntagmatic and situational compensation. The lover's situation needs to be well realized not only to challenge his metaphoric ingenuity to the fullest but also to ensure that his metaphors will be intelligible to the poem's readers. A brief digression to explain how metaphor works, and how it is that we find metaphors intelligible, will be needed to make this clear.

"Metaphor," as Jakobson explains in "Quest for the Essence of Language," "is the assignment of a *signans* to a secondary *signatum* associated by similarity . . . with the primary *signatum*."[1] For example the word "star," in its primary or proper meaning, refers to a celestial body, but in certain contexts this word is also used of a person. In such cases of transferred or figurative usage, there are conspicuous differences between the primary and the secondary *signatum*—differences in terms of fundamental semantic categories, like human/nonhuman. Because of these differences, we are forced, in the given context, to resort to marginal or secondary features of the *signans*—"shining," and perhaps also "high above," in the case of "star"—and to recognize that they are what it is being used to signify. In this connection Jakobson elsewhere cites Leonard Bloomfield's distinction between central or general meaning and contextual meaning: we will understand a word in its central meaning unless "the practical situation forces us to look to a transferred meaning."[2] A poem does not have a practical situation in the same way that a conversation does. In a poem, what will force us to look to a transferred meaning is the explicit verbal context of the word in question, the other words it appears in combination with: "When I died last, and, Dear, I die / As often as from thee I go."

Because the semantic features it enlists are peripheral, a metaphor always requires interpretation, and it may not be easy to interpret. Aristotle, remarks David Lodge, "acutely described metaphor as 'midway between the unintelligible and the commonplace.' "[3] The metaphoric application of "star" is commonplace enough to be found in the dictionary along with its primary or proper meaning, but if the metaphoric usage is more extraordinary, as it often is in poems, the risk of unintelligibility is greater. To interpret a poem's metaphors we may need to have recourse not just to what the speaker explicitly says but also to the motive for his saying it that we can infer from the poem as a whole.

> Oh stay, three lives in one flea spare,
> Where we almost, nay more than married are:

> I should have been a pair of ragged claws
> Scuttling across the floors of silent seas.

> The dice of drowned men's bones he saw bequeath
> An embassy.

In the first of these examples, the outlandish metaphor is motivated by the speaker's project of seduction. In the second, from Eliot's "Love Song of J. Alfred Prufrock," its motivating context is an unusual subjective state: Prufrock's metaphor expresses a painful acknowledgment of his own impotence to speak about his feelings to another person. But the third instance of metaphor, from Hart Crane's poem "At Melville's Tomb," is more difficult to interpret, because the speaker's motive or project cannot be inferred from its context.

In *The Modes of Modern Writing*, David Lodge explains that modernist poets like Hart Crane and T. S. Eliot coined unusual metaphors in order to challenge common sense and tamper with objective reality, on behalf of the achronic, alogical workings of the unconscious.[4] Their metaphors were disorienting and difficult, and they seemed to many readers to push metaphor too far toward unintelligibility. In a famous exchange between Hart Crane and Harriet Monroe that was published in *Poetry* magazine in 1926, Monroe professed herself unable to decipher metaphoric statements like "The dice of drowned men's bones he saw bequeath an embassy." In reply, Crane glossed his own metaphors. Dice bequeath an embassy, he explained, insofar as they have been "ground . . . in little cubes from the bones of drowned men by the action of the sea, and . . . finally thrown up on the sand. . . . These being the bones of dead men who never completed their voyage, it seems legitimate to refer to them as the only surviving evidence of certain messages undelivered. . . . Dice as a symbol of chance and circumstance is also implied." Monroe responded tartly that Crane's explanation did not justify or improve his poem, whose metaphors ought to have been intelligible without it, whereas they were not, even for "the most sympathetic reader." Crane put his finger on a different but related problem by admitting that he "may well have neglected to supply the necessary emotional connectives to the content featured."[5]

Donne's conceits are no less unusual than Crane's, but they are not in the same way obscure and disorienting, because he does always explicate them in the poem and/or supply the "necessary emotional connectives" to render them intelligible. The paradigmatic aberration is always well compensated syntagmatically, or well motivated by the poem's occasion, or both. In "The Flea," for example, the conceit that was quoted above is not only well motivated by the speaker's project, it is also given a highly redundant explication:

> Oh stay, three lives in one flea spare,
> Where we almost, nay more than married are:
> This flea is you and I, and this
> Our marriage bed, and marriage temple is;
> Though parents grudge, and you, we're met
> And cloister'd in these living walls of jet.
> Though use make you apt to kill me,
> Let not to that, self-murder added be,
> And sacrilege, three sins in killing three.

In its first, most condensed statement, the substitution of "lives" for "blood" and "married" for "flea-bitten" might well be unintelligible to most readers. But in view of the poem's occasion, it makes sense for the speaker to shock and puzzle his addressee a little bit, and then the third and fourth lines reiterate the conceit, in the form of an explicit equation. There follows a periphrastic restatement, which recasts each of the metaphors more vividly and takes in more of the situational context in concessive clauses. The series of moves will be more obvious if we disentangle the murder/sacrilege conceit from the marriage conceit and lay out their respective arguments one by one:

1. . . . three lives in one flea spare   (simple substitution)
2. This flea is you and I   (equation)
3. Though use make you apt to kill me,   (periphrastic
   Let not to that, self-murder added be,   restatement)
   And sacrilege, three sins in killing three.

1. Where we almost, nay more than married are   (simple substitution)
2.   . . . and this   (equation)
   Our marriage bed, and marriage temple is;
3. Though parents grudge, and you, we're met   (periphrastic
   And cloister'd in these living walls of jet.   restatement)

Repetition and elaboration do not serve to validate the metaphor as a description of reality, although the speaker pretends to be trying to do this. What they do is expand the situational and syntagmatic context of the bizarre substitutions, motivating them and giving them several chances to "take."

It is in general the case that whereas Donne's speakers seem to be justifying their metaphoric claims discursively, this is a facade of pseudo-reasoning. Often the conceit will take the form of an analogy or comparison, forms we ordinarily use to assert that A resembles B in x, y, z respects, or that they are structurally alike. But in Donne's analogies, common properties will be adduced between some A and some B on the strength of a metaphorical twist or play on words. The famous compasses conceit from "A Valediction: forbidding mourning" is a good case in point:

> If [our two souls] be two, they are two so   25
> As stiff twin compasses are two:
> Thy soul, the fix'd foot, makes no show
> To move, but doth, if the other do;
>
> And though it in the center sit,
> Yet when the other far doth roam,
> It leans, and hearkens after it,
> And grows erect, as that comes home.   32
>
> Such wilt thou be to me, who must,
> Like the other foot, obliquely run:

> Thy firmness makes my circle just,
> And makes me end where I begun.   36

By framing the metaphor as an analogy, Donne is able to make the metaphoric equation explicit, and to reiterate it several times. But his "proof" that souls and compasses are in the same way two-in-one would not be acceptable as a piece of scientific or philosophical reasoning. Souls do not "move" in the same sense that the legs of a compass do: the argument exploits this verb's flexibility between two different fields of discourse, physics and metaphysics. He describes the action of "our two souls" with verbs that are metaphorical with reference to compasses ("roam," "leans," "hearkens after," "comes home") but literally appropriate for human beings who are about to be separated, or else literal with respect to compasses ("grows erect") and metaphoric with reference to souls. Then as the focus shifts from "thou" to "me" in the last stanza, the metaphoric vehicle is taken hold of differently. "Thy" role having been depicted in terms of the opening and closing of the compasses, "mine" is depicted in terms of the tracing of a circle. Syntagmatic parallelism between the two stanzas creates the impression that to "end where I begun" is equivalent to coming home—coming back, that is, to where "I" am right now, within talking distance of "thee." But in terms of the compass metaphor, ending where I begun is not equivalent to coming home: the moving foot must remain at a fixed distance away from the fixed foot to draw the circle "just." In a lot of the writing that has been done about this poem, this shift to a different version of the compass metaphor has been registered as disconcerting or disappointing.[6] The problem is that the facade of dispassionate ratiocination makes it seem that an analogy is being made good, correspondence by correspondence, through three consecutive stanzas, but what we really have are two different metaphors, opportunistically conflated, for the lovers' mutual soul-action.

Compensation for the disparity between the terms of the metaphysical conceit takes several forms in Donne's poetry: explicit mention of both terms; reiteration in slightly different terms or from a different point of view; elaboration that incorporates more information about the circumstances that have motivated the speaker to invent it. All three are exemplified by the first stanza of "A Valediction: of weeping":

> Let me pour forth
> My tears before thy face, whilst I stay here,
> For thy face coins them, and thy stamp they bear,
> And by this mintage they are something worth,
> For thus they be
> Pregnant of thee;

The first two lines contain no metaphor except "pour," which is virtually a dead one. The startling conceit is initiated in line 3, and by that time we have inferred the situation that gives rise to it: lovers are about to be separated; he wants to make something very special of the occasion. Tears become coins in a sentence that presents both tenor ("my tears," "thy face") and vehicle ("coins," "stamp," "mintage") explicitly. The same conceit is twice repeated in line 3, restatement ensuring its intelligibility by making its context easier to visualize—we need to be clear that he is talking about the reflection of her face in his tear. Then a longer sentence reiterates the conceit once more, and also confirms the inference we had probably drawn already from the first two lines of the stanza—that the speaker is using this elaborate talk about tears to express to the lady how much he cares for her.

In the last part of the stanza, he uses different metaphors, still grounded in the notion that his tears reflect her face, to extend his perspective on their situation backward and forward in time:

> Fruits of much grief they are, emblems of more,
> When a tear falls, that thou falls which it bore,
> So thou and I are nothing then, when on a diverse shore.

Time-deixis is incorporated into the conceits themselves: "fruits of much grief" is retrospective, "emblems of more" proleptic. The last two lines, which explain what he means by "emblems of more," do two other things as well: they help to specify the context of his utterance more fully for the reader (the speaker is about to take a sea voyage); and they express the fear that has motivated the whole overingenious performance—the fear that their relationship will not survive this separation.

As a rhetorical strategy on behalf of the one who says "I" in Donne's lyrics, the metaphysical conceit uses metaphor to transform or transcend the context in which he finds himself. As a verbal structure within poetic discourse, it is a highly aberrant substitution that is very well compensated by metonymic devices. Because it is either very well grounded in a social situation or very well explicated by the poetic discourse, or both, the impression it creates is not of subjectivity, like modernist conceits, but of iconoclasm.

Notes

INTRODUCTION

1. In making a distinction between the "courtly" and the "popular" literature of the sixteenth century, G. K. Hunter attributes to courtly writers "the supposition that literature is a kind of courtship display of general secular capacity." (*John Lyly: The Humanist as Courtier* [London: Routledge, 1962], p. 33.) All the poetry I include in this study was written out of such a supposition. Shakespeare is a special case in relation to Hunter's courtly-popular distinction: whereas his plays are "popular," his sonnets and epyllions are courtly. From this it may be seen that the category designates not just the social status of the writer in question but a certain notion of what literature is, or is for.

2. C. S. Lewis coined the epithets "Drab" and "Golden" for the volume he contributed to the Oxford History of English Literature: *English Literature in the Sixteenth Century* (Oxford: Clarendon, 1954). He repeatedly asserted that he did not mean for these terms to have eulogistic/dyslogistic implications, but only to convey that the shift from Drab to Golden, in both poetry and prose, was a shift from simple, plain, temperate writing to rich, colorful, gorgeous writing, accompanied by a shift in attitude toward fiction-making such that the Golden poets celebrated the poet's prerogative to produce, not a realistic account of things as they are but what Sidney called "golden worlds." Lewis asserted that although there was "a great change in power (a change from worse to better)" as we move from the Drab into the Golden period (p. 323), this was *not* a function of the shift in stance and style. The poetry got better because by 1580 "men [had] at last learned how to write" (p. 65) in a vernacular medium whose pronunciation and stress patterns had only recently stabilized.

In an influential review of Lewis's book, which first appeared in the *Hudson Review* and was reprinted in *The Function of Criticism* in 1957, Yvor Winters accused Lewis of refusing to admit that he simply (and as far as Winters was concerned, perversely) preferred the flowery unreal landscapes and artificial rhetoric of Sidney and Spenser and their imitators over the kind of poetry the Drab poets had been writing—poetry that speaks directly and unostentatiously about matters of abiding human concern.

I would propose a different reason for Lewis's having resorted to epithets whose connotations he then backed away from. He saw that from one generation of writers to the next there had been an increase in quantity and an improvement in the quality of certain kinds of writing—the sonnet, for example, and pastoral. But he could not argue that it was directly related to the collective shift in attitude toward language and fiction-making, because he lacked a stylistic theory that could produce the relation between stance, style, and "power" in different kinds of writing.

3. For purposes of quotation from this essay, I have used Jakobson's *Selected Writings*, II (The Hague: Mouton, 1971), where it appears on pp. 239-59.

4. Jakobson indicates briefly in the "aphasia" essay how the metaphor-metonymy distinction might be applied to film or dream analysis, but does not himself elaborate these applications. Jacques Lacan, whose rereading of Freud has had an enormous impact on the psychoanalytic community in France, but in North America has been of interest primarily to literary theorists, makes a different correlation between Jakobson's two poles and the key terms of Freudian semiotics, as Anthony Wilden points out in *System and Structure: Essays in Communication and Exchange* (London: Tavistock, 1972; rev. 1980). (See also Malcolm Bowie, "Jacques Lacan," in *Structuralism and Since*, ed. John Sturrock (Oxford: Oxford University, 1981), pp. 116-53.) The difference between Lacan's version of Freudian semiotics and Jakobson's comes down to a decision as to which of several key terms in Freud is the privileged or fundamental pair: Jakobson classes "condensation" and "displacement" together in opposition to "identification"; for Lacan the crucial opposition is condensation versus displacement. Neither way of construing Freud's terms is simply mistaken, because condensation, the oneiric equivalent of synecdoche, is a metaphoric metonymy. For the application of Jakobson's categories to film studies, see Christian Metz, *Le signifiant imaginaire: Psychanalyse et cinéma* (Paris: Union générale d'Éditions, 1977). For classic instances of its application to literary studies, see Roland Barthes, *Elements of Semiology* (Paris: Seuil, 1964; trans. London: Cape Editions, 1967), and Gerard Genette, "Metonymie chez Proust," *Figures* III (Paris: Seuil, 1972).

5. It has also been criticized, deconstructed, and corrected, but so far Jakobson's model has held up very well against assailants and would-be revisionists. Martin Joos, in his 1957 review of the aphasia monograph in the journal *Language* (vol. 33, Part III, pp. 408-15), was the first to object that the bipolar model encourages us to overlook literary devices that combine metonymy and metaphor. Elmar Holenstein, who has written extensively about Jakobson, has argued that the opposition is not really symmetrical, phenomenologically, and other critics have agreed with him: see note 7 below. These are telling objections, but the model is coherent enough to withstand the second and, if carefully applied, to avoid the pitfalls foreseen in the first. The deconstructive approach taken by Paul de Man and Jonathan Culler has raised objections similar to these, but not so straightforwardly. Both de Man, in *Allegories of Reading* (New Haven: Yale, 1979), and Culler, in "The Turns of Metaphor" (*The Pursuit of Signs*, chapter 10 [Ithaca: Cornell, 1981]), introduce working definitions of metonymy that are slightly different from Jakobson's, and then argue on the strength of them that Jakobson's model is asymmetrical (Culler) or self-subverting (de Man). Hayden White, in *Metahistory* (Baltimore: Johns Hopkins, 1973), argues that although Jakobson's model has proven "fruitful . . . for the analysis of *linguistic* phenomena, . . . its use as a framework for characterizing *literary* styles is . . . limited" (p. 32). For his ideological analysis of nineteenth-century historical writing, White adopted a fourfold tropology for which he claims the sanction of "both traditional poetics and modern language theory." But although he cites Peter Ramus, Giambattista Vico, and Kenneth Burke as proponents of a fourfold classification (metaphor, metonymy, irony, synecdoche), he does not propose or invoke a systematic theory of

language to back it up—assuming that he did not mean to propose Vico's history of human cognitive development as a serious alternative to Prague School Linguistics. And his few remarks about Jakobson's model show that he did not understand how to use it to generate stylistic profiles: he seems to have assumed, for example, that metaphor and metonymy are mutually exclusive.

For a comprehensive bibliography up to 1984 of studies that "develop, define, or challenge" Jakobson's theory, see Willard Bohn, "Roman Jakobson's Theory of Metaphor and Metonymy: An Annotated Bibliography," *Style*, 18 (1984), 534–50.

6. *Style in Language*, ed. Thomas A. Sebeok (Cambridge, Mass.: MIT, 1960), pp. 350–77; *Selected Writings*, III (The Hague: Mouton, 1981), pp. 18–51.

7. It is certainly not obvious that co-occurrence in a sentence and co-presence in a situation are in the same sense instances of "contiguity" or of "combination." Alexander Gelley has argued (*NLH*, 11 [1980], 469–87) that Jakobson's model cannot be systematically applied, because syntactic and "phenomenal" contiguity are not really analogous. This was Holenstein's objection also (see, for example, "A New Essay Concerning the Basic Relations of Language," *Semiotica*, 12 [1974], 97–128). But Jakobson is entitled to suppose that they are analogous, on the strength of two related axioms of semiotic theory: (1) "Phenomenal" contiguity is linguistically mediated: situations are given to experience by language, and phenomenal contiguities are presupposed by formal syntactic contiguities, as of subject and verb, etc. (2) Language is a hierarchy of levels, and as we move up from the lowest (that of the bundles of distinctive features which constitute phonemes) to the highest (discourse units larger than the sentence) there is ever greater freedom of combination within the parameters of encoded usage; but this freedom never does become absolute. Surrealism calls our attention to this by producing ungrammaticalities at the level of the "situation." For a brief defense of Jakobson's "binarism," see Linda R. Waugh, *Roman Jakobson's Science of Language* (Lisse: Peter de Ridder, 1976), pp. 65–66.

8. "Shifters, Verbal Categories, and the Russian Verb" (Russian Language Project, Harvard University, 1957), *Selected Writings*, II, pp. 130–47. See also "Quest for the Essence of Language," *Diogenes*, 51 (Fall 1965), 21–37, and *Selected Writings*, II, pp. 345–59.

9. For further explanation of how, according to Jakobson, metaphor works and how it is that we find metaphors intelligible, see the "Postscript" to this volume.

10. *The Modes of Modern Writing: Metaphor, Metonymy, and the Typology of Modern Literature* (Ithaca: Cornell, 1977), chapter 6.

11. Cf. also Jonathan Culler, *The Pursuit of Signs*, p. 60: "a metaphorical world is separate but analogous, a member of a paradigm of conceivable worlds, while a metonymical world is contiguous with or part of our own, unexplored but governed by the same laws."

12. The theoretical orientation of "Linguistics and Poetics" is different from that of the aphasia paper, and its system of six linguistic functions cannot be directly correlated with the bipolar model elaborated there. But they are compatible: when he comes to define the poetic function in particular, Jakobson has recourse to the Saussurean dichotomy from which the earlier model is derived.

13. Jakobson approvingly cites William Empson, who insisted in *Seven Types of Ambiguity* (Norfolk, Conn.: New Directions, 1930; rev. 1947, 1953) on the polysemous character of poetic language. Empson did not offer any theoretical explanation of how "ambiguity" comes about in poems; his claim rests instead on the sheer quantity of instances he can persuade us to count as ambiguous in terms of one of his seven types.

14. Jonathan Culler used this poem to illustrate the interpretive conventions of "unity" and "significance" in *Structuralist Poetics* (Ithaca: Cornell, 1975). For both his purposes and mine it is useful because of being a notorious case of "the non-poem as poem."

15. *Idea*, sonnet 61, quoted from *Renaissance Poetry*, ed. John Williams (New York: Doubleday, 1963; repr. Norton, 1974), p. 219.

16. The most influential proponent of approaching Renaissance poetry by way of these poets' own training in logic and rhetoric was the late Rosemond Tuve. *Elizabethan and Metaphysical Imagery*, which was published just after World War II, was important in the 1950s and 1960s for American students not just of Renaissance poetry but of lyric poetry in general, because it exposed us to a science of language that was more sophisticated than the training our own "discipline" of literary studies had given us. Meanwhile, however, the new sciences of linguistics and semiotics were developing conceptual frameworks of comparable sophistication and greater coherence.

17. "What is Poetry?" *Selected Writings*, II, pp. 749-50. "What we have been trying to show," Jakobson continues, "is that art is an integral part of the social structure, a component that interacts with all the others and is itself mutable since both the domain of art and its relationship to the other constituents of the social structure are in constant dialectical flux." Jakobson echoes here an important essay of Tynjanov, "The Literary Fact," which was published in the Russian journal *Lef* in 1925. Ejxenbaum, in an essay that approvingly cites this same piece of Tynjanov's, makes it clear that the Formalists' early pronouncement about the autonomy of art had been made in reaction to the prevailing tradition of biographical-genetic studies, and also to "vulgar Marxist" attempts to posit direct, one-way causal links between economic and aesthetic developments. (Cf. Ejxenbaum, "Literary Environment," in *Readings in Russian Poetics: Formalist and Structuralist Views* [Cambridge, Mass.: MIT Press, 1971]. Cf. also Tynjanov, "On Literary Evolution," in the same volume.)

18. *Working With Structuralism: Essays and Reviews of Nineteenth- and Twentieth-Century Literature* (Boston: Routledge, 1981), p. 74.

CHAPTER 2

1. "Place and Patronage in Elizabethan Politics," in *Elizabethan Government and Society: Essays Presented to Sir John Neale*, ed. Bindoff, Hurstfield, and Williams (London: Athlone, 1961), p. 95. Cf. also Lawrence Stone, *The Crisis of the Aristocracy, 1558-1641* (Oxford: Clarendon, 1965), pp. 704ff.

2. *Tottel's Miscellany (1557-1587)*, ed. H. E. Rollins (Cambridge, Mass.: Harvard, 1928), I, 2: "The Printer to the Reader."

3. *Leicester, Patron of Letters* (New York: Columbia, 1955), p. 7. Cf. also Jan Van Dorsten, "Literary Patronage in England: The Early Phase," in *Patronage in the Renaissance*, ed. G. F. Lytle and Stephen Orgel (Princeton: Princeton University, 1981), pp. 191-206.

4. *The Posies of George Gascoigne, Esquire, corrected, perfected, and augmented by the Authour, 1575*, ed. J. W. Cunliffe (Cambridge: Cambridge University, 1907), pp. 3-14.

5. Ruth Luborsky's study of the work's elaborate editorial apparatus in "The Allusive Presentation of *The Shepheardes Calender*," *Spenser Studies*, 1 (1980), 29-67,

confirms that with this work Spenser and his friends were self-consciously ushering in the golden age of Elizabethan literature. In the same volume of *Spenser Studies*, Bruce R. Smith gives a succinct account of the reader-expectations that must have been fostered by E.K.'s introductory matter ("On Reading *The Shepheardes Calender*," pp. 85–86). The difference between this sort of apparatus, which calls attention to the poems' artfulness and to their place in an international poetic canon, and the editorial apparatus of *A Hundreth Sundry Flowers*, the first edition of Gascoigne's collected poems, is symptomatic of the shift from a metonymic to a metaphoric orientation for the lyric: the mid-century volume is also quite elaborately framed, but the purpose of its editorial apparatus is to assimilate the poems to particular social occasions. I will look more closely at this editorial strategy in chapter 4.

6. *The Posies*, p. 11.

7. *The Poetical Works of Edmund Spenser*, ed. J. C. Smith and E. de Selincourt (Oxford: Oxford University, 1912), p. 69.

8. *Miscellaneous Prose of Sir Philip Sidney*, ed. Katherine Duncan-Jones and Jan Van Dorsten (Oxford: Clarendon, 1973), p. 79.

9. Gladys Doidge Willcock and Alice Walker, editors of the Cambridge edition of *The Arte of English Poesie* (Cambridge University, 1936), have argued persuasively that although this work was published in 1589, much of it was actually written as early as 1569.

10. "Of Gentlemen and Shepherds: The Politics of Elizabethan Pastoral Form," *ELH*, 50 (1983), 435.

11. *Poetry and Courtliness in Renaissance England* (Princeton: Princeton University, 1978), pp. 51–52.

12. This is G. K. Hunter's term for mid-century poets like Gascoigne, Googe, and Turberville, who published editions of their own poems in apparent emulation of *Tottel's Miscellany*. See "Drab and Golden Poetry of the English Renaissance," in *Forms of Lyric*, ed. Reuben Brower (New York: Columbia, 1970). I am indebted here also to Hunter's notion of "aesthetic autonomy" as the hallmark of the lyric in the 1580s and 1590s.

13. Elaboration of this difference between mid-Tudor and Elizabethan poetics is the main business of chapter 5.

14. In chapter 6, differences in what I am here calling "erotic ideology" between the Tudor poets and the Elizabethans, and then also the shift that Donne makes in his secular lyrics, will be more fully demonstrated through close analysis of a series of lyric poems. Here my purpose is to sketch the bigger picture, both in political and in literary terms.

15. The classic study of Elizabeth's symbolic names is E. C. Wilson, *England's Eliza* (Cambridge, Mass.: Harvard, 1939).

16. *The Cult of Elizabeth: Elizabethan Portraiture and Pageantry* (London: Thames and Hudson, 1977). Cf. also John Phillips, *The Reformation of Images: Destruction of Art in England, 1535–1660* (Berkeley: University of California, 1973), p. 121.

17. *Astraea: The Imperial Theme in the Sixteenth Century* (Boston: Routledge, 1975), Part II, chapter 3: "The Triumph of Chastity."

18. *The Poems of Sir Walter Ralegh*, ed. Agnes M. C. Latham (Boston: Houghton Mifflin, 1929), p. 30. Cited by E. C. Wilson, pp. 239–40.

19. Cf. Strong, pp. 126–27; also Yates, *Astraea*, Part II ("The Tudor Imperial Reform"), and Edwin Greenlaw, *Studies in Spenser's Historical Allegory* (Baltimore: Johns Hopkins, 1932).

20. *Hemetes the Hermit* was performed at Woodstock in 1575; *The Lady of May* was

staged in 1578 or 1579, on Leicester's estate at Wanstead. See Wilson, p. 127; also *Miscellaneous Prose of Sir Philip Sidney*, intro. p. 13.

21. " 'Eliza, Queene of Shepheardes,' and the Pastoral of Power," *ELR*, 10 (1980), 164.

22. Cf. *Poetical Works*, p. 467: "Loe I have made a Calender for every yeare." The status of "total metaphor" or human microcosm is partly induced by the complete cycle of the months, and partly by the way in which the eclogues afford a schematic conspectus of human situations: solitary complaint; two-person moral debate; and "recreative" activities that involve the whole community.

Barnabe Googe, a mid-Tudor poet who will figure in chapter 4, wrote a set of pastoral eclogues (published 1563) that do *not* give shepherdhood the status of total metaphor in this way: Googe's shepherds belong to the contemporary real world, and suffer accordingly from the upheavals referred to above, which they comment upon with metonymic generalizations like "Nobility begins to fade, / And Carters up do spring."

23. In *The Making of the Tudor Despotism* (London: Nelson, 1928), the historian Charles Williams argued that "despotism" is the most appropriate term for Tudor government, even though it had some of the forms of constitutional monarchy.

24. Montrose, " 'Eliza, Queene of Shepheardes,' " p. 155.

25. FQ VII ("The Cantos of Mutabilitie"), *Poetical Works*, p. 406.

26. Cf. "A Letter of the Authors, Expounding his whole intention . . . To . . . Sir Walter Raleigh," *Poetical Works*, p. 407.

27. *The Countess of Pembroke's Arcadia*, ed. Albert Feuillerat (Cambridge: Cambridge University, 1912; repr. 1962), p. 179.

28. "Sir Walter Ralegh and the Literature of Clientage," *Patronage in the Renaissance*, pp. 165–87. Cf. also *England's Eliza*, p. 230ff.

29. Ralegh's "21st and Last Book of the Ocean to Cynthia" is a particularly interesting example of the metaphoric way of Elizabethan courtiership because it was a love poem addressed to the queen herself by a courtier whose livelihood depended on her favor. This poem's rhetorical strategy will be closely examined in chapter 6.

30. Malcolm Smuts explains, in "The Political Failure of Tudor Cultural Patronage" (*Patronage in the Renaissance*, pp. 165–87), that whereas Elizabethan state pageantry was rooted in "indigenous, half-medieval traditions," the Stuart court became more closely tied to the continent, and developed "a culture of monarchy rooted in the literature of Augustan Rome." Cf. also Norman Council, "Ben Jonson, Inigo Jones, and the Transformation of Tudor Chivalry," *ELH*, 47 (1980), 259–75.

31. *The First Anniversary: An Anatomy of the World*, in *John Donne: The Epithalamions, Anniversaries, and Epicedes*, ed. W. Milgate (Oxford: Clarendon, 1978), 11.215–38.

32. *The Breaking of the Circle* (Evanston, Ill.: Northwestern, 1950), p. 74ff.

33. For this exchange, see Milgate's introduction to *The Epithalamions, Anniversaries, and Epicedes*, xl.

34. I will look more closely at the rhetoric of Donne's *Anniversaries*, as a strategy for deconstructing the "Elizabethan World Picture," in chapter 6.

CHAPTER 3

1. Cf. Emile Benveniste, *Problèmes de Linguistique Générale* (Paris: Gallimard, 1966), trans. Mary Elizabeth Meek (Florida: University of Miami, 1971), pp. 219–20: "Lan-

guage has solved [the problem of intersubjective communication] by creating an ensemble of 'empty' signs that are nonreferential with respect to 'reality.' These signs are always available and become 'full' as soon as a speaker introduces them into each instance of his discourse. . . . Their role is to provide the instrument of a conversion that one could call the conversion of language into discourse."

2. In addition to two chapters in Benveniste's *Problèmes de Linguistique Générale*, the following three studies are the best, and almost the only, extended discussions of deixis as a topic in linguistics: Roman Jakobson, "Shifters, Verbal Categories, and the Russian Verb" (Harvard Russian Language Project, 1957), *Selected Writings*, II, 130–47. Charles Fillmore, *Santa Cruz Lectures on Deixis 1971* (Bloomington: Indiana University Linguistics Club, 1975); and Yehoshua Bar-Hillel, "Indexical Expressions," *Mind*, n.s. 63 (1954), 359–79.

3. *Structuralist Poetics: Structuralism, Linguistics and the Study of Literature* (London: Routledge, 1975), p. 165.

4. For this poem of Donne's I have used Theodore Redpath's second edition of *The Songs and Sonets* (New York: St. Martin's, 1984).

5. *Poetic Closure: A Study of How Poems End* (Chicago: University of Chicago, 1968), p. 15.

6. *A Glossary of Literary Terms*, 4th ed. (New York: Holt, Rinehart, Winston, 1981), p. 99.

7. This poem is ascribed to Ralegh in several Renaissance manuscripts, but their compilers probably got it from a printed collection where it was published anonymously. Ascription is a notoriously difficult problem where Ralegh is concerned, as Agnes Latham explains in her Textual Introduction to *The Poems of Sir Walter Ralegh* (Boston: Houghton Mifflin, 1929; repr. Cambridge: Harvard, 1951; 1985). In that edition, this is poem 15.

8. This is Jakobson's phrase from "Linguistics and Poetics," *Style in Language*, ed. Thomas A. Sebeok (Cambridge, Mass.: MIT, 1960), pp. 350–77.

9. Southall, *The Courtly Maker: An Essay on the Poetry of Wyatt and His Contemporaries* (New York: Barnes & Noble, 1964), p. 1.

10. The canon of Wyatt's poetry is notoriously problematic: R. A. Rebholz, editor of the Yale edition of *The Complete Poems* (New Haven, 1978), remarks in his Preface (p. 10) that modern editors and critics have tended to ascribe to Wyatt "every poem they like from the period." As I generalize about Wyatt's stylistic habits, I am no doubt guilty of this tendency myself; but all of my examples are chosen from among the poems that are "certainly" or "almost certainly" Wyatt's according to all modern editors.

11. For all quotations I have used Joost Daalder's edition of Wyatt's *Collected Poems* (London: Oxford, 1975). "It may be good" is poem 21, from the Egerton Manuscript. In the third line of the second stanza I have restored "hase" for Daalder's emendation to "has," to keep the possibility open that Wyatt's original word meant "hazard." That is John Williams's conjecture in his anthology, *English Renaissance Poetry* (New York: Doubleday, 1963), and Rebholz prefers it also to the "has" emendation.

12. *Tottel's Miscellany (1557–1587)*, ed. Hyder Edward Rollins (Cambridge, Mass.: Harvard University, 1928–29), I, 41.

13. *Petrarch's Lyric Poems*, trans. Robert Durling (Cambridge, Mass.: Harvard, 1976).

14. *The Courtly Maker*, pp. 43–44.

15. Stevens, *Music and Poetry in the Early Tudor Court* (London: Methuen, 1961), p. 208.

16. *Tottel's Miscellany*, p. 41.

17. In the Facsimile Reproduction of *Epitaphes, Epigrams, Songs and Sonnets (1567)*, intro. Richard J. Panofsky (Delmar, N.Y.: Scholars' Reprints, 1977), this poem appears on pp. 230–32 [101–3 in the 1567 edition].

18. I disagree, obviously, with the majority view that for twentieth-century readers Wyatt's poetry is irrecoverably obscure because of our distance from the world in which he composed and performed it. The most extreme statement of this view is Alastair Fowler's "Obscurity of Sentiment in the Poetry of Wyatt," in *Conceitful Thought: The Interpretation of English Renaissance Poems* (Edinburgh: Edinburgh University, 1975).

19. Another poem that is apt to strike us as Donne-like—partly because of the speaker's truculent colloquialism and partly because he is lying in bed as he speaks, like the lover in "The Sun Rising"—is Wyatt's often-anthologized "May Day" sonnet, "You that in love find luck and abundance" (Egerton, 92). But in Wyatt's poem there are no windows or curtains, no bed partner, no "unruly sun." The physical setting is no more than a strategic vantage point from which to refuse to join in any of the usual May Day celebrations: the day is more important than the place.

20. The standard modern edition of Surrey's poetry is *The Poems of Henry Howard, Earl of Surrey*, ed. F. M. Padelford (Seattle: University of Washington, 1920; rev. 1928). Where possible, I have consulted John Williams's anthology for help with the modernization of spelling and punctuation. In Padelford, this is poem 3.

21. *Rime*, 11: "Lassare il velo per sole o per ombra, / Donna, non vi vid'io."

22. For the same kind of tense-incoherence, cf. poem 11, "The sun hath twice brought forth the tender green."

23. *Tottel's Miscellany*, I, 10–11.

24. These are the first two poems in Padelford's edition.

25. The standard modern edition of Spenser's poetry is *The Poetical Works of Edmund Spenser*, ed. Smith and de Selincourt (London: Oxford, 1912). I have modernized only to the extent of minor adjustments in punctuation, changing *u* to *v*, and adding apostrophes where appropriate.

26. *Tottel's Miscellany*, II, 72.

27. *The Elizabethan Love Sonnet* (London: Methuen, 1956), pp. 48–49.

28. Douglas Peterson, in *The English Lyric from Wyatt to Donne* (Princeton: Princeton University, 1967), points out that Surrey has apparently followed "the biographical method of praise" as prescribed by contemporary handbooks of rhetoric, and remarks: "It is impossible to take seriously the concluding line in which Surrey suggests that he desires the love of the nine-year-old child. He is obviously directing his intentions to her parents" (p. 60).

CHAPTER 4

1. *A Hundreth sundrie Flowres*, ed. C. T. Prouty (Columbia, Mo.: University of Missouri Studies, 17, no. 2 [1942]), p. 51. The original spelling of this elaborate title rescues a pun, "Posy-Poesy," that may also be implicit in the simpler title of the second edition, even though its original spelling *(Posies)* does not call it to the reader's attention. I have reproduced the original spelling of the titles that were given to all of

these mid-century anthologies, partly because the meaning of certain generic terms that figure in them—"sonnet," for example—had not yet fully stabilized, and partly to save the double meanings of words like "outlandish" and "poesy." In quoting the poems themselves I have, as usual, modernized both spelling and punctuation. For these poets it is especially important to enhance readability, insofar as this can be done without changing the meanings of words, because the roughness and ineptitude of some of their work, as compared with the next generation of poets, has been exaggerated by the editions in which we have had to read them. None of these poets has had the benefit of an edition like William Ringler's Sidney, whose poems seem much more accessible and also more polished and carefully written, because of typographical adjustment and normalization that have rendered unmodernized spellings easier to read and, to a degree also, stabilized them.

2. The Scholar's Facsimile reprint (Gainsville, 1968) of the 1563 edition of Googe's poems (intro. Frank Fieler) carries this one on pp. 87–89. I have also consulted Williams's modernized version (cf. *Renaissance Poetry*, p. 96).

Where appropriate, I have changed the lineation of Googe's poems so that iambic pentameter quatrains emerge. Googe was one of the earliest and most successful practitioners of the English pentameter line.

3. *The English Lyric from Wyatt to Donne: A History of the Plain and Eloquent Styles* (Princeton: Princeton University, 1967), pp. 142–43.

4. *The Posies*, ed. John Cunliffe (Cambridge University, 1907), p. 38.

5. Facsimile edition, pp. 100–101. Cf. also Williams, p. 99.

6. In Panofsky's edition, these lines appear on p. 36. Panofsky (p. viii) explains that Turberville was "the first English poet to present amatory poems in a lengthy narrative series." Oddly enough, however, as Panofsky points out, these poems "do not appear in proper narrative order in the 1567 and 1570 editions that we know, although they can readily be rearranged to fit the story promised by 'The Argument.' "

7. "Drab and Golden Lyrics of the English Renaissance," in *Forms of Lyric: Selected Papers from the English Institute*, ed. Reuben Brower (New York: Columbia University, 1970), p. 8.

8. I have used an 1870 reprint (ed. J. P. Collier) of the 1576 edition.

9. Cf. *The Arte of English Poesie*, ed. Willcock and Walker (London: Cambridge, 1936), p. 188. Puttenham's example of mixed allegory is a poem of Gascoigne's, "The clouds of care have covered all my coast." "I call him not a full Allegory," Puttenham explains, "but mixed, because he discovers withall what the cloud, storm, wave, and the rest are, which in a full allegory should not be discovered, but left at large to the reader's judgment and conjecture."

10. Facsimile edition, p. 120. (In that edition the first line of stanza 5 reads: "Whiche two of us is best?")

11. *Elizabethan and Metaphysical Imagery* (Chicago: University of Chicago, 1947) pp. 106–8. This is a slightly longer passage than Tuve cites, from Googe's eighth *Eglog* (Facsimile edition). In reproducing this passage, where capitalization occurs haphazardly, sometimes involving adjectives as well as nouns, I have capitalized very sparingly, just where personification is indicated by the immediate context of a noun like "pleasure" or "vice."

12. Ibid., p. 101.

13. Kenneth Burke's discussion of metaphor as a "master trope" is closer to Puttenham in its orientation than Tuve's discussion of allegory, because Burke too is con-

cerned primarily with the socially and politically interested use of figures of thought. See "Four Master Tropes," *Kenyon Review*, 3 (1941), 421–22; also "Perspective as Metaphor," in *Permanence and Change* (New York: New Republic, 1935).

CHAPTER 5

1. *Shakespeare's Sonnets*, ed. Stephen Booth (New Haven: Yale, 1977): sonnet 73.

2. Samuel Daniel, *Poems and a Defence of Ryme*, ed. A. C. Sprague (Cambridge, Mass.: Harvard, 1930): *Delia*, sonnet 9.

3. *The Poetical Works of Edmund Spenser*, ed. Smith and de Selincourt (London: Oxford, 1912). I have modernized the spelling of Spenser's poems only to the extent of changing *u* to *v* and introducing apostrophes where appropriate.

4. Lisle Cecil John, *The Elizabethan Sonnet Sequences* (New York: Columbia, 1938), p. 9.

5. *Elizabethan Poetry: A Study in Conventions, Meaning, and Expression* (Cambridge, Mass.: Harvard, 1964), p. 136.

6. C. S. Lewis, *English Literature in the Sixteenth Century* (Oxford: Clarendon, 1954), p. 224.

7. "Early Elizabethan Sonnets in Sequence," *SP*, 68 (1971), 452.

8. J. W. Lever, *The Elizabethan Love Sonnet* (London: Methuen, 1956), p. 6.

9. Ibid., p. 39.

10. George Gascoigne, *The Posies*, ed. J. W. Cunliffe (Cambridge: Cambridge University, 1907), pp. 66–67.

11. Cited by Harris, p. 462: I have modernized the spelling.

12. *The Poems of Sir Philip Sidney*, ed. William A. Ringler (Oxford: Clarendon, 1962), p. 84.

13. *Sidney's Poetic Development* (Cambridge, Mass.: Harvard, 1967), p. 66.

14. Ibid., p. 63.

15. *Sidney's Poetry: Contexts and Interpretations* (Cambridge, Mass.: Harvard, 1965), p. 92.

16. *Poems and Dramas of Fulke Greville, First Lord Brooke*, vol. I, ed. Geoffrey Bullough (Edinburgh: Oliver and Boyd, 1939), sonnet 72. I have reproduced the capitalization of abstract nouns that imparts a hint of personification to certain of them, and the underlining which suggests that Love, in the last line, is the name of a powerful god as well as a feeling that ebbs and flows.

17. *A Treatie of Humane Learning*, in *Poems and Dramas*, I, 154–91.

18. *The Posies*, pp. 465–73.

19. *Poems and a Defence of Ryme*, p. 127ff.

20. Ibid., p. 155.

21. What Daniel is probably referring to, when he deprecates "that multiplicity of rhymes," is the number of different rhyme schemes that were currently being tried by his contemporaries.

22. *Poems*, p. 97: "Musophilus," 11.979–80.

23. "Musophilus," 11.981–88.

24. Michael Riffaterre, *Semiotics of Poetry* (Bloomington: Indiana University, 1978), p. 21.

25. *The Poetical Works of Edmund Spenser*, p. 475.

26. Ibid., p. 486.

27. Lever, p. 134.

28. This is George Puttenham's English translation of the term in *The Arte of English Poesie*, ed. Willcock and Walker (Cambridge: Cambridge University, 1936), p. 165. See also Sister Miriam Joseph, *Shakespeare's Use of the Arts of Language* (New York: Columbia, 1947), p. 164ff.

29. Quoted from sonnet 15, line 13.

30. Robert Durling, ed. and trans., *Petrarch's Lyric Poems* (Cambridge, Mass.: Harvard, 1976), p. 10. Cf. Lewis, *English Literature in the Sixteenth Century*, pp. 327–38. Cf. also Carol Thomas Neely, "The Structure of English Renaissance Sonnet Sequences," *ELH*, 45 (1978), 359–89.

31. Harris, p. 465.

32. I am indebted for this suggestion to Richard Panofsky's unpublished Ph.D. dissertation, "A Descriptive Study of English Mid-Tudor Short Poetry, 1557–1577" (U. of Cal. Santa Barbara, 1975). *DAI*, 36 (1976), 5324A.

33. *Poems*, p. 11, sonnet 2.

34. This is sonnet 35 and also sonnet 83 of the *Amoretti* sequence.

35. For a much more thorough treatment of calendrical and numerological patterns in the *Amoretti*, cf. A. Dunlop, "The Unity of Spenser's *Amoretti*," in *Silent Poetry*, ed. Alastair Fowler (Routledge and Kegan Paul, 1970); and esp. A. Kent Hieatt, "A Numerical Key for Spenser's *Amoretti* and Guyon in the House of Mammon," *YES*, 3 (1973), 14–27.

36. *Sidney's Poetry*, p. 122. For the text of the *Astrophil and Stella* sequence, I have used Ringler's edition of the *Poems* (pp. 165–237). In "The meeting of the Muses: Sidney and the Mid-Tudor Poets" (in *Sir Philip Sidney and the Interpretation of Renaissance Culture*, ed. Waller and Moore [Totowa: Barnes & Noble, 1984], Germaine Warkentin argues (p.18) for a direct influence of the mid-Tudor poets upon the *Astrophil and Stella* sequence: she thinks it was from reading their poetry that Sidney "absorbed a way of envisioning the poet-lover's experience [as] 'full, material, and circumstantiated . . .' "

CHAPTER 6

1. *Petrarch's Lyric Poems*, trans. Robert Durling (Cambridge, Mass.: Harvard, 1976), *Rime sparse*, No. 123, pp. 236–37.

2. Thomas Greene makes a similar point in his study of Wyatt's Petrarchan "imitations": cf. *The Light in Troy: Imitation and Discovery in Renaissance Poetry* (New Haven: Yale, 1982), p. 248ff.

The only study of Petrarch I have found that invokes Jakobson's terminology is Sandra Bermann's "Rhetoric and Consciousness in the Petrarchan Sonnet," *Romanic Review*, 72 (1981), 215–25. Bermann infers a *metonymic* bias from what she calls the "visible grammar" of Petrarch's lyrics. Briefly, our difference hinges on the way each of us has understood the poetic function of language in its relationship to metaphor and metonymy: thus I would argue that the poem she has used to demonstrate Petrarch's metonymic bias ("Solo e pensoso i piu deserti campi") is really an instance of the tendency in Petrarch's sonnets for metonymy to capitulate to metaphor as the lover's "story" unfolds—a tendency that is fostered by the sonnet form itself.

3. *Sir Thomas Wyatt and His Background* (Stanford: Stanford University, 1964), p. 199.

4. Thomas Wyatt, *Collected Poems*, ed. Joost Daalder (London: Oxford, 1975), poem 7.

5. *The Poems of Henry Howard, Earl of Surrey*, ed. F. M. Padelford (Seattle: University of Washington, rev. ed. 1928), poem 1.

6. *The Elizabethan Love Sonnet* (London: Methuen, 1956), p. 43.

7. Padelford, p. 207. Lever also cites this (p. 42) as a naive account of the difference between the two poems.

8. Hyder Rollins reprints Watson's translation in the notes to his edition of *England's Helicon* (Cambridge, Mass.: Harvard, 1935), II, 183.

9. *England's Helicon*, ed. Rollins, I, 179. This is an anthology of pastoral poetry that was published in 1600. Many of the poems that appeared there had already been published elsewhere.

10. All quotations in this chapter from the *Arcadia* are based on Albert Feuillerat's edition of *The Countess of Pembroke's Arcadia* (Cambridge: Cambridge University, 1922), where this poem appears on pp. 141–42.

11. I am indebted to William Empson's discussion of this poem in *Seven Types of Ambiguity* (Norfolk, Conn.: New Directions, 1930; 3d ed. rev. 1953), pp. 36–38.

12. Cf. chapter 1, pages 5–6, and notes 9 and 10.

13. Cf. Jon S. Lawry, *Sidney's Two Arcadias: Pattern and Proceeding* (Ithaca: Cornell University, 1972), p. 1: "If, as seems probable, the *Defence* [sic] was written after the *Old* was finished but before the *New* was seriously undertaken, the critical essay stands in a unique parental relationship to the two works." The classic study of the "New" *Arcadia's* conformity to Sidney's own account of heroic poetry in the *Defense* is Kenneth Myrick, *Sir Philip Sidney as a Literary Craftsman* (Cambridge, Mass.: Harvard, 1935), chapter IV: "The *Arcadia* as an Heroic Poem."

14. *The Poems of Sir Walter Ralegh*, ed. Agnes Latham (Boston: Houghton Mifflin, 1929), pp. 77–94. Latham reads 21th as 11th and 22 as 12, but this reading is not generally accepted. For my purposes, both sets of numbers are high enough that it hardly matters which Ralegh intended.

15. Lewis, *English Literature in the Sixteenth Century* (Oxford: Clarendon, 1954), p. 520.

16. Stephen J. Greenblatt, *Sir Walter Ralegh: The Renaissance Man and His Roles* (New Haven: Yale, 1973), p. 62.

17. Greenblatt, p. 190 (note 8).

18. In "Colin Clouts Come Home Againe," the poem in which Spenser expressed his gratitude for Ralegh's having sponsored him at court, Ralegh introduces himself to "Colin" as "the shepheard of the Ocean."

19. Cf. E. C. Wilson, *England's Eliza* (Cambridge, Mass.: Harvard, 1939), pp. 304–20.

20. G. K. Hunter, *John Lyly: The Humanist as Courtier* (London: Routledge and Kegan Paul, 1962), p. 151.

21. Cf. chapter 2, pages 22–24.

22. I am indebted to Jonathan Goldberg's study, *James I and the Politics of Literature* (Baltimore: Johns Hopkins, 1983), p. 28, for this quotation from Howard's letter to Harington. In the section of the book that begins at this point, Goldberg plays off James's Accession Day procession against Elizabeth's, in terms of its structure, its iconography, and the role played by the king as chief spectator, to illustrate the difference in style of rulership between the two monarchs. His reading of this differ-

ence meshes with Montrose's reading of the Elizabethan pastoral shows and with Roy Strong's *Cult of Elizabeth*, which I have already cited in chapter 2. Cf. also Graham Parry, *The Golden Age restor'd: The Culture of the Stuarts, 1603–42* (New York: St. Martin's, 1981), chapter 1.

23. Stephen Orgel and Roy Strong, *Inigo Jones and the Theatre of the Stuart Court* (London: Sotheby Parke Bernet; Berkeley and Los Angeles: University of California, 1973), vol. I, 7. "It is no accident," Orgel continues, "that perspective stages flourished at court and only at court, and that their appearance there coincided with the reappearance in England of the Divine Right of Kings as a serious political philosophy." Thomas Greene's brief remarks about the Jonsonian masque, in "Ben Jonson and the Centered Self," *SEL*, 10 (1970), 325–48, are highly suggestive along similar lines.

24. See Goldberg, p. 210ff., for a fuller treatment of Donne's relationship to the king.

25. Cf. Lawrence Stone, *The Crisis of the Aristocracy, 1558–1641* (Oxford: Clarendon, 1965), p. 488ff.

26. Cf. Parry, pp. 58–60. In his study *English Civic Pageantry, 1558–1642* (Columbia, S.C.: University of South Carolina, 1971), David Bergeron points out that whereas "in the Elizabethan period all the various kinds of civic pageants flourish, the same cannot be said of the later period. . . . With the death of Elizabeth the progress pageant suffers a demise, and there is nothing in the Stuart era comparable to the experiences at Kenilworth or Elvetham" (p. 5).

27. Bergeron, p. 72 and passim.

28. See especially, for example, the sermons preached on March 24, 1617 (anniversary of the king's Accession Day); on February 16, 1622, at Whitehall, which includes a defense of the Church of England; and on November 26, 1625, at Devonshire House, over the body of King James. All are to be found in *The Sermons of John Donne*, ed. Evelyn Simpson and George Potter (Berkeley and Los Angeles: University of California, 1953), 10 vols.

29. Barbara Kiefer Lewalski, *Donne's Anniversaries and the Poetry of Praise: The Creation of a Symbolic Mode* (Princeton: Princeton University, 1973), pp. 13–14.

30. Ibid., p. 46.

31. "To the Countess of Salisbury. August, 1614," *John Donne, The Satires, Epigrams and Verse Letters*, ed. W. Milgate (Oxford: Clarendon, 1967), pp. 108–9.

32. Lewalski, p. 161.

33. Zailig Pollock in " 'The Object and the Wit': The Smell of Donne's First Anniversary," *ELR*, 13 (1983), pp. 301–18, calls it a "radically indecorous" poem, and urges that we make its "irreducible oddness" the starting point of our reading, rather than try to explain it away.

34. *Dialogues/Roman Jakobson, Krystyna Pomorska* (Cambridge, Mass.: MIT Press, 1983), p. 134. These are interviews taken near the end of Jakobson's life by Krystyna Pomorska. In the "dialogue" from which this distinction is taken, Jakobson gives a brief informal account (pp. 125–36) of the origins and stages of articulation of what Pomorska refers to as "one of the principal propositions of your theory: that the concepts of metaphor and metonymy are diametrically opposed phenomena."

35. "The First Anniversary: An Anatomy of the World; Wherein, by Occasion of the Untimely Death of Mistress Elizabeth Drury the Frailty and the Decay of this whole World is Represented," *The Epithalamions, Anniversaries and Epicedes*, ed. W. Milgate (Oxford: Clarendon, 1978).

36. "The Second Anniversary: Of the Progress of the Soul; Wherein, by Occasion

of the Religious Death of Mistress Elizabeth Drury, the Incommodities of the Soul in this Life, and her Exaltation in the Next, are Contemplated." I have used the Clarendon Press edition of this poem, as above.

37. For this and all other quotations from *The Songs and Sonets of John Donne*, I have used Theodore Redpath's second edition (New York: St. Martin's, 1984).

CHAPTER 7

1. Douglas Bush, *English Literature in the Earlier Seventeenth Century: 1600–1660* (Oxford: Clarendon, 2d ed. 1962), p. 107.

2. Joseph Summers, *The Heirs of Donne and Jonson* (London: Chatto & Windus, 1970), pp. 39–40.

3. Richard Heigerson, *Self-Crowned Laureates: Spenser, Jonson, Milton and the Literary System* (Berkeley: University of California, 1983), p. 34.

4. Helgerson (pp. 104–7) cites Joseph Hall, Everard Guilpin, and Richard Barnfield to this effect.

5. *Ben Jonson: The Complete Poems*, ed. George Parfitt (Middlesex: Penguin, 1975; repr. New Haven: Yale, 1982), p. 52. I have used this edition for all of the poems of Jonson's that will be cited in this chapter, and also for *Timber* and the *Conversations with Drummond*, which Parfitt has included as Appendix I and Appendix II.

6. Cf. Parfitt's note to this poem, p. 490.

7. In Theodore Redpath's edition these are the first lines, respectively, of "The Canonization," "The Flea," "The Expiration," and "A Valediction: of the book."

8. J. L. Austin, *How to Do Things with Words*, 2d ed. (Cambridge, Mass.: Harvard, 1975), "Lecture I."

9. "The Good-morrow"; "Woman's Constancy."

10. "The Computation"; "Air and Angels"; "The Legacy."

11. Redpath (p. 241) cites James Reeves, editor of *Donne, Selected Poems* (Heineman, 1953).

12. Cf. Jakobson, in "Linguistics and Poetics" (1960): "This function, by promoting the palpability of signs, deepens the fundamental dichotomy of signs and objects."

13. I have already cited his famous objection to the encomiastic strategy of the *Anniversaries*, in chapter 1. According to another of his remarks to Drummond, "he esteemeth Donne the first poet in the world, in some things," and this is borne out by his epigram "To John Donne" (*Complete Poems*, p. 41), but he also averred to Drummond that Donne would perish "for not being understood."

14. In Wesley Trimpi's classic study of *Ben Jonson's Poems* (Stanford: Stanford University, 1962), there is a very good chapter given to playing off Jonson's Ciceronian poetics against the native tradition of the plain style, "the most distinguished early representatives of which were Wyatt and Gascoigne" (Trimpi, p. 115).

15. Cf. John Lemly, who remarks in "Masks and Self-Portraits in Jonson's late Poetry," *ELH*, 44 (1977), that he writes as if "the poetry itself cannot stand alone without the author's grotesque presence" (p. 249).

16. Cf. chapter 4, page 64 and note 7. The formulation is G. K. Hunter's.

17. *Complete Poems*, Appendix II, p. 461. If Jonson ever did write such a discourse, it has been lost.

18. Cf. Trimpi, who cites "the authority of syntax in the rhythmical construction

of the line" as being characteristic of Jonson's poetry.

19. *Miscellaneous Prose of Sir Philip Sidney*, ed. Katharine Duncan-Jones and Jan Van Dorsten (Oxford: Clarendon, 1973), p. 112; cited by Trimpi, p. 104.

20. Trimpi (pp. 120–21) plays off this passage from "Inviting a Friend to Supper" against a stanza from a poem of Chidiock Tichbourne's to illustrate the "authority of syntax" in Jonson's poetry.

21. *Complete Poems*, Appendix I, 11.2315–16.

22. Ibid., 11.2385–87.

23. Ibid., 11.2398–2400.

24. Ibid., 11.2362ff. Jonson's emphasis on "necessity" is reminiscent of Fulke Greville's *Treatise of Human Learning*, which was quoted in chapter 5, but Greville resorted to the language of Calvinist Protestantism to inveigh against the "Siren," Rhetoric. Jonson's formulation is more dispassionate and "Roman."

25. Trimpi (p. 203) quotes Henry Peacham's *Garden of Eloquence*, a contemporary Rhetoric, to the effect that *metonymia* "serveth aptly to brevity."

26. Don Wayne, building on Barbara Herrnstein Smith's discussion of the epigram in *Poetic Closure*, makes a related point about the epigram, whose generic hallmark is witty conciseness: "Inherent in the form is a tendency towards reduction and objectification of the 'matter' of the poem, its subordination to the authority of the poet as observer, commentator, and judge." ("Poetry and Power in Ben Jonson's *Epigrammes*: The Naming of 'Facts' or the Figuring of Social Relations?" *Renaissance and Modern Studies*, 23 [1979], 83.)

27. "To Sir Robert Wroth," 11.15–16. This poem was originally published in *The Forest*; it appears in the *Collected Poems* on pp. 98–101.

28. "An Ode. To Himself," stanza 6. This poem originally appeared in *Underwoods*.

29. "To Penshurst" was originally part of the *Forest* collection; it appears in the *Collected Poems* on pp. 95–98.

30. Edward Partridge, "Jonson's *Epigrammes*: The Named and the Nameless," *Studies in the Literary Imagination*, 6 (1973), 190–91.

31. Richard Peterson suggests that the word "head" carries three different meanings here: "well-spring," "father," and "a sculpted Roman ancestral bust." Peterson's discussion of this poem in his book-length study of *Imitation and Praise in the Poems of Ben Jonson* (New Haven: Yale University, 1981), pp. 56–61, brings out the close relationship between Jonson's encomiastic project and Camden's *Britannia*: Camden's project was partly, as Peterson explains it, "to construct a kind of Baedeker of living English virtue."

32. David Wykes points out, in an article in *Renaissance and Modern Studies*, 13 (1969), 76–87, that Camden had also written an etymological glossary of English names, with an accompanying disquisition in which he stressed the importance of names as means by which "the glorie and credite of men is . . . conveyed to the knowledge of posteritie."

33. Barbara Herrnstein Smith points out that a conclusion which is "hyperdetermined" in this way "will have maximal stability and finality" (*Poetic Closure: A Study of How Poems End* [Chicago: University of Chicago, 1968], p. 206). "Closure," as Smith has defined and analyzed it in this landmark study, is one of the most important instruments of what Jakobson calls "self-focus." Smith uses the epigram to illustrate closure at its most extreme, and many of her examples are Jonsonian.

34. "On Sir Cod the Perfumed" (*Collected Poems*, p. 40). "I scent" is a metaphor for "I discern," but it also means "I can smell him as he passes by."

35. "On Mill, My Lady's Woman," 11.15–16 (Collected Poems, p. 63).

36. This account of proper names was originally part of a 1950 paper entitled "Overlapping of Code and Message in Language," which was republished as the first section of "Shifters, Verbal Categories, and the Russian Verb" (Selected Writings, II, 130–48). Jakobson was indebted to C. S. Peirce's account of "indexical symbols," as well as to the English tradition of analytic philosophy, for his notion of how proper names differ from ordinary nouns on the one hand and indexical pronouns on the other. Russell's example is unfortunate if we refuse to let sleeping metaphors lie: "Fido" of course means "faithful" in Italian or in Latin.

37. George Parfitt's note to this poem, on p. 495 of the Collected Poems, explains that "the point of [lines 1–3] depends upon our linking Vere's Christian name with the Roman poet and his surname with Latin 'vere' ('truly')." My own reading of the pun works better in terms of "Roman sound": Vere does not sound the same as the Latin adverb "vere."

38. As Parfitt's notes point out, the lines in which Jonson explains how rare and valuable these virtues are have been adapted from Seneca and Pliny.

39. Complete Poems, Appendix II, p. 461.

40. His plays create a similar impression, according to Alvin Kernan's account of their episodic structure, whose parts are held together "only loosely by a central story or plot." Kernan finds in the plays "a world crammed with people and things, tending towards reduction and fragmentation." Cf. "Alchemy and Acting: The Major Plays of Ben Jonson," Studies in the Literary Imagination, 6 (1973), 2; and Wayne, p. 90.

41. That this is the central theme of the encomiastic epigrams is a point that was eloquently made by Thomas Greene in "Ben Jonson and the Centered Self," SEL, 10 (1970), 325–48. More recently it has been reiterated by Helgerson, Wayne, and especially Richard Peterson, who discerns a group of related tropes, all of which implicitly carry this theme: tropes of inclusiveness, transformation, fullness, columnar straightness, rootedness, etc. Both Greene and Wayne interpret this notion of the centered self as having political implications. "As Jonson aged," says Greene, "and watched the centrifugal forces in his society acquire increasing power, this sense of the beleaguered central self became more poignant" (p. 331). Wayne's reading is Marxist and forward-looking: he uses C. B. Macpherson's theory of the rise of "possessive individualism" to place Jonson at a historical moment in which "all social relations were undergoing transformation into relations of the market" (p. 98). My "post-Elizabethan" reading is closer to Greene's, but I am uncomfortable with the elegiac note he strikes with words like "poignant."

42. Jonathan Goldberg has developed the implications of this term as a characterization of Donne's poetic stance in very interesting and provocative ways: cf. James I and the Politics of Literature, p. 66; pp. 107–8.

POSTSCRIPT

1. Jakobson, "Quest for the Essence of Language," Diogenes, 51 (1965), 21–37; reprinted in Selected Writings (The Hague: Mouton, 1962–79), II, 355.

2. Jakobson, "Metalanguage as a Linguistic Problem," in The Framework of Language, Michigan Studies in the Humanities (1980), pp. 88–89, reprinted in Selected Writings (Berlin: Mouton, 1985), VII, 113–121. This essay was first delivered as a

lecture in 1956. Here as an example of figurative or "transferred" meaning, Jakobson cites the word "goose," which is sometimes used to refer to "a person who resembles the bird in stupidity." ("You silly goose" is a figurative expression if the deictic pronoun "you" refers not to a long-necked bird but to a person.) "Gander," when it is used as a verb with a human subject, is a more complicated instance of transferred meaning: in that case, Jakobson explains, we have "a metonymic transfer from the goose to its outstretched neck and goggling eyes in a metaphoric application to a human being" (p. 119).

3. Aristotle, *Rhetoric*, III, 1412a: cited by Lodge in *The Modes of Modern Writing* (Ithaca: Cornell, 1977), p. 112.

4. Lodge, pp. 117–18.

5. This exchange has been reprinted with the title "The Dynamics of Metaphor," in *The Modern Tradition: Backgrounds of Modern Literature*, ed. Richard Ellman and Charles Feidelson, Jr. (New York: Oxford, 1965), pp. 158–62. Crane glosses his metaphors very grudgingly, after defending the "apparent illogic" of modernist metaphor. It is his defense that makes the exchange an important document for the student of modernist poetics.

6. Theodore Redpath, who lists the alternative readings occasioned by it in a long footnote (pp. 265–66), concludes that if line 32 refers to the closing of the compasses, whereas line 36 refers to the completion of a circle, then "the ending of the poem is . . . not wholly satisfying." For an ingenious attempt to turn the disappointment to advantage as part of the poem's strategy of valediction, see David Novarr, *The Disinterred Muse: Donne's Texts and Contexts* (Ithaca: Cornell, 1980), chapter 2.

Index

Abrams, Meyer: definition of lyric, 33
Acrostic poem, 162–63
Alighieri, Dante, *Vita Nuova*, 99
Allegory: in mid-Tudor poetry, 67–75; mixed, as metonymic device, 67; as social performance, 73–75, 150; Spenserian, 70
Aphasia, 2, 3–4, 131–32
Aristotle, on metaphor, 172
Auto-anthologies, 19, 59–60, 63–67, 155, 181 n. 12. *See also* Mid-Tudor poets
Autobiography as metonymic device, 83, 154
Axis of selection. *See* selection function

Blazon, as metaphoric device, 54–55
Benveniste, Emile, 182–83 n. 1
Bermann, Sandra, 187 n. 2
Bloomfield, Leonard, 172
Burke, Kenneth, 185–86 n. 13
Bush, Douglas, 143

Chivalric romance, 20, 22–23, 115
Combination, axis of, 3–4
Commonplaces: in mid-Tudor poetry, 62; in Wyatt's poems, 43–44
Contiguity-relation, 3
Continued metaphor. *See* Allegory
Correlative verse, 85–86
Couplets and the axis of combination, 157
Crane, Hart: "At Melville's Tomb." 172–73; on modernist metaphor, 173, 193 n. 5
Culler, Jonathan, 31, 178 n. 5, 179 n. 11, 180 n. 14

Daniel, Samuel: metaphoric sonneteering exemplified by, 78–79; on monumentality, 95–96, 102, 105; and the poetic function of language, 20, 92–95; recuperation of diachrony into synchrony by, 80, 111. Works: *Defense of Rhyme*, 92–95; *Delia*, 100–102, 104–5; "Musophilus," 95
Deixis: defined, 31, 182–83 n. 1; in Donne's poems, 31–32, 149; metaphoric, 54; as metonymic strategy in poems, 31–34, 55–57, 108–11; in Wyatt's and Surrey's poems, 34–57, 119
Donne, John: as apologist for monarchy, 133, 189 n. 28; anti-Elizabethan stance of, 1, 27–28, 133–36, 168–69; iconoclasm of, 133, 135–36, 140–41, 145; metaphor in the poems of, 147–53, 171–76; metonymic deixis in, 31–32; metonymic strategy of, compared to Gascoigne, 75, 150; compared to Wyatt, 45–46; performatives in the poems of, 146; strategy of compliment, 134–36; transaction of major lyrics, 150–53. Works: *Anniversaries*, 27–28, 133–35, 137–39; "The Canonization," 140–41, 151–53; "The Ecstasy," 148; "The Flea," 149, 173–74; *Songs and Sonets*, 139–40, 145–53; "The Sun Rising," 31–32, 147–48, 150–51, 161–62; "A Valediction: forbidding mourning," 146, 174–75, 193 n. 6; "A Valediction: of weeping," 146, 149–51, 175–76
De Man, Paul, 178 n. 4

Drayton, Michael, as metonymic poet, 9–11, 111

Drummond, William. *See* Jonson, *Conversations with Drummond*

Drury, Elizabeth. *See* Donne, *Anniversaries*

Durling, Robert, 99

Dyer, Edward, 132

E.K., editor of *The Shepheardes Calender*, 11, 16, 17, 23–34

Eliot, T. S., and modernist metaphor, 172

Elizabeth I of England: cult of, 20–24, 26–28, 96–97, 131–132; as Cynthia, 26, 127–28, 131–32; as Eliza Queen of Shepherds, 23, 26; as Gloriana, 18, 25, 26; as Laura, 21–22; and literary patronage, 26; summer progresses of, 20

Elizabethan poetry: as ideological apparatus, 1, 15, 115–16, 132; as national institution, *see* English poesy; love in, 115, 127–32; metaphoric bias of, 15–20, 127

Elizabethan World Picture, 28, 136–37; deconstruction of, 137–39

Empson, William, 179 n. 13, 188 n. 11

England's Helicon, 123, 188 n. 9

English poesy, 16, 141, 144

Epic, Elizabethan. *See* Chivalric romance

Epigram: closure in, 191 n. 33. *See also* Jonson, Ben

Epitaph. *See* Jonson, Ben

Faeryland, as total metaphor, 17–18, 159

Fowler, Alastair, 184 n. 18

Frequentative present tense, 49, 108

Gascoigne, George: editorial apparatus of, for self-publication, 16, 17, 59–60, 64–65, 181 n. 5; and metaphor as social gambit, 65–67, 71–75, 150; and moral conversion by metaphor, 68–69, 70–73, 75; and the poetic function of language, 91–95, 157; and the sonnet, 80, 83–84, 110. Works: *Adventures of Master F.J.*, 17, 60, 64–67, 73–75, 100; "Certain Notes of Instruction," 20, 80, 91–95, 157; "Gascoigne's Good Night," 68–69; "Gascoigne's Woodmanship," 71–73, 75; *Hemetes the Hermit*, 23, 181 n. 20; *A Hundreth sundrie Flowres*, 59–60, 64–66; *Posies*, 16, 17, 60, 62, 65, 91–92; "sonnets in sequence," 81–83, 99

Gelley, Alexander, 179 n. 7

Googe, Barnabe, 59, 61–63, 67–70, 185 n. 2; "Epitaph for Nicholas Grimald," 60–61, 63; and the pentameter line, 185 n. 2; pastoral eclogues of, 69–70, 182 n. 22. *See also* Mid-Tudor poets

Goldberg, Jonathan, 188 n. 22, 192 n. 42

Greenblatt, Stephen, 127, 129

Greene, Thomas, 187 n. 2, 189 n. 23, 192 n. 41

Greville, Fulke: friend of Daniel, 92; sonnets of, 88–89, 110; *Treatise of Human Learning*, 89–90

Hardison, O. B., 134

Harris, William, 81, 99

Headnotes, as metonymic device, 64, 67

Helgerson, Richard, 143–44, 155, 192 n. 41

Henry VIII of England, court of, as setting for lyrics, 35, 41–42

Holenstein, Elmar, 178 n. 5, 179 n. 7

Hunter, G. K., 64, 132, 155, 177 n. 1, 181 n. 12

Iconoclasm. *See* Donne, John

Jakobson, Roman: on aphasia, 2, 3–4; on metaphor, 5, 171–72, 192–93 n. 2; on metonymy, 4–5; on the poetic function of language, 6, 8; on proper names, 166; and the Russian Formalists, 8, 12, 180 n. 17; semiotic theory: essentials of, 3–6, 8; limitations of, 11–13; critiques of, 178 n. 5, 179 n. 7; applications of, 12, 178 n. 4, 187 n. 2; relationship to Freudian semiotics, 178 n. 4

James I of England, as literary patron, 1, 26–27, 92, 132–33, 168

Javitch, Daniel, 19

John, Lisle, 80

Jonson, Ben: as critic of Donne's iconoclasm, 27, 153, 190 n. 13; as critic of Spenserian archaism, 159; encomiastic strategy of, 144–45, 163–69; "facts" in the poetry of, 154, 160, 166, 168; on metaphor, 159–60, 191 n. 24; metonymic strategy of, compared to mid-Tudor poets, 153, 155, 156, 190 n. 14; metonymy as moral action in the poetry of, 160, 191 n. 26; and monumentality, 144–45; and the poetic function of language, 156–57; post-Elizabethan stance of, 1, 133, 144, 157, 168–69, 192 n. 41; proper names in the poetry of, 155, 163–68; satiric strategy of, 154, 165; self-presentation of, 154, 190 n. 15; and the Stuart masque, 133, 189 n. 23; syntax in the poetry of, 157–58, 191 nn. 18, 20; topicality in the poetry of, 145, 154. Works: *Conversations with Drummond*, 27, 153, 156–57, 159, 168, 190 n. 13; *Epigrams*, 163–68; epitaphs, 162–63; *Herologia*, 168; "Inviting a Friend to Supper," 155–56, 158; "To Penshurst," 160–61, 169; *Timber*, 158–59

Joos, Martin, 178 n. 5

Kalstone, David, 88, 105
Kernan, Alvin, 192 n. 40

Lacan, Jacques, 178 n. 4
Latham, Agnes, 183 n. 7, 188 n. 14
Lawry, Jon S., 188 n. 13
Lemly, John, 190 n. 15
Lever, J. W., 56, 81–82, 97, 122, 188 n. 7
Lewalski, Barbara Kiefer, 134
Lewis, C. S., 1–2, 61, 81, 99, 127, 177–78 n. 2; on Drab and Golden poetry, 1–2, 177–78 n. 2
Lodge, David, 2, 12–13, 172–73
Luborsky, Ruth, 180–81 n. 5
Lyric poem, as metonymy, 32, 40; as social performance, 63–64, 91–92; standard definitions, 33

MacCaffrey, Wallace, 15, 20
Masque, as royal tribute, 132–33
Meta-linguistic statement, 33
Metaphor, 5, 113, 171–72, 193 n. 2; as act of aggression, 147–48; Aristotle on, 172; in Donne's poems, 147–53, 171–76; as linguistic necessity, 70, 90, 159, 191 n. 24; modernist, 172–73, 176, 193 n. 5; and moral conversion, 68–69, 70–73, 75; and simile, 5; and subjectivity, 113, 122; "total," 6, 124, 127, 137, 179 n. 11, 182 n. 22; used to strengthen metonymy, 161
Metaphoric bias, 2, 4, 5–6; and monumentality, 20; of "The Ocean to Cynthia," 130–31; of pastoral, 6; in poems, 55; and the printed book, 19, 156; of Romanticism, 12; of the sestina, 124, 128; of the sonnet, 77–80,

90–91; of surrealism, 12
Metaphoric way, 4, 6–7. *See also* Metaphoric bias
Metaphysical conceit, 171–76. *See also* Donne, metaphor in the poetry of
Metonymy: defined, 4–5; and brevity, 191 n. 25; as moral action, *see* Jonson, Ben; poem as, 8–9, 31–32; and realist writing, 5–6
Metonymic bias, 4–5; and cubism, 12; ideological implications of, 137; in poems, 8–10; in prose fiction, 4–5; and realist writing, 12
Metonymic way, 4–5, 6. *See also* Metonymic bias
Mid-Tudor poets, 59–75, 80–84, 99–100; love poem sequences of, 100, 185 n. 6; metaphor in the poems of, 67–71; metonymic bias of, 15, 60–64, 67–69; poetics of, compared to Ben Jonson, 153, 155, 156, 190 n. 14; proper names in the poems of, 62–63; and the sonnet, 80–84, 99–100; and *Tottel's Miscellany*, 19, 44–45, 59, 63, 81. *See also* Auto-anthologies
Monroe, Harriet. *See* Hart Crane
Montrose, Louis, 19, 23, 24
Monumentality, 95–96, 105, 141, 144, 145; and the printed book, 156
Myrick, Kenneth, 188 n. 13

Narcissus, as archetype of the lover, 102–3, 118
Nicolson, Marjorie Hope, 27
Novarr, David, 193 n. 6
Numerology, 95, 104, 105, 187 n. 35

Occasion of a poem, 32
Orgel, Stephen, 133, 189 n. 23

Padelford, F. M., 122, 125
Panofsky, Richard, 185 n. 6, 187 n. 32
Paradox, 7, 153
Partridge, Edward, 163, 165
Pastoral, 6, 20, 22–24; and the cult of Elizabeth, 20; as metaphoric fictional mode, 6
Pastoral situation: in the *Arcadia*, 124–26; in "The Ocean to Cynthia," 127, 132; in *The Shepheardes Calender*, 182 n. 22
Peacham, Henry, on metonymy, 191 n. 25
Peirce, C. S., 2, 31, 192 n. 6
Pembroke, William, Earl of, as dedicatee of Jonson's *Epigrams*, 163–64, 166

Performatives, in Donne's poems, 146
Peterson, Douglas, 61, 184 n. 28
Peterson, Richard, 191 n. 31, 192 n. 41
Petrarch, and his early commentators, 118; as precursor for the Elizabethan poets, 16, 21–22, 101–2. Works: *Rime sparse*, 99, 103, 114–18; *Trionfi*, 21; "Una candida cerva . . . ," 117; "Zephira torna . . . ," 121–23, 125
Petrarchan elegy, 134
Petrarchan erotic paradigm, 115–18, 120–21, 126
Petrarchan imitation and translation: by Elizabethan poets, 101–2, 115; by Wyatt and Surrey, 38–40, 48–49, 80–82, 115–22
Petrarchan time-sense, 99, 107, 118, 120–21
Poetic function of language: defined, 6, 8, 190 n. 12; and meter, 6; and rhyme, 6; and self-focus, 6–8
Proper names, 3, 166–67, 192 n. 36; as metonymic strategy in mid-Tudor poetry, 62–63; in Jonson's epigrams, 163–68
Puttenham, George (*Art of English Poesy*): on allegory, 67, 70–71, 185 nn. 9, 13; on literary decorum, 19; on pastoral, 23
Pollock, Zailig, 189 n. 33

Quintilian, on "custom," quoted by Jonson, 158

Ralegh, Sir Walter, as Timias in *The Faerie Queene*, 131; "On the Life of Man," 33, 43; "The Ocean to Cynthia," 26, 127–32, 188 n. 14; "A Vision upon his Conceit of the Faery Queene," 21–22
Rebholz, R. A., 183 nn. 10, 11
Refrain poem, 46–48
Redpath, Theodore, 193 n. 6
Riffaterre, Michael, 95–96
Ronsard, Pierre, as precursor of Elizabethan sonneteering, 101
Rosenberg, Eleanor, 16
Rudenstine, Neil, 87

Satire, 143
Saussurean model of language, 3
Schemes; defined, 11; Sidney's use of, 87–88
Selection function, 3–4, 128
Self-focus: defined, 6; illustrated, 7–8; in "The Canonization," 153; and Elizabethan poesy,

127; in Jonson's poems, 145; and the poetic function of language, 6; and the printed book, 19; and the sonnet, 77, 79, 84–88, 104
Selfhood in Jonson's epigrams, 169
Sestina, 123–24, 128
Set toward the context, 5–6, 9; in *Astrophil and Stella*, 105–11; and deixis, 34; in Donne's poems, 146; in Jonson's epigrams, 145; in Wyatt's poems, 34–35
Shakespeare's sonnets: compared with *Astrophil and Stella* sonnets, 107–8, 111; and the metaphoric way, 6–8, 77–78, 113–14; monumentality of, 96; recuperation of diachrony into synchrony in, 80, 102–5; syllepsis in, 97–99
Shifters. *See* Deixis
Sidney, Sir Philip: as creator of English poesy, 1, 16, 18–19; deconstructive sonneteering of, 88, 110–11, 141, 157; double sestina of, 123–24; metaphoric bias in the early sonnets of, 10, 85–88, 111; revision of the *Arcadia*, 25–26, 124–27, 188 n. 13; schemes in the poetry of, 87–88; treatment of love by, 123–27. Works: *Arcadia*, 24, 25–26, 124–27; *Astrophil and Stella*, 80, 88, 105–11, 141, 157; *Defense of Poesy*, 1, 11, 16, 18–19, 73, 113, 127, 157; *The Lady of May*, 23, 181–82 n. 20
Similitude, as metonymic strategy, 62, 67–69, 150
Smith, Barbara Herrnstein, 33, 191 n. 33
Smith, Bruce R., 181 n. 5
Smith, Hallett, 81
Smuts, Malcolm, 182 n. 30
Sonnet: Elizabethan poets and the, 84–97, 157; Gascoigne's definition of the, 80; impact of Wyatt and Surrey on the, 80, 81–82; and introspection, 114; metaphoric bias of the, 6–8, 9–10, 77–80, 128; mid-Tudor poets and the, 80–84, 99–100; Petrarchan form of the, 81, 82, 106; Shakespearean (English) form of the, 77, 81, 83; Spenserian form of the, 79–80, 84–85; used metonymically, 9–10, 109–10
Sonnet sequences, Elizabethan, 80, 99–105
Southall, Raymond, 34, 41–42
Speech-act theory, 146
Spenser, Edmund, archaizing diction of, 20, 97, 159; as creator of English poesy, 16–17;

and the cult of Elizabeth, 23–24, 25; erotic idealism in the poetry of, 54–55, 102–3; as exponent of monumentality, 96–97; as poet laureate, 22, 97; recuperation of diachrony into synchrony in the poetry of, 18–19, 84–85, 104. Works: *Amoretti*, 10, 54–55, 79–80, 84–85, 102–5; "Colin Clouts Come Home Againe," 188 n. 18; *The Faerie Queene*, 17–18, 25, 27, 70, 131; *Ruines of Time*, 96; *Shepheardes Calender*, 1, 13, 16–17, 23–24, 137, 159, 180–81 n. 5, 182 n. 22; *Teares of the Muses*, 96–97. See also Faeryland

Spenserian sonnet form, 79–80, 84–85
Spenserian stanza, 20, 97
Stevens, John, 42
Strong, Roy, 21, 23, 133
Summers, Joseph, 143
Surrey, Henry Howard, Earl of, 48–54, 55–57, 120–22; edited by Tottel, 53; metonymic strategy of, 56–57; Petrarchan imitation and translation by, 16, 39, 48–49, 82, 115, 119–22; spatial deixis in the poems of, 34, 51–54; verb-tense incoherence in the poems of, 48–51, 184 n. 22; and Wordsworth, 54. Works: "Alas, so all things now do hold their peace," 53–54, 120–21; "Description and Praise of his Love, Geraldine," 55–57; "So Cruel Prison," 51–52; "The soote season," 53, 121–22
Syllepsis, 97–99, 153
Synecdoche: cognitive implications of, 137; explained as metaphoric metonymy, 136–37; ideological uses of, 137

Tennenhouse, Leonard, 26
Thomson, Patricia, 118
Topical references, as metonymic strategy, 108–9, 154
Tottel's Miscellany, 1, 15–16, 19, 59, 63, 80–81; emendation of Wyatt and Surrey in, 35–36,

53; influence of, on mid-Tudor poets, 44–45, 59, 63, 81
Trimpi, Wesley, 157, 190 n. 14, 191 nn. 18, 19, 25
Troilus, as archetype of the lover, 100, 102
Tropes, defined, 11
Turberville, George, 1, 44–45, 59, 60, 64. See also Mid-Tudor poets
Tuve, Rosemond, 70, 180 n. 16, 185 n. 13

Warkentin, Germaine, 187 n. 36
Watson, Thomas, 80–81, 122
Wayne, Don, 168, 191 n. 26, 192 n. 41
Whetstone, George, 60, 66. See also Mid-Tudor poets
White, Hayden, 178–79 n. 5
Williams, Charles, 182 n. 23
Williams, William Carlos, as metonymic poet, 8–9, 10
Winters, Yvor, 177–78 n. 2
Wykes, David, 191 n. 32
Wyatt, Sir Thomas (the elder), 1, 15, 16, 34–38, 63, 80–82, 111, 115–19; compared with Donne, 34, 35, 45–46, 148, 184 n. 19; deictic manipulation of verb tense in the poems of, 34, 36–39; imitation and translation of Italian poetry by, 16, 38–40, 40–45, 80–82, 115–16, 116–17, 118–19; impact on the sonnet, 80–82; obscurity in the poetry of, 34, 42–43, 184 n. 18; and his original readers, 42–43; and problems of ascription, 183 n. 10; refrain poems of, 46–48; and Tottel's emendations, 35–36. Works: "In eternum," 47, 48; "It may be good," 35; "Me list no more to sing," 42–43, 48; "Whoso list to hunt," 118–19

Yates, Frances, 21
Young, Nicholas, as translator of Petrarch, 122–23
Yeats, W. B., "Prayer for my Daughter," 129